Branding

FOR

DUMMIES

A Wiley Brand

2nd Edition

by
**Bill Chiaravalle and
Barbara Findlay Schenck**

FOR

DUMMIES

A Wiley B

Branding For Dummies®, 2nd Edition

Published by: **John Wiley & Sons, Inc.,** 111 River Street, Hoboken, NJ 07030-5774, www.wiley.com

Copyright © 2015 by John Wiley & Sons, Inc., Hoboken, New Jersey

Published simultaneously in Canada

For general information on our other products and services, please contact our Customer Care Department within the U.S. at 877-762-2974, outside the U.S. at 317-572-3993, or fax 317-572-4002. For technical support, please visit www.wiley.com/techsupport.

Wiley publishes in a variety of print and electronic formats and by print-on-demand. Some material included with standard print versions of this book may not be included in e-books or in print-on-demand. If this book refers to media such as a CD or DVD that is not included in the version you purchased, you may download this material at http://booksupport.wiley.com. For more information about Wiley products, visit www.wiley.com.

Library of Congress Control Number: 2014945062

ISBN 978-1-118-95808-7 (pbk); ISBN 978-1-118-95809-4 (ebk); ISBN 978-1-118-95810-0 (ebk)

Manufactured in the United States of America

10 9 8 7 6 5 4 3 2 1

Contents at a Glance

Table of Contents

Introduction

Congratulations! You're about to take control of your brand.

If you're thinking, "I don't even have a brand," then this book is definitely for you. It's also for anyone who wants to build a better brand, repair a broken brand, extend the power of a valuable brand, or start from scratch and create a brand-new brand.

Branding is a red-hot topic (pardon the pun) that keeps increasing in importance for good reason: Brands pave the way for marketing success.

When people hear your organization's name — or your personal name, in the case of personal brands — thoughts pop up that influence what they believe and how they buy. Those thoughts, held in the minds of others, are the basis of your brand. They may be the result of direct associations with you or your organization, but chances are even greater that they're the result of web searches, online reviews, word-of-mouth comments, or other impressions that you're making even when you're nowhere in sight.

This book is all about defining the vision and idea of your desired brand image and then making sure that the impressions you're making lead to the positive set of thoughts you want people to have, trust, and believe about who you are and what you stand for.

Count on this book to guide you through the branding process and to lead you to a better, stronger brand that can compete successfully in the big, branded world around you.

About This Book

When the publisher *For Dummies* books, one of the world's most recognized book brands, first asked us to write a book on branding, we knew we were looking at a tall order and sky-high standards to live up to. Since the original edition of this book was published in 2006, *Branding For Dummies* has been read by thousands upon thousands of readers, translated into multiple languages, and excerpted in hundreds of other books and sites. Now, eight years later, we're happy to introduce this heavily updated second edition.

Branding For Dummies, 2nd Edition, is still the only plain English, do-it-yourself guide to branding we've seen, and we've looked high and low. What's changed is that this second edition includes new chapters on personal branding and one-person business brands, digital communications, and social media, which has emerged at rapid speed to become today's all-important brand-communication channel. Plus nearly every page of this book has been brought up-to-date with current advice, examples, and step-by-step instructions to follow.

As with all *For Dummies* books, this one can be used as a reference, so you can jump around and still make sense of the information, even if you haven't read all the chapters that precede it. Sidebars, the shaded boxes of text, cover bonus content that's interesting but not essential, so you can skip them if you're in a hurry.

Here's our pledge: You don't need an MBA or even a marketing or business background to make sense of this book. All you need is an interest in the topic of branding and a curiosity about what it is and how to do it. We take care of the rest.

You probably already know that branding works. This book shows you how to make it work for you.

Foolish Assumptions

First things first: Anyone smart enough to want to know more about branding is no fool. Thanks for entrusting us with your interest. We've done back flips to make sure that this book includes everything you need to know about branding, all presented with easy-to-understand translations for every technical term.

In writing this book, we made a few assumptions about you and the many others we hope will use this book.

- You're not a marketing professional — or if you are, you're looking for a branding refresher course for yourself or to share with those you work with. To make this book useful to every reader, we gear our explanations and advice to those who are charting new territory as they enter the branding arena.

- You're interested in building or strengthening a brand — for your company, for a nonprofit organization, for your new business, for a campaign (fundraising, political, social, you name it . . .), or for yourself by making your name into a respected resource, a local personality, or a small-scale celebrity. Regardless of your branding objective, we're guessing that you're not expecting to become the next Nike or Apple, but we think it's a safe bet that you'd like to acquire some of their branding strength. Who wouldn't!

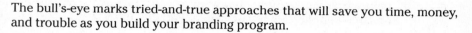 You're willing to invest effort to achieve the returns that result from a good branding program. To help, we include worksheets, charts, and sets of how-to instructions to guide the research, planning, positioning, design, implementation, and management involved in fueling your success with the power of a great brand.

Icons Used in This Book

This book wouldn't live up to the *For Dummies* brand promise without the symbols that sit in the outer margin alerting you to valuable information and advice. Watch for these icons:

The bull's-eye marks tried-and-true approaches that will save you time, money, and trouble as you build your branding program.

It's one thing to read advice and steps to follow. It's a whole other thing to read a true story of how an actual business tackled an issue topic successfully. This icon flags great branding examples and lessons.

When there's a danger to avoid or just a bad idea to steer clear of, this icon sits in the margin like a flashing yellow light.

This icon points out branding's golden rules. Watch for them throughout the book.

Beyond the Book

In addition to what you'll find in this book's 300-plus pages, you can also access the *Branding For Dummies* Cheat Sheet at `www.dummies.com/cheatsheet/branding`. It contains at-a-glance guidance and additional information you can put to work as you develop your brand and branding program.

Plus, we've posted some more useful material at `www.dummies.com/extras/branding`, including a bonus Part of Tens list featuring traits common to the world's greatest global brands and articles that summarize important and easy-to-reference advice from each of the parts in this book.

Where to Go from Here

True to the *For Dummies* format, you can start this book on any page. Every portion of the book is a self-standing component, which means that you don't have to read sequentially from cover-to-cover to make sense of the content. (If you have time and the inclination to read every word on every page, start-to-finish, however, we'd love nothing more!)

If you're new to the field of branding, count on Chapter 1 for a good overview of the contents of the entire book as well as a crash-course on the topic, language, and process of branding. If you're in a hurry because you're facing a crucial branding issue or wrestling with a branding problem, the table of contents or index guides you straight to the advice you need. If you already have a branding program but want to polish the luster of your brand or even do some rapid brand repair, skip to Parts IV and V.

For now, get started by using this book from start-to-finish or by cherry-picking the contents. So long as you end up with a clear brand identity that you project consistently in your market, your approach will have worked. So turn the page — and start branding!

Part I

Getting Started with Branding

In this part . . .

- Get clear about what brands are, why they're such a big deal, how they power success, and what it takes to build the brand image you want for your business, your product, your organization, or yourself.

- Familiarize yourself with clear-cut definitions of branding terminology and learn the differences between brands and commodities, including what it takes to move your offerings into the coveted brand category and far from the budget-breaking realm of generic contenders.

- Follow proven steps for building your brand from essence to esteem. Zero in on your brand vision, get real about your current brand identity and awareness level, assess your strongest brand assets, set your branding goals, make your branding to-do list, and assemble the resources you need build, manage and protect your brand — including your branding budget and your all-important brand-building team.

- Get the lowdown on how to power up your personal brand and — if you're a freelancer, consultant or one-person business owner — your solo-business brand as well.

Chapter 1

Putting Brands and Branding in Perspective

. . . .

In This Chapter

▶ Orienting yourself to what brands are all about

▶ Understanding the power of branding

▶ Committing the necessary people, resources, and time to build a brand

. . . .

Maybe you're gearing up to brand a new business or a product. Maybe you have an established brand and it's time to undertake some brand updates or brand extensions. Maybe your brand needs repair. Or maybe you're planning for a minor-to-major overhaul or the drastic move of a full-fledged rebranding.

Perhaps you simply want to come up to speed — in a hurry — on the whole topic of branding and how to do it best. Or, maybe you aren't quite sure whether or not you even *have* a brand, but you're pretty sure you need one and you want to know which steps you should take to end up with the brand you set out to build.

You've chosen the right book. Of the thousands of resources out there on the topics of brands and branding, you've opened the one that's branded with the *For Dummies* promise: *Making Everything Easier.*

The primary job of branding is to transform a complex message into simple and clear communication. This chapter gets you going with a simple and clear overview of the reasons brands matter, branding steps to follow, and how the brand value you develop far exceeds the time and effort you invest.

Wake-Up Call: You Probably Have a Brand, Whether You Know It or Not

When people encounter your name, they conjure up impressions and memories that determine their beliefs about you. Their notions may be the result of direct dealings with you or your organization or they may stem from web-search results, good or bad publicity, word-of-mouth, online reviews and ratings, or any other mentions that plant thoughts about you in their minds.

People may have a deep well of perceptions about you, or your slate in their minds may be nearly clear of any impressions whatsoever. Regardless of whether the beliefs people hold about you are many or few, good or bad, or accurate or inaccurate, they comprise the image of your brand, influencing how customers think and buy. Branding is the route to making sure that your brand image in the minds of others is perfectly aligned with the brand image you want them to have.

What Are Brands, Anyway?

Brands are promises. More complete definitions follow, but as you venture into the world of branding, keep those three words and these three truths in mind:

- ✔ **You establish your brand by building trust in a one-of-a-kind promise.** Your promise conveys who you are, what you stand for, and what unique and meaningful benefits you deliver.

- ✔ **You build your brand by living up to your promise every time people come into contact with you, your name, your message, or your business.** It makes no difference whether that contact is through a web search, your website, social media, advertising, publicity, word of mouth, the buying experience, customer service, billings, returns, or any other form of communication. Every encounter affects how others perceive your brand.

- ✔ **You strengthen your brand by constantly reinforcing your brand promise.** If encounters with your brand aren't in line with what people expected, those experiences essentially break your promise, breaking your brand and risking your reputation as a result.

Building brands takes focus, passion, persistence, and diligence. Plus, brand building requires effort and commitment. The payoff, and it's a big one, is that strong brands power personal and business success. The following sections shed light on what brands do and why they're such a big deal.

It's about perception, not the logo

We want to clear up a branding misconception: A logo isn't a brand. A logo is a symbol that represents a brand. Your brand isn't how you look or what you say or even what you sell. Your brand is what people trust and believe you stand for. For example:

- Starbucks sells coffee and, increasingly, other beverages. It stands for daily inspiration.

- Apple sells computers. It stands for thinking differently.

- Disney sells animated and amusement-park family entertainment. It stands for imagination, wholesome fun, and making dreams come true.

Your brand lives in consumer minds. Branding is the process of developing consumer beliefs and perceptions that are accurate and in alignment with what you want your brand to be.

What brands do

Brands create consumer trust and emotional attachments. As a result, they foster relationships between consumers and products that withstand pricing wars, transcend offers from new competitors, and even overcome rare lapses in product or service excellence, as detailed in the next few sections.

Great brands aren't just known and trusted. They're loved.

For examples of brands that enjoy strong bonds with customers, the next time you're stuck in traffic, look at the logos posted in the windows of the cars around you. Each time you see a logo decal, try to think of that brand's chief competitor. Then ask yourself, "What's the chance that a buyer of the competing brand would display the brand's logo with such pride?" Only brands that strike deep emotional chords with customers make their way into hearts, minds — and car windows. Chapters 13 and 14 provide a playbook to follow as you cultivate brand enthusiasts inside and outside your organization.

As you develop your brand and it gains strength and loyalty in your market area, look forward to reaping the following benefits.

Brands make selling easier

People prefer to buy from companies they feel they know and can trust. Brands put forth that assurance.

Whether you're selling products to consumers, investment opportunities to stockholders, job opportunities to applicants, freelance or consulting services to clients, or ideas to constituents, a brand paves the way for success by establishing positive awareness of your unique and meaningful promise before you ever present your sales proposition.

When people are aware of your brand and its unique and positive attributes, they understand what you stand for and what unique value they can count on you to deliver. As a result, when it comes time to make a sale, brand owners can concentrate on the wants and needs of the consumer because they don't need to explain themselves.

Without positive brand awareness, you have to build a case for the value you deliver every single time you get ready to make a sale. While brand owners are closing the deal, those without strong brands are still introducing themselves.

Brands prevail over no-name offerings

In the marketplace, you have either a one-of-a-kind brand or a one-is-as-good-as-any-other commodity.

- ✔ **Brands are products defined by and chosen for their unique distinguishing attributes and promise.** Consumers are willing to spend extra effort and money to obtain the brands they believe in.

- ✔ **Commodities are products that are easy to substitute and hard to differentiate.** Oil, coffee beans, wheat flour, and milk are commodities. Consumers buy commodities because they meet minimum standards and are available when and where they're needed and at the lowest price. Only commodity items that are distinguished by a unique attribute and promise — think of Pillsbury flour as an example — develop into strong brands.

As proof of how brands pave the way for positive decisions, imagine you're setting out to buy a computer and you see one emblazoned with a known logo — the face of a known brand. It's likely that your next step is to dive into a discussion with the salesperson of how much memory the particular model you're viewing contains, how the machine can be customized to your needs, what software is included, and other details that will move you to the purchase decision. On the other hand, if you see a no-name model — even at a dramatically lower price — you're likely to first try to assess the quality of the manufacturer. You may ask the salesperson where the computer was made, how long the manufacturer's been in business, whether the manufacturer is reliable, whether other customers have been satisfied, and other mind-calming questions about consumer satisfaction levels, warranties, and return programs that you wouldn't raise when dealing with the known entity of an established brand.

Selling a no-name item is a costly route to a sale in a brick-and-mortar setting, and it's even a tougher proposition online, where no one is standing by to offer explanations, inspire confidence, counter resistance, or break down barriers for your consumers.

Flip to Chapter 2 for more on outselling budget-busting commodities with your brand.

Brands build equity

Brands that are preferred and valued by consumers deliver a long list of business benefits that translate to higher sales, higher profit margins, and higher owner value. Consider these brand advantages as proof:

- People are willing to pay more to buy brands that they believe deliver outstanding and desirable benefits. This is true for business brands, product brands, and personal brands, which are the focus of Chapter 4.

- Consumers stay loyal to brands, buying them more often, in greater volume, and without the need for promotional incentives.

- Retailers provide brands greater store visibility because they know that brands drive sales and result in higher store revenues.

- Brand owners can grow their businesses by leveraging their brands into product and line extensions rather than having to introduce new products from scratch.

- Brand owners find it easier to attract and retain good employees because applicants believe in the quality of the workplace based on advance knowledge of the caliber of the brand.

- Brand owners run more efficient operations because they align decisions with the mission, vision, and values that underpin the brand promise.

- Brand owners benefit from increased market share, increased investor support, and increased company value.

Why brands are a big deal

With more new businesses and products than ever before, and with a competitive arena that — thanks to the Internet — stretches all the way around the world, brands are more necessary today than ever before. Here are a few of the reasons why:

- **Brands unlock profitability.** Today's marketplace is full of more products than ever before, and, overwhelmed by the selection, people choose and pay premium prices only for products they've heard of, trust, and believe deliver higher value than the others. If consumers think all products in a category are virtually the same and no offering is better or distinctly different from the others, they simply grab whichever one is available at the lowest price. That's a profit-squeezing reality that brand marketers gratefully avoid.

✔ **Brands prompt consumer selection.** For the first time in shopping history, consumers can shop and buy without any geographic limitation. The Internet and other at-home shopping options allow far-reaching access to any product, anywhere. With a few clicks or keystrokes, consumers find and select products with names they know and promises they trust. In this boundless marketplace, brands rule and no-name products barely survive.

✔ **Brands build name awareness.** For good reason, new businesses and products increasingly go by invented names instead of by known words. For one thing, more than three million U.S. trademarks are already registered, so any marketer who wants to protect a new name practically needs to create a never-before seen word in order to succeed. For another, 99 percent of all words in the English dictionary are already reserved as Internet addresses and are therefore unavailable to new marketers. As a result, most new offerings are launched under invented names, and invented names require strong and diligent brand development in order to achieve consumer awareness, recall, and meaning. (Chapter 7 is full of advice for naming your brand.)

✔ **Brands increase the odds of business survival.** New businesses and new products are being launched at an unprecedented pace. Only those that ride into the market on the strength of an established brand or those that are capable of building a brand name in a hurry can seize consumer awareness, understanding, and preference fast enough to survive.

Brands have been around for centuries, as the sidebar "The red-hot history of branding" explains. But they've never been more important — or more essential to business success — than they are today.

Gaining Your Branding Bearings

People confuse branding with designing a logo. Or they think branding is a matter of creating a great website, great ads, and consistently great marketing messages. But branding is way more than any of that.

Deciphering branding lingo

Following are some need-to-know terms:

✔ **Brand:** The essence and idea of what you stand for. Your brand starts with a vision and grows into a promise about who you are and what you stand for that gets reinforced every time people come in contact with any facet of your business or organization.

✔ **Brand identity:** The name and visual marks that present your brand, usually in the form of a logo, symbol, or unique typestyle, as well as all other identifying elements including colors, package shape, even sounds and smells associated with your brand.

✔ **Brand image:** The beliefs about what your brand is and what it stands for that exist in the customer's mind as a result of all encounters, associations, and experiences with any aspect of your business or organization.

✔ **Branding:** The process of building positive perceptions in your customer's mind by consistently presenting the vision and idea of your brand so others understand and believe what you stand for and the promise you invariably make and keep.

✔ **Brand position:** How your brand fits in with and relates to various other brands within your competitive market.

✔ **Brand management:** Controlling the presentation of your brand identity, message, and promise across your entire organization and through all communication channels, and protecting your brand identity against infringement or misuse.

✔ **Brand equity:** The value of your brand as an asset based on its qualities, reputation, recognition, and the demand, loyalty, and premium pricing it generates.

Armed with an understanding of the above terms, you can navigate branding conversations just fine. Plus, throughout this book we introduce other terms — brand message, brand promise, brand strategy, brand extension, brand revitalization, rebranding, and many others — that will be useful as you take specific branding steps. Use the index to beeline to other definitions.

Branding's essential ingredient

Originally we titled this section "Branding's essential ingredients." Lucky for you, we changed the plural to a singular. Brands are built around four fundamentals: differentiation, relevance, esteem, and knowledge. But the magic ingredient that converts those fundamentals into a branding success story is *consistency.*

In branding, consistency is the single most important ingredient for success. Here's why:

✔ If you bring consistency to your branding program, you build a brand that stands head and shoulders (no branding pun intended) above the others.

✔ If you have a clear and passionate vision about what you stand for and project messages to your target market that constantly reinforce how your offering is different and relevant, you build knowledge and, eventually, esteem.

✔ As a result of your consistency, you win out over businesses that shift with the wind, regardless of how beautifully they've polished their identities or their marketing materials.

Too many companies develop award-winning logos and marketing materials only to have their brand images go sideways when the customer has an actual brand experience. In Chapter 2 we make the analogy that treating branding like a skin-deep solution is like putting lipstick on a pig: False promises don't work. Your brand must be an honest, accurate reflection of who you are.

Turn to Chapter 6 for assistance as you define your brand and put your desired brand image into words you can live up to. Then turn to Chapter 14 for help developing a brand experience that ensures consistent presentation of your brand through every single customer encounter.

Branding's altered environment

What a difference a decade makes. Since 2006, when the first edition of *Branding For Dummies* hit bookshelves, the world in which brand-builders operate has undergone seismic shifts. Although the definition of what brands are and do remains unchanged, the expectations of today's always-screen-connected consumers have vastly affected branding tactics. Here are the new realities:

✔ **Every brand needs an online home base.** Even if your customers are among the rare few who don't go online for information, those who influence them do. Without a fast-loading website or major social-media pages that you control and keep updated, you lack an essential brand-building tool. Chapters 10 and 11 outline steps to take.

✔ **Online search results make or break brand images.** In the now-famous words of former *WIRED* Magazine editor Chris Anderson, your brand is what Google says it is. Before they meet you in person or consider a purchase of your products or services, people in ever-greater numbers check you out online. Their search results often form the first impressions of your brand. And even after making initial contact, they tune into and trust word-of mouth-comments and online rants, raves, and mentions more than they trust (or tune into) your marketer-generated communications. Your brand has to be visible, engaged, and interactive online to stay part of the dialog. Chapter 11 makes the job easier.

✔ **You have only seconds to pull people to your brand, no matter the communication channel.** Only good branding can turn your name and logo into a familiar face that wins a second glance, and only messages that reach out and grab interest can convert that interest to action. Make Chapter 12 your guide as you plan ads, promotions, and publicity efforts.

✔ **Customers expect a consistent experience whether they're encountering your brand online or in-person.** They expect your brand to look, act, and deliver on the same promises whether they're dealing with your website, social-media pages, brick-and-mortar location, products, promotions, or staff — before, during, or after the purchase. And they expect your online and offline locations to interact seamlessly, with web pages offering one-click phone contact and arrival directions and physical locations supporting online purchases. Turn to Chapter 13 for help building, auditing, and strengthening an across-the-board brand experience capable of winning and keeping customers and loyalty.

The never-ending branding process

Chapter 2 walks you through the steps involved to build a brand from the essence of an idea to the esteem of a known and trusted offering. For a glimpse of what's involved, look at Figure 1-1.

The red-hot history of branding

People associate the word *brand* with ranching in the Old West, but the history of branding goes way farther back in time.

Archaeologists trace the concept of branding back to marks on 5,000-year-old Babylonian and Greek pottery shards, and relics from the medieval age show makers' symbols seared onto everything from loaves of bread to gold and silver products.

In the 1800s, brands emerged as a marketing force when manufacturing breakthroughs led to mass production that generated a glut of products vastly beyond the needs of any one local market area. Manufacturers who were used to presenting, explaining, and selling their goods to friends and neighbors were suddenly shipping products off to fend for themselves in distant locations. Realizing that their goods were leaving home accompanied by little more than their product labels, manufacturers worked to gain far-reaching awareness and belief that their names stood for quality, distinction, and honesty. In short order, the concepts of branding, publicity, and advertising gained momentum.

Two centuries later, when eight out of ten purchases are influenced by information found on websites and 80 percent of people research and establish the credibility of businesses and individuals through web searches, online visibility of brands has become a prerequisite for business and personal success.

Through it all, the purpose of branding remains the same: To build, maintain, and protect a positive image, high awareness, and product preference in consumers' minds.

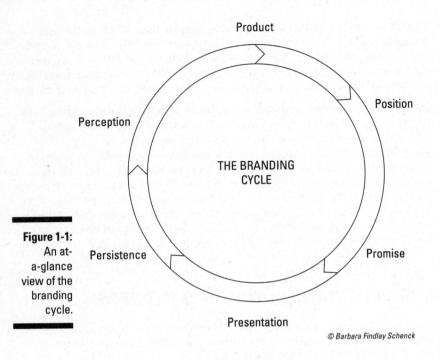

Product

Position

Perception

THE BRANDING CYCLE

Promise

Persistence

Presentation

© Barbara Findlay Schenck

Figure 1-1:
An at-
a-glance
view of the
branding
cycle.

Branding is a circular process that involves these actions:

1. **Product definition:** You can brand products, services, businesses, people, or personalities. The process starts by defining what you're branding and whether your brand will be your one-and-only or one of several in your organization. Chapter 2 provides assistance with this beginning step.

2. **Positioning:** Each brand needs to fill a unique, meaningful, and available spot in the marketplace and in the consumer's mind. To determine your brand's point of difference and the unique position it (and only it) fills in the marketplace, see Chapter 5.

3. **Promise:** The promise you make and keep is the backbone of your brand and the basis of your reputation. Chapter 6 helps you put it into words.

4. **Presentation:** How you present your brand can make or break your ability to develop consumer interest and credibility in your offering. Start with a great name and logo (see Chapters 7 and 8), and then launch communications that establish your brand, convey a compelling message, engage your audience, and foster the kind of two-way brand communication and interaction demanded by screen-connected and empowered consumers. The chapters in Part III tell you when, where, and how to send your brand message into your marketplace.

5. **Persistence:** This is the point in the branding cycle where too many brands lose steam. After brands are established, brand owners often begin to improvise with new looks, new messages, and even new brand personalities and promises. Just when consistency is most necessary in order to gain clarity and confidence in the marketplace, brands that lack persistence go off track. To save your brand from this pitfall, turn to Chapters 8 and 17 for help writing and enforcing brand presentation and management rules.

6. **Perception analysis:** In a consumer's mind — which is where brands live and thrive — a brand is a set of beliefs about what you offer, promise, and stand for. Great brands continually monitor brand perceptions to see that they're in alignment with the brand owner's aspirations and in synch with consumer wants and needs. (Chapter 16 provides advice for conducting this assessment.)

Based on the results of perception analysis, brand owners begin their loop around the branding cycle again, this time adjusting products, fine-tuning positioning statements, strengthening promises, updating presentations, rewriting brand-management rules, and, once again, monitoring perceptions in preparation for brand realignments and revitalizations.

Assembling your branding team

Brands grow from the top down and from the inside out. What that means is that your brand needs commitment and clarity from the highest levels of leadership _and_ support from employees at every point in your organization.

Involving your whole organization

Whether you have a one-person team or a 1,000-person team, every person in your organization has to be involved in building and maintaining your brand. Here are the key players:

1. **Organization leaders:** Enlist the leadership and buy-in of those whose names appear at the very top of your organizational chart. Great brands are expressions of the vision, mission, and core values established by leaders, and therefore leaders need to head up the branding effort.

2. **Marketing team:** This group takes on the day-to-day responsibility for advancing, maintaining, protecting, and fine-tuning the brand. From this team, name one person to serve as your brand manager and chief brand protector, choosing a top-level executive who has the authority and commands the respect necessary to oversee what, in time, will become your organization's most valuable asset — your brand.

3. **Team of brand champions:** If one person fails to uphold your brand promise — at any point from an initial inquiry to a post-purchase product or service concern — the strength of your brand is weakened. That's why great brands begin with internal launches that achieve team understanding and support (see Chapter 9). They also include ongoing brand orientations and training sessions to ensure flawless brand experiences (see Chapters 13 and 14).

Enlisting help from branding professionals

Brand development requires professional expertise and effort from those within and outside your organization. Pick and choose from the following professional resources:

- ✔ **Brand consultants:** These firms specialize in soup-to-nuts creation, building, and management of brands. They're experienced at positioning, naming and trademarking, logo development and all aspects of launching and managing brands. If you're seeking to build a brand that reaches into large markets or competitive fields, the expertise of a brand consultant can be worth the expense many times over.

- ✔ **Public-relations specialists:** New brands are newsworthy. An experienced PR professional can help you develop the right news hooks and angles to get your story into circulation. Depending on the size and ongoing nature of your needs, a public-relations freelancer may be able to handle your task as a one-time assignment. If brand publicity is an ongoing objective, a PR firm with greater staff and media resources may be the way to go. (Flip to Chapter 12 for more on public relations.)

- ✔ **Brand identity (logo) designers:** If you need help only with logo development or refinement, hire a graphic designer who specializes in brand identity who has a proven track record and a portfolio of success. Ask to see samples to be sure the caliber of design matches up with your expectations. Then use the advice in Chapter 8 as you manage the logo-development process.

- ✔ **Advertising agencies:** Some ad agencies specialize in brand development. Others focus on creation of print, broadcast, or interactive advertising. Yet others are known for award-winning packaging, and even for their public-relations departments. Chapter 13 includes guidance for determining your needs, locating the right resources, and working with the professionals you hire.

When interviewing professionals, ask to see case studies to determine whether those you're considering have the experience you seek. Many companies present themselves as brand developers when, in fact, they handle only one aspect of the branding process, such as logo development or brand advertising.

When selecting a firm, use these 3 Cs to help determine if they are right for you:

  ✔ **Are they competent?** In other words, do they have the experience?

  ✔ **Is the chemistry right?** Do they get us?

  ✔ **Do their compensation needs fit within our budget?**

Gulp! How much does it cost?

Branding budgets run the gamut depending on whether you're building a brand that will face only moderate competition in a small geographic region or a brand that aims to elbow out major competitors in the global marketplace. What's more, budgets vary depending on whether you can reach your market through digital communications and social media or whether you need to invest in traditional media and marketing channels.

A glance at branding budgets

Table 1-1 shows a lineup of the major tasks involved in brand development along with the range of price tags involved. Brace yourself: The high-end figures are apt to cause heart palpitations.

Table 1-1	Professional Brand-Development Fees	
Task	**Low-End Fee**	**High-End Fee**
Name development	$10,000	$75,000
Brandmark (logo) creation	$3,500	$150,000
Core brand presentations (website and brand marketing materials)	$10,000	$250,000+
Advertising	$10,000	Millions annually
SEO (website search-engine optimization	$1,000 monthly	Thousands monthly
Social media	Your time	Hundreds of thousands annually
Signage, vehicles, packaging	$20,000	$250,000+ annually

As Table 1-1 verifies, there's a huge range between the low-end costs involved to build a professional brand that competes on a local or regional level and the high-end costs involved to build a powerful brand that can flex its muscle nationally or internationally.

As you start tallying up the costs to your business, avoid the temptation to strike out certain line items that you think you can handle on your own without incurring outside costs. Businesses that start with do-it-yourself logos and presentation materials achieve false savings. They economize on the front end, for sure, but they also cost themselves the benefit of a strong, competitive, professional first impression.

If your goal is to build a brand that you can grow, leverage, and even sell in the future, invest the money required to get off to a good start. By the time you amortize your start-up expenses, the cost will be minimal in comparison to the value received.

In lieu of big bucks . . .

In case you're clinging to your billfold or balance sheet, shaking your head and wondering how you can build a brand on your kind of budget, remember this truth: *In essence, your business is your brand and your brand is your business.*

If you don't have the budget to develop the most powerful brand identity, triple or quadruple your efforts to design and deliver the most consistent brand experience. Follow these suggestions:

- ✔ **Spend extra time and effort to define your brand and what it stands for so that everyone in your organization knows exactly the promise you're making and keeping.** Defining your brand involves creating your mission and vision statements, defining your brand promise, developing your brand definition and core brand message, and deciding on the brand character or personality that you'll put forth with every brand communication. Chapter 6 covers these tasks.

- ✔ **Develop a brand experience that never fails or fluctuates.** If you can't have the most dazzling brand identity and presentation, aim instead to have the most amazing and amazingly consistent brand encounters. Chapters 13 and 14 help you deliver a brand experience that never lets consumers down and never leaves them wondering what you stand for.

When people choose your offerings, what they really buy into is your brand. How well you define and deliver your brand determines the ultimate value and success of your business. View branding not as an expense but as an investment that delivers value over the long haul.

Pop Quiz: Are You Ready to Brand?

Is branding the right next step? If you answer "yes" to a good many of the following questions, you have good reason to turn the page and get started!

- ✔ Are you launching a business, product, or personal effort that will benefit from a clear identity and high awareness?

✔ Have you been in business for a while but feel you lack consumer awareness and understanding about who you are and what you stand for?

✔ Do you worry that prospects don't know your name or the distinct benefits you offer?

✔ Do you feel that people in your own organization are unclear about how to explain your offerings, your distinctions, your target market, and how you excel over competitors?

✔ When you study your marketing materials, personal presentations, and the ways that people encounter you or your business, do you see inconsistencies in the look, message, and personality being presented?

✔ Is the leader of your organization prepared to devote time, staff, energy, and dollars to develop, launch, and grow a brand?

And the final question is "Can you think of even one reason why people should choose your offering over competing solutions?" If so, turn the page and start building your brand!

Chapter 2

Why, What, How, and When to Brand

More than 5,000 branding books and millions of branding websites give proof to the fact that brands are a hot topic surrounded by a deluge of information — and confusion. To clear up the facts, here are a few easy definitions.

A *brand* is the essence and idea of what you stand for. It starts with a vision and grows into a promise that's reinforced every time people come into contact with you or any facet your business or organization.

Branding is the process of positioning, packaging, and presenting the vision and idea of your brand so that others understand and believe what you stand for and the promise you invariably make and keep.

Branding isn't a veneer that you slap on (usually in the form of a new logo) to mask or transform a product offering. Treating branding like some skin-deep solution is like putting lipstick on a pig: People see through the makeup. Instead, successful branding goes all the way to the core of who you are and what you stand for. When it does, it signifies, simplifies, clarifies, unifies, and magnifies what you are and do. And it adds considerable value as a result.

This chapter gives you a look at when and how to brand and why branding is worth every bit of the effort it involves.

Why Bother with Branding?

To brand or not to brand, that is the question. Or at least that's the question that hangs in the air until people who aren't quite sure about whether they really need a brand hear this truth: More than any other quality — even more than strong financial statements, great management, or terrific product or service ideas — brands are the key to winning long-term growth and success.

By building a brand, you cast a strong, clear vision of what you stand for. Without a brand, you blur into a dime-a-dozen, one-seems-just-like-another category called *commodities*. In a sea of similar choices, branding differentiates and elevates your offering, paving the way for awareness, preference, selection, and profitability.

If you can think of even one way your offering is meaningfully different and better (not just different, but *meaningfully* different and better!), then you have at least one reason to build a brand that moves it into the prestigious realm of people, products, businesses, and organizations that stand out as distinctly different, preferable, and more valuable than all the others.

Branding to avoid the budget-busting commodity trap

Warren Buffett, widely regarded as the 20th century's most successful business investor, sums up the formula for business success in four frequently quoted words: *Buy commodities, sell brands.*

- ✔ **Commodities** are offerings that customers can't differentiate from one another because they all seem to serve the same need, solve the same problem, and deliver the same value. If people can't see a clear reason to buy one product over another — if they think that they all deliver the same value and quality — they buy whatever's available at the lowest price, which is hardly a formula for business success.

- ✔ **Brands** are the opposite of commodities. A commodity becomes a brand when those in the marketplace understand and value compelling characteristics that make it different and better than others in its category. Branding is a powerful tool that differentiates an offering in ways that develop consumer preference and deliver *pricing power* — the power to raise prices without losing business.

Airline tickets, laptop computers, and strawberry jam start out as commodities. All competitors address basically the same need in basically the same way, and if customers see no reason to choose one over the others, they simply opt for the one with the lowest price. Yet every day, customers make conscious decisions to buy the offering of one airline or computer manufacturer or jam maker over the others because of the unique attributes they trust to be true about their choice. Maybe they're won over by the frequent flyer club options, service or warranty program, organic ingredients, or any of a zillion other distinguishing characteristics — the *brand promises* — that they understand and believe are worth premium pricing.

As proof that brands lift offerings out of crowded commodity categories, look at the following examples:

Commodity	*Brand*
Soft drinks	Coca-Cola
Water	Evian
Sneakers	Nike
Technology	Apple
Razor blades	Gillette
Internet search	Google
Online retail	Amazon
Logistics	UPS
Coffee	Starbucks
Lingerie	Victoria's Secret

When you build a brand, you develop value, trust, preference, and the potential for higher prices and profit margins.

Branding to cast your vision

Your brand reflects the vision of the good that you aim to achieve. Just as the images on a country's flag symbolize the core of what's important to that culture and nation, your brand reflects the core of what's important to you and your organization. It's the banner that signifies what you're passionate about, your fundamental values, what you aspire to achieve, and the promise on which you stake your reputation.

A well-defined vision is important whether you're building a personal brand or an organizational brand:

- **If you're developing a personal brand,** your vision clarifies the qualities and characteristics for which you want to be known. It keeps you on track and steers the presentation of an authentic, well-aligned voice and presentation in all personal communications, whether online and offline.

- **If you're developing a product, business, or nonprofit brand,** your vision defines — for every person in your organization — why you're doing what you're doing and the ultimate good you want to achieve through your success. Establishing a clear vision keeps your entire team on track and makes branding an almost-transparent process. You don't have to tell people why upholding the brand promise is important. By understanding the long-term vision you're working to achieve, the brand promise becomes a commitment that's caught, not taught, throughout the organization. Chapter 6 guides you through the process of putting your brand into words.

Great brands stem from the beliefs, personalities, and values of those leading the brand. They result in a brand culture that's authentic and heartfelt.

Branding to win trust and increased value

Amid a deluge of unfamiliar options, brands stand out as friends you can count on. That trust leads to selection, purchase, and, for the brand-builder, profitability.

Instinctively, you've proven the influence of brand trust thousands of times over. Think of the last time you reviewed job applicants, or scrolled through screen-after-screen of shoe choices, or scanned reviews for movies playing in town. You had to make a choice, and chances are good that you opted for the offering you thought you could trust. Branding, or lack thereof, led to your selection.

If you viewed all the choices as similar and fairly risk-free, you probably let convenience or low price tip your decision. That's because no single offering inspired your trust or presented distinguishing benefits, so you went with the quickest, least-expensive option. (The section on commodities earlier in this chapter has more on the topic of undifferentiated offerings.)

But if, after scanning all your options, you settled on an offering that took you out of your way or caused you to pay a little or a lot more, your decision was likely based on a sense that the one you selected was worth the price or the trouble because you believed it wouldn't let you down. That trust, almost certainly, was the result of good branding.

So, What Do You Want to Brand?

You can build a brand for a product or service, a small or huge company, or a nonprofit organization. You can build a brand for yourself, called a *personal brand,* which is a brand category so hot that we've given it its own chapter (Chapter 4). In this section we give you an overview of all the kinds of brands you can build.

Product brands

Products are tangible, physical items that you can hold in your hands or see with your own eyes before you make the purchase.

If a product lacks any perception of distinct quality or value, it's known as a *commodity* (think salt). When a manufacturer wins awareness in the marketplace that its product has characteristics that make it different and better than others in the product category, that commodity turns into what's known as a *consumer brand* (think Morton's). (Refer to the preceding section for more on commodities.)

Branding is a powerful way to differentiate a product in ways that create consumer preference and premium pricing.

Service brands

People buy services sight-unseen. Unlike tangible, three-dimensional products that shoppers can see and feel and try out before buying (or at least look at on your website), people buy services purely based on their trust that the person or business they're buying from will deliver as promised.

If you sell a service or run a service business, you absolutely, positively need to develop and manage a strong brand image for the following reasons:

- **People buy your service based entirely on their belief in your brand promise.** People need to have faith in you, your ability, and your reputation before they decide to commit their business.

- **Before signing on the dotted line to purchase a service, customers need to believe that their expectations will be met.** If they know nothing about you or lack confidence in the quality of your service, they'll take their business elsewhere.

Examples of globally recognized service brands include Google, eBay, H&R Block, Charles Schwab, and FedEx. For examples of local-level service brands, think of your region's leading law firm, best hair salon, most innovative homebuilder, or most trusted medical clinic. Each earned its reputation by building a clear identity and consistently conveying a believable promise that people trust in while they wait for the purchased service to be performed and their high expectations to be met.

Business or corporate brands

Many large companies and corporations build product or service brands in addition to their business brands. (The section later in this chapter titled "Brand Architecture 101" describes how business and product or service brands relate to each other.)

Procter & Gamble, for example, has a corporate brand in addition to a portfolio of consumer brands. On a smaller scale, you probably can think of a local land developer that builds product brands for each new residential community in addition to a brand for the land development company that holds the individual brands.

Table 2-1 summarizes how product or service and business brands differ from and complement each other.

Table 2-1   Comparison of Business Brands and Consumer Brands

Business Brand	*Consumer Product or Service Brand*
Builds trust with stakeholders, including investors, associates, and employees	Builds emotional attachment with customers
Helps prospective stakeholders decide: Is this business organized to deliver on its promises? Is the leadership strong and trustworthy? Is the business innovative?	Helps prospective customers decide: How is this product or service relevant to my life? What does it mean to me?
Projected through marketing tools and especially through personal contacts	Projected through product packaging, labeling, digital communication, and advertising
Results in lasting investor, employee, customer, and stakeholder relationships	Results in consumer choice, purchase, and loyalty

If you build only one brand — and that's the advice we give to any business with limited marketing expertise or budget — build a business brand because business brands accomplish the following:

- Lead to awareness, credibility, and good reputations
- Pave a smooth road for product introductions
- Inspire employees
- Attract the interest of job applicants, investors, and business reporters

✔ Contribute to customer preference for your products and services, often accompanied by a willingness to pay more for the association with a leading, high-esteem business

Branding individuals (namely, yourself)

Individual brands are a hot topic and the focus of Chapter 4. They come in two types: personal brands and personality brands.

✔ *Personal brands* reflect personal reputations. They differentiate individuals by creating awareness of who they are, what they stand for, what they do best, and how they contribute to the world around them. By developing your personal brand, you establish yourself for your expertise, enhance visibility, develop preference, gain influence, and power success toward your personal goals. You prepare yourself to take every opportunity to make a great first impression.

✔ *Personality brands* are personal brands gone big-time. They're individual brands that are so well-known that they not only become celebrities (think Oprah, Kobe Bryant, Donald Trump, and, like 'em or not, any of the Kardashians) but also create significant value when associated with products or services (for example, think of George Foreman, David Beckham, Beyoncé, LeBron James, and a long list of other celebrities who launch or endorse product brands). But personality brands aren't exclusively for the uber-famous and ultra-rich. For example, community leaders become local personalities whose endorsements of projects or fundraising campaigns turn otherwise obscure efforts into overnight successes.

Whether you aspire to be a successful job applicant, a sought-after speaker, or a star in your community or industry, start by building a personal brand. Chapter 4 gets you started. Then look into Susan Chritton's book *Personal Branding For Dummies,* 2nd Edition (Wiley) for in-depth guidance.

Branding: A Bird's-Eye View

Branding starts before most brand-builders even know it. As soon as people form an opinion about you or your business, product, or service — perhaps based on real-world or online encounters you don't even realize are happening — they form the basis of your brand image in their minds, which is where brands live. Branding is the process that aligns the opinions people hold about your brand with the image you want them to believe.

The path from brand essence to esteem

This section covers major branding steps and where to turn in the upcoming chapters for step-by-step branding advice.

Step 1: Decide what you're going to brand

Are you branding a product, a service, a company, or an individual? If the distinctions are a bit blurry, flip back to the section in this chapter titled, "So, What Do You Want to Brand?"

As part of your decision about what you're going to brand you need to decide if the brand you're developing will be your one-and-only or if it will live alongside or under the umbrella of other brands in your organization. The upcoming section on *brand architecture* helps you plot, plan, and decide the relationship between your business and your brand or brand.

Step 2: Do your research

When you're clear about what you're branding, the next step is to analyze your offering and the market in which it will compete. Think of this as your discovery phase, which is comprised of two major steps:

1. **Find out everything there is to know about your market.**

   Begin by researching your prospective customers — who they are, where they are, and what motivates their buying decisions. Then analyze your competition to discover what solutions already exist in the marketplace and exactly how the offering you're branding is different and better.

2. **Find out everything there is to know about your product or service.**

   You need to know what makes your offering unique, what attributes make it excel over competing alternatives, and how it solves your customers' wants or needs.

Flip to the first pages of Chapter 5 for help with this fact-finding mission.

Step 3: Position your product or service

Positioning defines how you'll differentiate your brand and how you'll slot it into an available space in the market and in customer minds.

Determining your brand's position is an essential early step in the branding process because people will make mind space for your offering only if you can convince them, in a split second, that you provide unique solutions to problems or needs that aren't already being addressed by competing solutions.

To determine your market position, follow these four steps:

1. **Determine which distinct and meaningful consumer needs or desires only your product or service addresses in the marketplace.** Don't try to take an already established position away from a competitor unless you have the budget, expertise, and time to do so.

2. **Communicate your point of difference.**

3. **Win a unique position for your offering in the market and in the consumer's mind.**

4. **Perform so well that no competitor can compete against or unseat your position.**

Chapter 5 takes you on a step-by-step walk through the positioning process, including how to locate your market position, how to communicate your position, how to win your position in your consumers' minds, and how to protect your position so that your brand can claim and own the defined niche in which it will live and grow.

Step 4: Write your brand definition

Your *brand definition* is a true statement about what your brand stands for. It describes what you offer, why you offer it, how your offering is meaningfully different and better, the unique benefits your customers can count on, and the promise or set of promises you make to all who work with and buy from your business.

You have to know your brand definition before you begin to develop and project the public presentation of your brand. Otherwise the external face of your brand — everything you present through marketing efforts — won't match up with the internal base of your brand, and your brand will lack credibility.

Figure 2-1 uses an iceberg to represent the relationship between the base and face of your brand:

- ✔ **The external face of your brand** rises into public view in the form of your name, logo, website, ads, packaging, promotions, and marketing messages that everyone from employees to consumers, suppliers, friends, and colleagues can quickly and easily see, understand, and believe. Like the tip of the iceberg, the face of your brand is only a representation of the larger brand base that lies out of consumer view.

- ✔ **The internal base of your brand** is the substance of what your brand is and stands for. It includes your services, products, culture, mission, vision, and values, as well as the leadership, management, and organization that together create the strong basis for your brand.

As you define your brand, turn to Chapter 6 for help with every step involved.

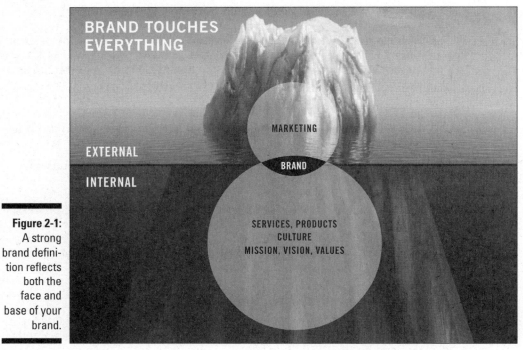

BRAND TOUCHES EVERYTHING

EXTERNAL

INTERNAL

MARKETING

BRAND

SERVICES, PRODUCTS
CULTURE
MISSION, VISION, VALUES

Figure 2-1:
A strong
brand defini-
tion reflects
both the
face and
base of your
brand.

Illustration courtesy of Bill Chiaravalle, Brand Navigation

Step 5: Develop your name, logo, and tagline

This is the point where branding gets exciting. The minute you give your brand a name and face — or logo — you can watch managers, employees, and others inside the company start to buy into the branding process. Here's a brief introduction to these important brand elements:

- ✔ **Name:** Your name is the key that unlocks your brand image in your consumer's mind. Turn to Chapter 7 for help creating or revising your brand name, including advice for how to recognize qualities of a great name, pick or create the name, test the appropriateness and availability of the name you want, and turn the name you choose into a vehicle that conveys your brand promise and contributes to brand value.

- ✔ **Logo:** Your *logo* is the mark or symbol that serves as the face of your brand on your signage, packaging, stationery, websites, advertising, sales material, and every other communication vehicle that carries your name into the marketplace. Coauthor Bill is the guru on this subject, and he's filled Chapter 8 with information on how to develop a great logo, avoid logo design taboos, apply your logo with consistency throughout your marketing program, change your logo when and if it's time for a revamp, and manage your logo so that no one tampers with or misuses it.

✔ **Tagline:** Your *tagline* is the memorable phrase that provides consumers with a quick indication of your brand position and promise. Some marketers make their taglines an essential part of their identities, whereas other marketers don't create taglines at all. Taglines are particularly useful, though, for brands with names or logos that don't clearly convey their brand position or personality and for businesses that rely heavily on communications in which logo presentation isn't possible. See Chapter 8 for help deciding whether or not your marketing would benefit from a tagline and, if so, how to create one for your brand.

Step 6: Launch your brand

Your brand launch happens in two phases and in this order:

1. **Internal launch**

   Whether you're launching a new brand or relaunching a revitalized brand, be sure to launch from the inside out. Before you even think of introducing your brand to prospects, explain it to all the people who have or feel that they have a stake in your business, including the following:

   • **Shareholders, managers, and employees:** These are the people most invested in your business and most apt to serve as ambassadors for your brand. Be ready to answer questions like "Why are we spending money on this?" and "How will this strengthen our business?" by linking your branding program to your business mission and goals. By all means, take extra care with those who sell your product, providing them with a complete set of tools to help them present your brand position and story to prospects and customers (turn to Chapter 9 for advice).

   • **Key partners and major customers:** Before loyal supporters and clients see your new or revised brand identity on packaging or in ads, give them a preview. Chapter 9 helps you plan your approach.

2. **External launch**

   Your brand goes public when you unveil your name, logo, and slogan and when you begin to tell your market the story of how your brand reflects what you stand for. Coauthor Barbara is the marketing guru on our author team, and she's designed Part III to guide you as you write the marketing plan for building awareness for your brand through digital communications, social media, advertising, publicity, promotions, sales materials, and all other communications that carry the announcement and story of your brand into your marketplace.

Step 7: Manage, leverage, and protect your brand

This is the "care and feeding" phase of the branding process. This stage also requires the most persistence, and it's where too many brands lose steam. Just like good parenting, good branding management can be summed up in a single word: consistency.

✔ Display a consistent look.

✔ Project a consistent message and tone.

✔ Deliver a consistent level of quality through all communications, products, and services.

✔ Be diligent about consistently protecting your brand from misuse.

✔ Stay consistently true to your brand.

Begin managing your brand from the moment you introduce it for the following reasons:

✔ The minute your name or news of your offering enters the marketplace, you begin making first impressions of your brand, whether they're the ones you intend to make or not.

✔ By etching your brand onto a blank slate in the marketplace, you don't have to undertake the difficult task of erasing erroneous impressions and rewriting your brand image.

The chapters in Part IV begin with advice for keeping a tight rein on the way people encounter your brand, called your *brand experience,* followed by chapters full of tips for creating brand allegiance and loyalty, leveraging value, and, when the time's right, revitalizing your brand by giving it a partial or full makeover to fit market or business conditions, tastes, and trends.

The chapters in Part V focus on how to protect your brand by establishing and standing up for your legal rights. They also help you create usage rules that protect your brand from well-meaning but misguided attempts by staff members, freelancers, printers, sign makers, and others who are all too willing to help you "refine" or "tweak" your brand image, which usually leads directly to an erosion of the consistency you're fighting to maintain. And, should conditions rock your brand strength, Chapter 18 helps you take action through both preemptive actions and, if necessary, crisis communications.

Step 8: Realign your brand to keep it current

When you hear people talk about their (or your) need to rebrand, think long and hard before tuning into the conversation or signing them on as your branding consultants. In all but the most extreme cases, when people talk about rebranding what they really need is a brand update, also called a *brand refresh* or a *brand realignment.*

✔ **Rebranding** involves abandoning the essence of what a brand stands for and starting from scratch to build a brand new brand. Rebrands are rare and costly and should be approached only with the greatest of care. Chapter 16 can help you make the decision.

✔ **Brand realignments** begin with recognition that your brand is the essence of what you or your business stands for. You can't just change essence; you can't just change your brand. What you can (and should) be willing to change is how your brand is presented. Market trends and conditions change. Purchase behaviors change. Design looks or cultural aesthetics change. When they do, brand realignments refresh your brand by updating its look and message — but *not* by changing the essence of the brand or the brand promise.

Here are some examples of successful brand realignments and rebranding efforts:

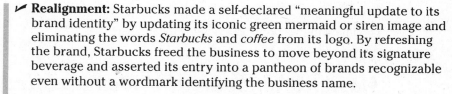

✔ **Realignment:** Starbucks made a self-declared "meaningful update to its brand identity" by updating its iconic green mermaid or siren image and eliminating the words *Starbucks* and *coffee* from its logo. By refreshing the brand, Starbucks freed the business to move beyond its signature beverage and asserted its entry into a pantheon of brands recognizable even without a wordmark identifying the business name.

✔ **Rebranding:** Responding to environmental concerns, British Petroleum changed its wordmark to the initials BP to signify *Beyond Petroleum*. It also unveiled a logo featuring a bursting flower, explaining that the changes reflect "the revolutionary quality of our business."

When and if your brand presentation gets out of step with its market, work hard to keep the brand esteem you've carefully built as you refresh and realign your brand presentation to match the market's evolving interests.

The branding process at a glance

If you're a visual person, Figure 2-2 lays out the branding process in a diagram that presents the eight steps involved to develop a brand from the essence of a vision to an understanding and preference that results in choice, marketplace esteem, and greater success.

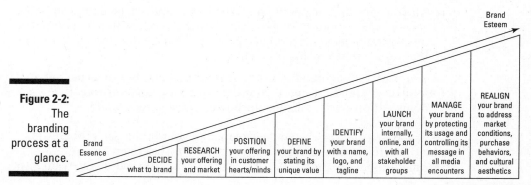

Figure 2-2: The branding process at a glance.

© Barbara Findlay Schenck

Brand Architecture 101

The verbal and visual relationship between your business brand and your product brand — also described as the relationship between your parent and subsidiary brands — is called *brand architecture*. Most brands follow one of two types of brand architecture:

- Master (or parent-dominant) brand architecture, resulting in a *branded house*
- Multiple (or product-driven) brand architecture, resulting in a *house of brands*

The following sections describe each category.

Master brand/parent-driven architecture: A branded house

Businesses that follow master-brand architecture introduce each product under the strong brand identity of the parent organization. FedEx is an example of a parent-dominant brand. Whether you choose FedEx Express, FedEx Ground, FedEx Office, or any other FedEx offering, the FedEx parent brand dominates.

Adopt a master brand strategy if any of the following situations apply to your business:

- **Your business has a modest marketing department and budget.** If your resources are limited, build one strong parent brand to represent your core business and then introduce each new offering under the umbrella of your business identity. By doing so, you eliminate the need to create and manage the identity of multiple self-standing brands, which requires an intense investment of time, people, discipline, and dollars.

- **All your products support your business brand image and promise.** For example, if your business brand issues a promise to deliver top-tier quality to the most discerning customers, you can't introduce a product that serves the bargain-basement market.

- **You want to heighten the value of your business brand as part of a long-term plan to prepare your business for growth or sale.** Parent-dominant products enhance the equity of the parent brand.

Unless you're a deep-pocketed megamarketer, your brand will probably fall under the category of master brand/parent-driven brand architecture. We feel so strongly about the practicality of creating a single brand that we dub it the

Rule of One. Heed the rule by building a single business brand. If you need to brand individual products or services, build parent-e subsidiary brands under your single, strong business brand.

Multiple brand/product-driven architecture: A house of brands

A multiple or product-driven brand architecture is used by companies that offer a range of products within a single or various market segments. For example, Tide and Pampers are among major brands owned by Procter & Gamble, yet P&G is virtually invisible as each brand is presented to consumers.

To consumers, subbrands are brands, period

A *subbrand*, also known as a parent-endorsed subsidiary brand, is a brand that's closely tied to a parent brand but that has its own identity and values, which distinguish it from the attributes of the top-level brand. If that definition confuses you, imagine what the concept of a subbrand does to the consumer!

Often a brand introduces a subbrand as a way to offer a lower-priced line without harming the esteem of the top-level brand; Four Points by Sheraton and United Airline's Ted are examples of subbrands.

Coauthor Bill Chiaravalle tells his clients to proceed cautiously with subbrands. For one thing, brands (whether top-level brands or subbrands) need esteem to succeed, and it's hard to build esteem out of an identity that begins as subordinate to something else. For another thing, subbrands confuse consumers and weaken brand management.

Bill goes so far as to say that there's really no such thing as a subbrand, at least not in the consumer's mind, which is where brands live. To the consumer, a brand is a brand, not a subset of a brand. As a brand manager, you should look at it the same way.

Bill's stance is reinforced by plenty of other brand thought leaders. James Burgin and Jon Ward, coauthors of *Branding For Profit* (Trump University Press), put it this way: "When it comes to brands, the consumer can only count to one." In today's overloaded marketing environment, the human mind takes in and remembers only so much, including one brand at a time.

For example, the consumer sees Diet Coke either as its own brand or as a flavor variety of the Coke brand, not as a subbrand of Coke. Likewise, consumers see Jetta and Passat either as their own brands or as flavors of VW.

The consumer keeps it simple, and as a brand manager, you should, too. When developing the branding strategy for a new product, rather than creating some second-cousin-once-removed relationship, ask "Does this product fit best as a flavor or variation of our established brand? Or does it have a unique enough set of attributes, or fit into a unique enough product category, that it should live under its own brand?" In any case, consider "subbrand" the wrong answer.

Multiple brand or product-driven brand architecture is the most costly branding strategy. You need to build a strong, stand-alone brand for each and every product, *plus* you need to build a corporate or business brand that carries its weight in the financial and corporate worlds while also serving as a magic carpet for each brand to ride in on until it establishes itself as a seemingly independent entity in the marketplace.

When to Rev Up Your Branding Efforts

The upcoming sections spotlight major times that businesses launch or work to strengthen their brands.

Launching a business

When you launch a business, branding needs to be an essential part of your business plan (if that term just threw you into a panic, run — don't walk — to get a copy of *Business Plans Kit For Dummies,* 4th Edition, by Steven Peterson, Peter E. Jaret, and Barbara Findlay Schenck [Wiley]).

As you blueprint how to brand your business, follow the first seven steps in the branding process outlined in the preceding section of this chapter and detailed throughout this book, taking special care with these steps:

✔ Spend extra time figuring out how you'll position your business within the competitive landscape you're entering (Chapter 5 helps).

✔ Finalize your name, brandmark or logo, stationery, website, sales material, and other brand presentation tools before launching your brand and introducing it to funding partners, prospective employees, business partners, and customers.

Everything you've ever heard about first impressions is doubly true when launching a brand. You don't get a second chance. Have your brand identity ready before you throw open the doors or launch your website.

Introducing a product

When introducing a product, begin by deciding whether it will enter the market under your business brand or as its own brand, with or without a visible link to your business brand. (For more on this decision, refer to the earlier section "Brand Architecture 101.")

If you decide to introduce your product as an altogether new brand, follow the seven steps in the branding process outlined in this chapter, giving special consideration to the Step 2 discovery phase that determines your product position, point of difference, and marketing approach.

If you decide to introduce your product as a new offering under your business brand, your product introduction can gain leverage from the established visibility and value of your brand in the marketplace. However, take a few steps to ensure that the product enhances your brand as much as your brand can enhance the product introduction. Consider these questions:

✔ Does the new product support and extend your established brand image?

✔ Have you done a competitive analysis to be sure that the product is distinctively different and better than existing products and that it will contribute to rather than weaken your brand image in your marketplace?

✔ Have you developed a product name and logo that fits with the image of your business brand?

✔ Have you created product advertising and sales materials that conform to your business brand image and graphic identity?

The Rule of One is worth repeating here: Unless your business has strong marketing expertise and a well-funded marketing budget, limit the number of brands you build to one and introduce all products under that strong, single brand. The price of getting too ambitious is marketplace confusion and erosion of brand understanding and trust in your marketplace.

Turning your gig, consulting, or freelancing into a business

Projections have it that by 2020, more than 40 percent of the American workforce will be freelancers, contract workers, or temporary employees. No question about it, if you're working independently, you're up against stiff and growing competition. But here's the good news: Research by the Freelancers Union finds that freelancers who think like entrepreneurs and turn their services and talents into branded businesses earn higher rates and work more hours.

Branding yourself and your solo business is so important that in this second edition of *Branding For Dummies* we've devoted a whole new chapter to the topic. If you're a one-person business, turn to Chapter 4 for help building your brand and presenting the brand story that can serve as the deciding factor in winning business and achieving success.

A brand is stronger than a giving request

Founded in 1980, Make-A-Wish grants the wish of a child with a life-threatening medical condition once every 38 minutes. "We have an audacious vision to grant the wish of every eligible child every year, and right now we're halfway there," reads a letter posted online by the organization's president. That clear, compelling organization-wide commitment is backed by an equally clear summary of the organization's brand story: "Wishes make life better for kids with life-threatening medical conditions. This simple, but powerful belief inspired the founding of Make-A-Wish and drives everything we do."

Make-A-Wish generates emotional connection, trust, belief, and support simply by delivering on its vision every day. In addition to sharing "wish impacts," it posts announcements of all wishes on its website and videos of wishes granted on its YouTube channel.

In 2013, when Make-A-Wish turned San Francisco into Gotham to grant the wish of a 5-year old San Francisco boy who wanted to be Batkid for a day, the response was met with an uprising of interest, volunteerism, global media coverage, a 20,000 person crowd, and President Obama' first-ever Vine posted on Twitter. Also part of the spontaneous response: Philanthropic contributions that covered all city costs and a deluge of individual donations — in spite of the fact that no giving request was ever issued.

Announcing or fundraising for a nonprofit

Successful nonprofit efforts and fundraising campaigns operate under the auspices of well-known, well-regarded, well-branded organizations. Jim Collins, author of the bestselling management book *Good to Great* (HarperBusiness), actually names brand reputation the key link in social sectors, where potential supporters need to "believe not only in your mission, but in your capacity to deliver on that mission."

In a sentence, nonprofits need strong brands.

Before launching a fundraising campaign, establish credibility and trust by building a brand image that prospective donors can trust and believe in. Follow all the steps in the branding process detailed in this chapter, taking extra effort to build a strong, emotional story that builds belief in the cause you're seeking to fund and confidence among supporters that you will leverage donated dollars into good works.

Taking a business public

Brand first. Go public second. Don't even consider launching an *initial public offering*, or IPO, until you have a well-established and well-regarded brand. Investors buy into businesses they trust to be innovative, successful, and capable of rising to even higher levels of growth and profitability, and brand strength factors heavily into the decision.

For proof that the sequence of branding before going public works, look no farther than the IPOs of Facebook and Twitter. Both built brands so strong that when shares were made available investors scrambled to buy, even though Facebook profits had dipped and Twitter profits had yet to materialize.

Opening markets or going global

Maybe you're expanding into an adjacent regional market. Maybe you want to sell in international markets. Or perhaps you're establishing a global business with operating presences in a range of countries. If your brand is going to travel, it had better be up to the task. Before your company opens markets or crosses borders, take these steps:

- **Create or realign your brand to fit the realities of the cultures it will enter.** Be sure that your name translates favorably, that the colors and shapes in your logo create positive impressions in the new environment, and that your brand messages are consistent with the culture of your new market. (Chapter 16 can help you make these adjustments to your brand.)

- **Plan, budget for, and launch a brand introduction in each country or market area.** Winning market share in a new market is a big task that begins with gaining name familiarity and belief in your business. Make it your aim to quickly achieve the reputation of a trusted business with whom those in your new market want to work. (Chapter 9 offers advice for accomplishing this step.)

Raising capital

Venture capitalists look to invest in companies with strong leadership, strong business concepts, and strong positions in growing market arenas.

Don't even think of approaching venture capitalists until you have

- Clearly defined and differentiated technology and products

- A business model capable of delivering predictable streams of revenue

- A management team with proven capability that's relevant to the size and kind of businesses you're trying to fund

- A distinctive brand story and the ability to personally represent your brand by making an impeccable first impression

Use your business plan — the prerequisite to every venture-capital request — to present your business and explain your brand. But also be prepared to make your personal presentation the embodiment of your brand personality. The old phrase *walk the talk* goes hand-in-hand with the advice to *be your brand* to communicate and gain trust in your brand story.

Merging with another business

There's really no such thing as a brand merger. Combining Brand A with Brand B doesn't result in Brand A + B. It either results in a retooled version of Brand A, a retooled version of Brand B, or an all-new Brand C.

Entering a merger is entering a politically sensitive area. As part of the merger negotiations, address the following questions:

- ✓ Is the merger actually a takeover? If so, one culture and one brand will be subsumed by the other.

- ✓ Is the reason for the merger to acquire brand strength or to acquire physical attributes? If it's to acquire brand strength, then the stronger of the two brands is the one that must prevail.

- ✓ Can you afford the loss of established brand equity if you decide to create an altogether new brand as a result of the merger?

Depending on your answers to these questions, move into branding action by either revising and reintroducing the surviving brand (turn to Chapter 16 for steps to follow) or starting from scratch to build an altogether new brand, following every step described in this book. Either way, dedicate time, effort, and funding to gain understanding and buy-in from the staffs and stakeholders of both organizations before taking the retooled or new brand public.

Chapter 3

Gearing Up to Brand or Build a Better Brand

In This Chapter

▶ Determining what you want your brand to accomplish

▶ Evaluating your existing brand identity and assets

▶ Incorporating branding into your business plan

▶ Assembling and leading your branding team

*B*rands are indelible. When they're seared into customers' minds, they're long lasting and durable. That's why this chapter is so important. It walks you through the steps of figuring out what you want your branding program to accomplish, what kind of brand identity you're seeking, and what reaching the branding success you seek will take.

If you don't have a brand — if you're starting a business or launching a new product — this chapter can help you plan your brand from scratch so you get your brand identity, image, and strategy spot-on from the get-go.

If you already have a brand — if people already know your name and have impressions about what you stand for — use the information in this chapter as you assess whether your current brand image accurately reflects who you are and adequately appeals to marketplace tastes and trends. If not, you have two choices: You can bring your brand into alignment, following all the advice in Chapter 16. Or, you can take what we call a *branding mulligan* and work to rebrand your business — making the rare and drastic decision to throw out all the vestiges and value of your current brand and starting from scratch to build a new brand following every step in this book.

You Are Here: Marking Your Brand-Development Starting Point

Whether you're launching a new brand or refining an existing brand, you have to start by figuring out what people think when they hear your name or think about the industry or business arena you're entering. When you're clear about how people currently perceive your identity, you have the information necessary to understand the brand assets you have to build upon, the misperceptions you want to overcome, and the brand identity, in your dreams, you want to achieve.

Getting real about your brand identity

The best starting point for brand development is a true and candid look at what people currently think of your brand and offerings in the marketplace.

If you're starting a business and don't yet have a brand to analyze, instead assess the image of the business arena you're entering. For instance, if you're starting a children's museum, think about the mental images people have about museums in general and children's museums in particular. When you know the preconceived notions you're dealing with, you're in a good position to develop a strategy that leads to a brand image that fills a unique position (there's way more on positioning in Chapter 5) and reflects the distinct attributes and differentiating aspects of the brand you're establishing.

The point of your brand assessment is to determine answers to the following questions:

- ✔ What do people like or dislike about you, your business, or your business arena?

- ✔ What do they trust or distrust?

- ✔ Who do they think you are and what do they think you do?

- ✔ Why do they choose you or your offering?

- ✔ How do they think you compare with your competitors?

- ✔ How do they think you affect their lives for better or worse? Do they find your offering relevant and a good fit with their lives and needs?

To arrive at your answers, first conduct a self-assessment and then reach out to learn the opinions of others.

Self-assessing your brand image

Don't rely solely on your own judgments or those of your top management team as you aim to get a clear idea of your brand image. Include the opinions of those who work on the front line of your business and the people who answer incoming calls, take product orders, field complaints, and fix service problems. Ask the following questions:

- ✔ How would you quickly describe your brand as the elevator doors are closing? If you have only seconds, what would you say you do, and what makes you different and better?

- ✔ What brand promise do you always try to keep?

- ✔ What five key messages can you boldly declare about your brand?

- ✔ Who are your customers and what do they care about?

- ✔ Who are your top competitors and what are their distinct differences from you and your offerings? What one thing makes you better?

- ✔ What five words best describe your brand? For example, *cool, innovative, irreverent, hip, serious, friendly, elegant, fast, youthful, sophisticated, gourmet;* the list goes on and on.

- ✔ Which major brands are closest to your brand style? Assemble logos of international, national, regional, and local brands in your category. Let people choose which they think are closest to your brand personality and promise.

- ✔ If your brand were a car, what would it be and why?

- ✔ If your brand were a celebrity, who would it be and why?

- ✔ What phrase tells the people you serve who you are and what you stand for? Chapter 7 includes information on developing taglines, but for now just dive in and quickly take a crack at summarizing the benefits of your brand in a few words.

- ✔ If you absolutely had to be the person who comes up with a symbol to represent your brand, what would that symbol look like? Quickly sketch an idea for your logo.

Seeing your brand through the eyes of others

Start by opening a search engine and entering your name and the name of your business. See what others see when they look you up, including whether or not you dominate the first screen of results and whether links lead to information consistent with the image you want to project. The section on ego-surfing in Chapter 10 gives tips to follow.

Then talk with customers or prospective customers. If your customer base is large or geographically far-flung, pose the questions through surveys. Turn to Chapter 5 for advice on how to conduct customer research and when to call in professional assistance.

The following questions help you collect information without making you or those you're interviewing feel self-conscious about their answers. If you're developing a personal brand, adjust the questions to address your personal qualities:

- ✔ In a sentence, how would you describe our business? What simple idea captures the essence of what we stand for?

- ✔ How would you describe our products or services?

- ✔ What one reason, above all others, causes you and others to buy from our business?

- ✔ When you consider buying from our business, what three other companies or brands do you also consider?

- ✔ What one reason, above all others, do you think causes people to buy from one of our competitors?

- ✔ Would you say there is high or low awareness of our brand in the marketplace?

- ✔ Do you see clear and distinct differences between our offerings and those of our competitors? If so, what are a few of the distinct differences that make our offerings unique or more desirable?

- ✔ If you were to compare our brand to a car, what car would it be and why? What car would you associate with each of our three top competitors?

- ✔ If you were to compare our brand to a celebrity, who would it be and why? Who would you associate with each of our three top competitors?

Compare how your brand is perceived within and outside your organization. By understanding where there are perception gaps, you'll have the information you need to develop a branding program that aligns your desired brand image with the image in your marketplace and consumer minds.

Knowing and protecting brand assets

Before planning adjustments to your brand image, get clear about what contributes to the value of the brand you currently own.

For a well-known example, consider the brand assets of Coca-Cola: the red packaging, the Coca-Cola script, the bottle shape, the name, the formula. Coca-Cola can evolve any one of those brand assets to fit emerging cultural attitudes and tastes, and so long as consumers feel that the brand assets they love remain intact, the changes only increase brand value by enhancing relevance to changing marketplace tastes and trends. Witness how the name Coca-Cola became Coke in marketing campaigns.

What brands can't do, without diminishing value, is to take beloved assets away. Were you around when Coke triggered consumer backlash by daring to fiddle with its formula? Or do you remember when Gap unveiled a "sexy and cool" new logo that was so reviled on social media that the design was pulled within a week of its preview?

Use the worksheet in Figure 3-1 as you assess the strength of each of your brand assets, based on your own opinions and on the opinions you collect from those in your company and customer base. Chapter 16 has advice for turning to professional researchers for help if you're realigning a widely known brand that will have significant range and value in the future.

BRAND ASSET ANALYSIS WORKSHEET

Assess the strength of your brand assets by assigning a rating of 1–5 (with 1 indicating poor value and 5 indicating outstanding value) in each of the following areas. Then determine whether your brand strength would be reduced if the brand asset were altered.

Brand asset	Is it well-known?	Is it well regarded?	Is it well managed?	Would your brand strength be reduced if this asset were changed or eliminated? Yes	No
Your brand name				☐	☐
Identifying elements					
Logo				☐	☐
Logotype/script				☐	☐
Slogan/tagline				☐	☐
Color scheme				☐	☐
Packaging				☐	☐
Your core message				☐	☐
Your dominance in a key market niche				☐	☐
Your relationship with key customer groups				☐	☐
Other				☐	☐
Other				☐	☐

Figure 3-1: Assess the current strengths of your brand assets and prioritize which assets to develop part of your branding strategy.

© Barbara Findlay Schenck

After you decide which elements of your brand have significant value, you'll know which assets that you should protect or evolve and which assets have little recognition or regard and can go by the wayside with little or no loss of brand strength or value.

In your dreams! Defining what you want out of branding

WARNING!

Branding isn't a game of leapfrog. You can't ask people to jump past what they currently believe and immediately land on a new perception about what you stand for. You have to nudge their beliefs in a new direction by building on the images they currently hold and helping them to adopt new beliefs about you and your offering.

Use the chart in Figure 3-2 to assess how well your brand currently fares in each major brand capability: Awareness, emotional connection, distinction, credibility and trust, and purchase motivation. Use the right-hand column to rank which capabilities most need strengthening in order to reach your near-term branding goals. For example, if you're launching a new brand, developing awareness will be a top priority. Your responses will help you determine the priority you should place on revitalizing or enhancing perceptions of each attribute in your branding strategy.

Prioritizing Your Branding Goals

To build a brand or fine-tune the brand you have, you first need to know where you want to arrive. Which of the following brand functions best describe what you aim to achieve through branding?

- ✔ Build awareness
- ✔ Create an emotional connection
- ✔ Convey distinguishing attributes
- ✔ Gain credibility and trust
- ✔ Achieve buyer preference

Some brand builders, especially those representing big, hugely funded companies or top-tier celebrities, aim above all else to establish and entrench top-of-mind awareness to ensure that the spotlight in their category shines brightly and fully in their brand's direction. Others want to forge or deepen emotional connections with customers, to differentiate their products from competing offers, or to develop the kind of preference and motivation that prompts purchase decisions and makes cash registers ring. Some brand builders want their brands to do all of the above.

BRAND STRENGTHS, WEAKNESSES, AND PRIORITIES WORKSHEET					
FUNCTION	✔ Your brand's strength in this area				PRIORITY for enhancement to meet branding goals
	Poor	Fair	Good	Excellent	
Awareness How well-known or noticed is your brand in its market?					Low Medium High
Emotional Connection How deeply and emotionally do people relate to your brand?					Low Medium High
Distinction How well do people understand the attributes or promises that set your brand apart from competitors?					Low Medium High
Credibility and Trust How well do people believe and trust in you and your promises? How good is your reputation?					Low Medium High
Purchase Motivation How well does your brand inspire preference and pave the way for a purchase decision?					Low Medium High

© Barbara Findlay Schenck

Figure 3-2: Assess how your brand is currently perceived and to prioritize which brand functions need to be strengthened to meet your branding goals.

TIP

Use the worksheet in Figure 3-2 as you set your branding goals. It lists the five key brand functions, which we describe further in the upcoming sections, and provides space to rate your brand's strength in each area before prioritizing the functions you want to enhance through your branding strategy.

Build awareness

Brands large and small put awareness building at the top of the branding to-do list for these reasons:

✔ **Awareness leads to marketplace dominance.** The most powerful brands owned by the biggest companies and celebrities hold their competitive positions based largely on how widely they're known and noticed. That's why marketers with the biggest brand names constantly reinforce their images through advertising, promotions, publicity, and ever-expanding social-media followings. They know that in order to maintain market dominance, they must continuously broaden brand awareness and notice.

✔ **Awareness makes selling easier.** Marketers who aren't branded with names like Nike or Beyoncé still need to build awareness, not to become the best-known brands in their marketing worlds but to build sales, pure and simple. Without brand awareness, you spend the lion's share of every ad, presentation, or sales call introducing your business and explaining why it's better than the alternatives. With established brand awareness, you can spend that time advancing information that moves the customer to a purchase decision.

Brand awareness acts like a proxy for your business. When you can't be somewhere in person, brand awareness stands in your stead, winning attention and conveying your core message and promise on your behalf.

Create an emotional connection

Not all brands rely on emotional connections. Some brands succeed based on their high levels of credibility or on their abilities to distinguish themselves based on unique benefits that customers can't get from competing companies. They win based on factual comparisons. They appeal to what people think; they involve decisions of the mind. Brands that rely on emotional connections appeal to what people feel; they involve decisions of the heart.

Consider the last time you bought dish soap. You looked at the array of bottles, glanced at the prices, saw that a soap brand you'd heard of was competitively priced, and made your selection. Your decision was a rational one. You weren't looking for a happy marriage between you and the dish soap — you just wanted to know you were choosing a good product for a decent price. Emotions didn't come into play. On the other hand, think of what you went through the last time you bought a car; gave to a charity; helped your son or daughter select a university to attend; or decided on a new home, or even expensive sunglasses. Suddenly, your emotions came into play. In addition to function, you weighed whether or not your choice would *feel* good — whether it would instill confidence, pride, or even a coolness factor. Your emotions steered you toward your choice more than your mind did.

In setting your branding strategy, make emotional connection a top objective if any of the following apply:

✔ Your product is selected for the sense of satisfaction or security it delivers, the self-image it enhances, or the experience it provides — as much or more than for its factual attributes.

✔ Your product involves a major financial investment or contributes to the customer's ego or lifestyle. Not all high-priced items involve emotional connection (root canal, anyone?) but many do, including those that affect how buyers feel about themselves and how they appear to others.

✔ Customer loyalty is essential to your success. Face it, people stick with brands they love — and love, above all others, is a strong emotion.

Differentiate your product

If you're not 100 percent sure of how you stand apart from the competitive pack — or if your customers don't appear to find the distinction clear, meaningful, or motivating — then product differentiation needs to move up on the list of what you want to accomplish through your branding strategy.

Would you date your brand?

Branding and online dating follow the same path to success: Make a head-turning impression, stand out, establish connection, and then — as quickly as possible — issue invitations that move budding relationships out of the competitive environment and toward lasting commitments and long-term loyalty. But the cardinal rule, in the words of OKCupid co-founder Christian Rudder, is to be "really, really hot" because you're going to be up against what Dan Slater, author of *Love in the Time of Algorithms* (Penguin), calls *choice overwhelm.*

In branding or dating, you have to seize attention and win interest before gaining preference, selection, and, finally, a positive decision. You have to get people to buy in before they'll buy.

David Ryan Polgar, author of the e-book *Wisdom in the Age of Twitter,* says that brand builders would benefit from the playful exercise of creating an online dating profile: What are your brand's hobbies? What music does it like? What does it do on weekends? Who does it aim to attract?

Be honest and accurate about how you present who you are and what you do, because although half of all online dating profiles contain lies, exaggerations, or airbrushed photos, your brand has to be authentic and capable of living up to its promises through every encounter — from first infatuation through forever-after. "Once people fall in love," Polgar says, "the Velcro effect lasts even after initial attractions fade. Brand love can withstand a few errors. Especially if those errors don't shatter the core beliefs people have and hold dear."

Product differentiation is particularly important if you're facing any of these marketing challenges:

- ✔ Customers fail to see your offering as unique and distinctly beneficial.

- ✔ Your market environment is crowded with similar offerings.

- ✔ To win sales in your competitive environment, you frequently revert to a reliance on low pricing or discounting strategies rather than high value.

Sometimes, simply fine-tuning your brand promise and marketing message is enough to win differentiation in the customer's mind. (Chapter 6 is full of information on these topics.) More often, though, you need to undertake at least some level of product or service modification to add meaningful and differentiating attributes and benefits. Additionally, you many need to update how your product is packaged and presented to magnify important distinctions that will reel customers in at the point of purchase. (If repackaging is in the cards, turn to Chapter 12 for information.)

Create credibility and trust

Brands essentially result from promises made and consistently kept. If your brand fails to win on these two counts — if it fails to appear credible or trustworthy — it fails altogether.

All brand builders need to develop and maintain credibility and trust, but developing or enhancing trust needs to be a top priority if you're introducing a new business or product, if you're selling a service (because services are bought entirely based on trust), if you're selling online (where familiar and trusted brands win out over all others), or if you're facing a credibility crisis because you've failed to deliver on brand promises or customer expectations.

To rate your brand's credibility and trust levels, ask yourself these questions:

- ✔ Do people believe we're credible and trustworthy?
- ✔ Do we appear credible and trustworthy?
- ✔ What promise do we make to customers, and do we keep that promise without fail?
- ✔ What guarantee or assurance do we extend?
- ✔ What additional promises can we make to build higher levels of trust?

Your answers help you determine the emphasis you need to put on heightening credibility and trust in your branding strategy.

Achieve preference and motivate selection

Brands are like great advance teams that establish interest, appeal, confidence, preference, and purchase motivation in a customer's mind before you or your product ever enters the arena.

Using a dating analogy (see the sidebar "Would you date your brand?"), think back to the social scene of your high school days. Which would you have preferred: a date with a person whose name you knew and regarded highly, to whom you were attracted, and with whom you felt trust and a sense of pride in the potential association; or a blind date who didn't even come with an assurance from a good friend? The answer's a no-brainer.

Faced with a selection, you and nearly everyone else opt for the safe choice. And the safe choice is the one you've heard of (awareness), the one that makes you feel good (emotional connection), the one with uniquely positive attributes (distinction), and the one you can rely on (credibility and trust).

Together, the brand functions combine to create preference and to motivate selection and purchase, although all don't play equally in all branding strategies. If you're launching a brand, your initial emphasis will probably focus on developing awareness and differentiating your offering. If you're refining or realigning an existing brand, you probably have established strength in at least some of the branding functions. Therefore your future branding strategy will direct your efforts toward gaining strength in areas of weakness. The worksheet in Figure 3-2 helps you prioritize your efforts.

Crunching Numbers: Budgeting Realities

Ask homebuilders how much it costs to build a home and, no surprise, they'll tell you the cost depends on the home being built. The same is true when the question is, "How much does it cost to build a brand?" The variables involved in the cost of brand building include

- ✔ **The amount of your own time and expertise you can commit:** Especially if your brand is local or your business is small, you can probably research your current brand image, define your desired brand image, determine the value of your brand assets, set goals, and oversee development for your brand — all without professional help.

- ✔ **How far your brand will travel:** If your brand will represent you in distant markets when you're personally nowhere to be found, it will almost certainly require you to make a more sizeable investment in branding than that required by a very small business with a small and geographically limited clientele.

✔ **The nature of your competition:** If you intend to compete with well-known and superbly developed brands, be prepared to invest in a brand that's up to the task in terms of how it looks, how well it's known, and how highly it's regarded. Making it in the major league requires major-league talent. Unless you're an accomplished designer, for example, a do-it-yourself logo is out of the question.

As you assemble your budget, flip to Chapter 1 for a look at the range of costs involved in each phase of the brand development process. Then earmark allocations for each of the following brand-development phases:

1. **Brand strategy and positioning**

   This phase involves market research, brand-identity research, and development of the positioning and branding strategies you'll follow to reach the branding success you seek. (If you plan to do a good portion of this work yourself, check out Chapters 5 and 6.)

2. **Creating brand identity elements**

   Professionals are worth their weight in gold when it comes to creating, selecting, and protecting your name; designing your logo; devising your tagline; and developing the core marketing message and materials that will carry your brand into the marketplace.

If you don't have the heaviest hammer . . .

The old saying marketing pros use when dealing with small-budget clients is, "If you don't have the heaviest hammer, use the sharpest nail." Here's how that same logic relates to branding: If you don't have the biggest budget (or anything even close to a big budget), develop the most sharply targeted branding program. Don't try to reach people outside your target market (Chapter 5 has a worksheet that will help you define your target market), and don't confuse those in your target market with multiple messages or a blurry brand identity. Follow this advice:

✔ See that every communication — online or offline, in person or through media — carries your brand identity without variation so that you etch a single, crystal-clear brand image.

✔ Put identical versions of your name and logo on absolutely everything that represents your brand in the marketplace — online and offline.

✔ Add a tagline or slogan (see Chapter 8 for help) if your name doesn't adequately convey who you are, what you do, and why you're great.

Building a brand doesn't have to cost a fortune, but building a brand that doesn't cost a fortune *does* require target marketing and utmost consistency.

If you're developing a name and logo for a business that faces only moderate competition in a local market area, plan on a moderate investment. On the other hand, if you're dreaming up a name and logo that will travel online and over state and international borders to a marketplace of hundreds of thousands or even more, invest more heavily in an identity that will deliver rewards for years to come.

3. **Implementation of your brand strategy**

   When you've set your brand strategy and established your brand identity, implementing your branding program becomes part of your existing marketing program — and your existing marketing budget. Branding and marketing aren't separate in terms of message *or* money. Your brand strategy becomes the foundation for your marketing strategy, just as it becomes the basis of your business plan (see the next section).

Committing to the Branding Process

Think of entering the branding process as entering a marriage. You have to agree that you're in it for the long haul. You have to start with a unique and desirable identity, establish connection, develop trust, cultivate positive interaction, and propose an offer worth accepting. Then you have to deepen the mutual commitment, consistently stay true, and forever live up to what you promised — every single day and through every experience and encounter.

No wonder the result of successful branding is called *brand love*. Google the term and you'll get hundreds of thousands of results, many featuring this two-word first step: Know yourself.

Brands that inspire love start by knowing their missions and visions, and build their brands and all their brand actions around the core values of their companies.

Aligning your mission, vision, and brand identity

Your brand is a reflection of your own (if you're building a personal brand) or your company's mission and vision. So you'd think that identifying your brand and starting the branding process would be piece of cake. But it rarely is. Perhaps you've never crafted your mission and vision statements. Oops. Or, if you have, the statements may no longer reflect what you want to achieve and stand for. If either of these scenarios sound sounds familiar, Chapter 6 offers step-by-step guidance for putting your statements into words.

But first, because the terms *mission, vision,* and *brand identity* confuse even the pros, here are some definitions:

- ✔ **Your mission** is your broad purpose and the positive effect you or your business will have on others.

- ✔ **Your vision** is your long-term aspiration. It's what you want to achieve through your success.

- ✔ **Your brand identity** is a tangible expression that reflects and represents both your mission and your vision.

Here's a quick way to put the three in context: Your mission is the heart of your brand, your vision is the eyes, and your brand identity is the face. Chapter 6 helps you put all three into words.

Including branding in your business plan

Whether you're planning for job-search success, success of a one-person business, or the launch or growth of a small-to-huge business, your brand plays a starring role. It reflects your mission, vision, and values. It impacts your product development plans. It guides your market segmentation, customer targeting, and competitive-strategy decisions. It determines what you do and say and how you present yourself in the marketplace. It keeps you true to your business promise.

That's why branding needs to be a key consideration throughout your business plan. (Okay, moment of truth: Do you have a business plan? If not, here's a lineup of what you need to cover and a recommendation to pick up *Business Plans Kit For Dummies,* 4th edition [Wiley]).

Include your brand statement and branding strategy in each of the following business plan components:

- ✔ **Your business overview,** which includes your mission, vision, values, key products and services, and major goals

- ✔ **Your business environment,** which includes an overview of your business arena or industry, customer profile, competitive analysis, and current image and awareness levels

- ✔ **Your business description,** which details attributes of the products and services you offer, strengths of your business or personal capabilities, and major changes you aim to achieve

- ✔ **Your business strategy,** which includes your business model (translation: how you'll make money), goals, marketing plan, and growth strategies

When you build your business, essentially you're building your brand, and vice versa. The two are interdependent and mutually beneficial.

Who's on First? Suiting Up Your Branding Team

Unless you're building a personal brand, to paraphrase an old coaching adage, there's no "I" in the branding team. Everyone in your organization plays an important role because your brand is reinforced or weakened every single time people come in contact with any facet of your organization.

The following tips help you when putting together a cohesive branding team:

- ✔ **Start by gaining buy-in from owners and leaders.** Without participation and leadership from those in a position to make strategic business decisions, a brand is in danger of a credibility train wreck.

- ✔ **Involve and enlist the support of top-level executives.** A brand needs to be reinforced through every business decision. For that reason, it needs to have the interest and engagement of those who call the shots to keep the company true to its brand premise and promise.

- ✔ **Gain organization-wide brand awareness and commitment.** Every single person who has any form of customer contact — whether before, during, or after the purchase — is in a position to strengthen or weaken brand trust and belief in your brand promise. Gain all-important commitment by educating everyone from the CEO to part-time or freelance contractors about your brand strategy, promise, identity, and presentation guidelines. Turn them into brand champions (use Chapter 13 as your playbook) and ensure that they know the rules for presenting your brand by following the advice for managing your logo in Chapter 8 and staying true to your brand promise in Chapter 14.

As you set out to create or revamp your brand, include representatives from all areas of your organization. Then, at key milestones along the way, involve your entire team in updates and to share the rewards of a brand well built. Commit the time and effort it takes to put everyone on the same branding page — because what they don't know *can* hurt you.

Chapter 4

Powering Up Your Personal and One-Person Business Brands

In This Chapter

▶ Tilting the odds for success in your favor by developing a personal brand

▶ Getting an off-target personal brand image back on track

▶ Winning business and revenue by branding your one-person business

Developing brands for yourself and your services involves all the steps listed in Chapter 2 and described in every chapter that follows. But personal and one-person business brands get their own chapter in this edition of *Branding For Dummies* for two reasons. First, they're the brands that most people tend to put off, and that's a big mistake we want you to avoid. And secondly, with more people than ever checking you out online and within their business and social circles before ever meeting you or considering your offerings, a well-projected brand has never had a bigger impact on personal success. Just look at the numbers:

✔ Google handles more than a billion name searches daily.

✔ Nine of ten job recruiters use social networks to find candidates, and three of four check search results and social-media profiles when making hiring decisions.

✔ Ninety percent of Internet users say online reviews impact their purchase decisions.

✔ Nearly everyone now gathers information online or through word-of-mouth when pursuing personal or business relationships.

Whether you're building a reputation for your one-person business, angling for a promotion, vying for office, or working to make it onto the speaker circuit or the A-team of your business or social world, the impressions you make and the personal reputation you develop profoundly affect your ability to succeed. Personal branding tilts the odds greatly in your favor.

Taking Ownership of Your Personal Brand

The concept of building personal brands around individual assets took hold in the late 1990s, when individuals increasingly wanted to stand out as talented free agents with desirable personal qualities and positive images that could travel with them as they migrated from one job opportunity to another. Rather than marketing themselves as representatives of an employer, as in decades past, they began to build what management leader Tom Peters termed "The Brand Called You."

Today, online searches or word-of-mouth comments etch impressions before individuals ever introduce themselves in person, so there's no question as to whether or not you need a personal brand. You already *have* a personal brand: It's whatever other people see, hear, and believe about you. If they think you're always late, that's part of your brand. If they can't find anything about you in online searches, their impression is that you aren't a key player. If someone they trust says you do better work than anyone else in your field, your brand stands for outstanding quality.

How's your connectivity quotient?

Think about how you react to a LinkedIn connection invitation. If you know and think well of the person, you probably accept with no second thoughts or, if the person is someone you hold in high regard, you probably accept with pride in the association.

If you've never heard of or barely know the person, and especially if the invitation wasn't customized to make a positive impression, you probably hesitate. Perhaps you scan the person's profile looking to see if you share interests or connections, noting accomplishments and recommendations, and following links to help you form opinions before finally accepting or ignoring the invitation.

Your response to the invitation is based on what you believe about the other person's reputation and possible impact on your life and goals. Your connection decision is the result of the other person's success or failure at developing a positive personal brand image in your mind.

But enough about other people, let's talk about you: What do people think when they see or hear you or your name? What do they learn if they ask around or search for your name online? How do they perceive your brand image? The answer impacts your personal success and, if you have a business, the success of your business as well. Just as product and service brands are built on a reputation based on experience, so your personal brand is a reputation built on how others consistently experience you.

Personal branding is how you manage your reputation and interactions to develop positive impressions in the minds of those you want to influence. Through personal branding, you positively affect how people react to you, how they fit you into their hierarchy of interests and needs, and how they view you as an asset, a leader, a star in your field.

This chapter helps you buy into the fact that your personal brand is your very most important brand because it affects your success in every aspect of your life. For even more advice, pick up Susan Chritton's book, *Personal Branding For Dummies* (Wiley).

Benefits of a strong personal brand

The obvious benefit of a strong personal brand is the power of a positive, highly regarded reputation that precedes and paves the way for you whether you're submitting a resume, asking for a date, making a sales call, leading a negotiation, offering a book for sale, contending for a plum keynote speech role, or prevailing in any other encounter.

The less-apparent benefit of personal branding is the sense of self-direction it instills. Age-old wisdom has it that the oracle of Delphi told Socrates and all ancient Greeks that the most important life task is to "know thyself." When you know your personal brand, you gain laser focus about who you are, how you want to present yourself, and and how you aim to succeed.

Personal branding as a marketplace force

Through personal branding, you help others to know and trust the following information about how you factor into the marketplace:

- **Who you are and what you stand for,** eliminating the need for time-consuming introductions before each interaction.

- **Your expertise and credibility,** leading to increased interest in what you have to say. Think about how you scan your news feeds and status updates, stopping when you see names or photos of those you trust to have meaningful information to share, or how you respond more favorably to an introduction that includes a recommendation or referral from a trusted associate or mention of impressive credentials or mutual associations.

- **Your unique benefits and value,** leading to competitive advantage, higher interest and demand, preference, selection, and higher pricing.

- **What you do best** and whether what you offer fits with what they seek and need, speeding decisions and sparing you both from an inappropriate fit.

Personal branding as an internal force

In addition to helping others know you, personal branding helps you know yourself. Through branding, you determine

- ✔ **What you're best at** and what unique attribute — what big thing — you want to be known for. (See the sidebar "Personal branding starts with a wish.")

- ✔ **The personal brand image you're working to etch;** what you want others to believe and trust when they encounter you or your name.

- ✔ **The roadmap you're following** to reach your goals.

- ✔ **How you want to present yourself,** whether in person, in writing, on social media, in business, or in social settings.

- ✔ **Self-confidence** in your strengths, your goals, your target audience, and the unique personality, expertise, and message you want to consistently cultivate and convey.

Personal branding keeps you on track. It helps you define your assets, your audience, and your objectives. From there, you can relax and present your authentic self with consistency. Awareness, trust, credibility, value, consumer preference, purchase decisions and pricing, and even invaluable buzz and word-of-mouth support will follow.

What's more, strong personal brands deliver the valuable benefit of consumer lenience. On the off chance you slip up with an errant tweet, a social *faux pas,* or some other misstep that could irreparably harm someone else, the great reputation and positive image others hold for you — thanks to personal branding — improves your ability to make amends and move on with strength.

Personal branding starts with a wish

Jimmy Fallon set his sights early: He wanted to be on *Saturday Night Live.* "That was my goal since I was probably 14 or 15," he told host Terry Gross during an interview on NPR's *Fresh Air.* "If I ever blew out candles on a cake or wished upon a falling star or threw a coin into a well, I'd say, 'I wanna be on *Saturday Night Live.*'"

And he knew the route he intended to follow to his goal: "Celebrity impressions. That was my big thing. I wanted to be the next Dana Carvey."

What's your "big thing"? Who do you want to be? Where do you want to go? Your answers become GPS coordinates on your road from here to there, whether your aim is the corner office, a stronger voice in your family, your city's A-list, neon-lights stardom, political office, or making a difference in your industry or community. Personal branding helps you plot your route.

Launching the personal-branding process

Chapter 6 helps all brand builders define the qualities, character, promise, core message, and essence of their brands. Every step of that chapter is essential to your personal branding success as well. But personal brands benefit from the following additional considerations.

Mapping your starting point

Creating a personal brand begins with productive navel-gazing: What do you want people to believe and trust about you? What's your idea of success? What will it take to get your personal brand image from where it is to where you want to be? As part of your self-searching, take these steps:

1. **Choose an idol.** Follow what internationally acclaimed personal branding coach Liz Goodgold, author of *Red Fire Branding* and *DUH! Marketing*, calls the "cheater route" by picking a celebrity you'd like to emulate. "I wanted to be the Suze Orman of branding," she says. Jimmy Fallon wanted to be the next Dana Carvey. Who do you want to be — or be like — and why?

2. **Assess your core competencies.** After you name your role model, list the attributes you want to replicate, indicating which strengths you have in the bag and which you'll need to acquire. Personal brands reflect who you *are*; not who you want to be. To get where you want your image to go, you need to become the person you want people to believe you are.

3. **Solicit input.** List five words you'd like associated with your image and then determine how well those align with what people currently believe about you. Look through recent compliments, testimonials, endorsements, and recommendations, pulling out words others use when describing your strengths. If you work for a firm that does formal reviews, look through recent evaluations and pull out the positive descriptors. Then ask people you know and work with to quickly name the first five words that come to mind when they think of you. Find the words that others use frequently. Whether they're the words you want to be known for or not, they represent what people believe about you.

If the words people use when describing you are in line with those you want associated with your image, pat yourself on the back; your personal branding effort is off to a good start. If not, your first goal is to redirect your brand image from where it is to where you want it to be.

Redirecting an off-target personal brand image

If those you need to influence hold erroneous or outdated beliefs about you, it's your job to help them connect the dots between what they currently believe and what you want them to think and trust. You can't expect them to make a leap of faith on your behalf.

Al Franken connected the dots as he migrated from comedian to senator by explaining to voters that politics and comedy have a lot in common: both help people and make lives better. On a local level, we know a surgeon who left the operating room to run for state office, leveraging his ability to diagnose, prepare, perform, and lead medical interventions into proof of his readiness to take on and treat the acute issues facing government budgets and programs.

Whether you're orchestrating a career U-turn, breaking into a new arena, or overcoming current misperceptions, realize that people aren't going to simply abandon their beliefs about you. You have to build a bridge to transport their opinions from what they thought to what you want them to believe.

Differentiating yourself from the crowd

Competition for every job opening, freelance assignment, or plum opportunity is fierce. What makes you stand out?

✔ **What do and don't you do?** No one expects you to excel at everything, and if you say you do, you lose credibility from the get-go. Take time to list what you do better than those you're competing with. Also list what they do and you don't. Your lists will lead you to a definition of the market niche you serve. They'll also lead to a more powerful personal reputation for excellence in a clearly defined arena.

✔ **What about you turns heads?** What makes someone pull your résumé out for closer review? What makes you a good source for a news story? What makes people want to meet you? Find the accomplishment, the ability, or the entry on your resume that sets you apart — that makes you cool and makes others want to learn more — and build your personal brand statement, your social-media description, and every personal introduction around it.

✔ **What makes you recognizable and memorable?** When people describe you, what do they say? When they see you, what do they expect? What about you looks and sounds meaningfully different? Johnny Cash was the man in black. Mark Zuckerberg is the hoodie-wearing CEO. Hillary Clinton describes herself as a "pantsuit aficionado." Each has developed a presence people have grown to expect and trust. What's yours?

Whether online or in person, in writing or over the phone, present yourself uniquely and consistently to acquire the brand strength and trust you seek.

Setting personal branding goals

Developing a personal brand is a lot like entering coordinates into a mapping app. You have to know your starting point, which this chapter and Chapter 5 help you mark, and you have to know where you want to go.

Following are examples of personal branding goals:

- ✔ Establish yourself as an expert in your field.
- ✔ Enhance your visibility and reputation within your community or industry.
- ✔ Differentiate yourself based upon your unique style and talents.
- ✔ Gain influence in social or business arenas.

Chapter 6 leads you through the process of setting goals and putting your brand into words. Chapter 11 is full of advice for developing your personal brand through social-media networks.

Growing into a personality brand

You don't have to be in Hollywood to be a star. Your personal brand becomes a *personality brand* when you acquire such awareness and regard that those in your industry, community, or interest area seek you out with confidence that they'll benefit from the power of association with you. A personality brand makes you a celebrity in your world.

- ✔ **Industry celebrities:** Leaders in a professional field are most in demand as keynote speakers, most sought out for recommendations or opinions, and most quoted in industry news coverage.

- ✔ **Community celebrities:** The endorsements of local A-listers are sought for major hometown projects or fundraising events, their thoughts influence regional policies and programs, and their names appear on every major invitation list.

- ✔ **Online celebrities:** Some people have huge followings on Facebook, YouTube, Twitter, Tumblr, Vine, and Instagram. The biggest online celebrities — many with names known only online — reach millions daily, winning clicks, buzz, and jackpot-sized payouts from corporate brands in return for product placements and sponsored posts. A few leverage Internet stardom into Hollywood-style celebrity (Justin Bieber or PSY) or into lucrative corporate contracts (teenager Bethany Mota leveraged fashion and beauty videos into a contract with Aéropostale). Most, however, become online personalities in niche market segments, gaining influence that leads to dominance in their business arenas and awareness that leverages into publicity, speaking and publishing opportunities, and new business.

Here's how personality brands and other brands connect with each other:

- ✔ **Some celebrities are launched by business or product brands.** For example, the late Dave Thomas of Wendy's became a celebrity as a result of the Wendy's brand marketing campaign. He then leveraged his celebrity to create attention for his Foundation For Adoption. Other examples: John Schattner of Papa John's, and Jonathan Goldsmith, "The Most Interesting Man in the World," for Dos Equis.

- ✔ **Some celebrities launch business or product brands.** For example, Newman's Own grew out of the celebrity brand of Paul Newman. The George Foreman Grill capitalized on the fame of George Foreman. Oprah leveraged her powerful brand into a recommended reading list, her own TV network, and most recently a chai latte brand at Starbucks. The Olsen twins, the Kardashians, Paris Hilton, and other celebrities have launched apparel brands, and almost every sports brand has a line built on the strong brand of an athletic superstar.

- ✔ **Some business or product brands launch celebrities, who go on to launch new business or product brands.** For example, Walt Disney Studios and Disneyland led to the globally recognized Walt Disney celebrity brand, which now shines over an array of Disney products, sub-brands, and services.

Although only the most visible personalities turn their names into supersized celebrity brands, anyone — including you — can set a goal to build a personality brand that develops into a community, industry, or online star.

Branding Your Freelance or Consulting Services

If you're a solopreneur — a freelancer, a consultant, or a one-person business dynamo — building a personal brand, essential as it is, may not be enough to fuel your success. You might also want to turn your talents into a branded business that others know and trust, especially if you want to compete with established businesses or if you have plans to grow your one-person business into a larger enterprise you can someday sell to a new owner. In that case, you need to build two brands at once.

Benefits of a one-person business brand

By most forecasts, one of three people now work as freelancers or on contract, and over the next decade the contingent of self-employed is on track to include nearly half of us. If you're aiming to succeed selling service or talent, full time or as a side gig, you're up against stiff competition that's only going to keep getting more intense.

That's why freelancer or one-person business brands are advantageous. They prepare you to convince the person you're trying to sell that you're serious about what you do, that your offerings are different and decidedly better than other choices, and that you can be counted on today, tomorrow, and well into the future to serve as a supplier and to stand by your work.

Thinking like an entrepreneur

By turning freelancing into a branded business, you turn yourself into an entrepreneur, and freelancers who think like entrepreneurs work more hours, make more money, are more optimistic, and enjoy more success than free-lancers who provide services without an entrepreneurial or business-owner mindset. Those facts come from findings in the 2012 Freelance Industry Report, based on responses from 1,500 freelancers worldwide.

Branding to win business

Participants in the Freelance Industry Report survey were asked to name their most effective method for finding and landing clients. The leading answers: Referrals (27 percent), word of mouth (26 percent), and networking (17 percent).

By building a trustworthy brand for your one-person business, rather than treating your work as a series of assignments or side activities, you develop the trust and confidence that inspires referrals, positive word-of-mouth, and networking success — online and in person.

One-person brand-building steps to follow

Branding freelancing or consulting services tends to differ from branding any other kind of business in one big (and dangerous) way. People who set out to build multi-person or high-growth businesses know they need to estab-lish their businesses as trustworthy brands from day one, whereas people launching one-person businesses too often think they can wing it for now and develop a branded business later. As a result, they get off to a slower start, make weaker first impressions, command lower prices, and compete at a lower level than competitors who appear more structured, professional, and established.

The minute you decide to turn your freelancing into a business, pave the foundation for a business brand by taking the following steps:

1. **Define your business.** Include its point of difference, target audience, and competitive position (see Chapter 5).

2. **Define your business brand and how you'll present it online and in-person.** Chapter 6 is your how-to guide.

3. **Formally establish your business.** Choose and register a business name (Chapter 7 details steps to follow). Also, establish business accounts that separate your business and personal finances. (It's hard to develop a credible business brand when you're paying business expenses with personal checks.)

4. **Prepare to market by developing your business brand identity and making your business findable online through a website and social-media pages.** See Chapters 8, 10, and 11 for advice.

Especially if your business serves businesses rather than individuals, realize that clients prefer to work with credible professionals they can count on well into the future rather than with individuals who work on a piecemeal basis and may leave to take a job or pursue another opportunity on a moment's notice. Branding your one-person business gives it the necessary edge.

Balancing Personal and Business Brands

If this chapter's done its job, you're now convinced you need to build a brand for yourself and, if you own a business — even a one-person, part-time business located in a corner of your living room — you need to build a brand for your business as well. On top of that, you have to keep the strength of each brand in check with the other.

Keeping your personal and business brands in balance

You're reading a book that's all about enhancing the image, visibility, credibility, and trust of brands, so this next sentence may surprise you: You have to be careful not to overdevelop your personal or your business brand. You have to keep each one in sync with the other and with your goals.

Here are examples of what can happen when one brand eclipses the other:

✔ The personal brand of George Zimmer was so synonymous with Men's Wearhouse that when he and the business parted ways, news reports called it "the firing heard around America." Zimmer had closed countless ads with the line, "You're going to like the way you look. I guarantee it." The business promise had become his personal promise and his abrupt departure shook investor confidence in a way that might have been avoided had the business shifted brand visibility before transitioning its powerfully branded founder to "a smaller role at the company."

- A restaurant owned by award-winning chefs famous for leading the sustainable-dining movement is for sale at a price the owners feel is in line with the fame and following they've acquired. Last we checked, a buyer hadn't been found. A million dollars is a lot to pay for a restaurant people love primarily for the brilliance of its owners — and fear that when they're gone there'll be no "there there," as the saying goes.

- A business owner — or a business employee — who is such a strong business brand ambassador that her title and company affiliation is the overarching theme for everything from her LinkedIn profile headline to her social encounters to her appointment to local boards fails to create a personal brand that serves as a transportable identity. As a result, when it's time for a change, she literally has to rebrand herself with the personal brand she never adequately developed during her business stint.

Imagine your personal and business brands are riding a teeter-totter. Does one outweigh the other? The next section helps you make a quick assessment.

Keeping your personal and business brands in check

If you're building brands for yourself and your business, consider these questions:

- **Do your brands share equal levels of awareness, or is one significantly more powerful than the other?**

  - Put each name into a search engine (Chapter 10 includes a section on ego-surfing, with tips for how to make sure your search history doesn't skew the results). Are results for each name equal in terms of quantity, quality, and how well they reflect your desired brand image?

  - Review recommendations, publicity, online mentions, and comments by others. If they refer to you personally, do they also mention your business name, and vice versa?

- **Does each brand support but also stand independently of the other?** Would each brand have credibility even if the other disappeared?

  - Is your business brand strong enough to survive without the power of your personal brand? If you sold or left your business tomorrow, would its brand be dramatically diminished by your exit?

- Conversely, are you, personally, adequately visible within your business brand? People humanize businesses and go where they can't, such as to networking events and into community or leadership positions. Is your personal brand strong and visible enough to boost the power of your business?

Based on your findings, you may need to take one of two steps:

- ✔ **If your personal brand is weak in comparison to your business brand:** Follow the brand-building steps in this book to develop your awareness and value in your business arena, industry, community, and online. Make personal branding a priority — power up your personal identity, awareness, and credibility — especially if your business could benefit from a more personal face or if you're planning to pursue personal opportunities outside your business.

- ✔ **If your business brand is weak in comparison to your personal brand:** Start reducing the emphasis on you and your own name and turn the spotlight onto your business and its name, team, processes, and assets. Make business branding a priority especially if you plan to grow or sell your business or if you want fare better in competitions against seemingly stronger and well-branded businesses. If your business doesn't have a website, launch one. If you don't have a business logo, get one and feature it in your personal email signature and on personal online pages where business contacts might reach you.

Cross-promoting your two brands

When you build personal and business brands, you establish two sets of positive images in the minds of others. Your business name unlocks one set of images and your personal name unlocks the other. By consistently linking your brands through cross-promotion, you make each brand an asset of the other, fortifying each brand and extending the reach of both.

Connecting your brands can be as easy as presenting the logo, web address, Twitter handle, or other identifiers for your business brand on your personal sites and clearly establishing yourself as the business founder or owner in all business introductions. The result is greater reach and credibility for both brands.

Using our two names as examples:

- ✔ A Google search for "Bill Chiaravalle" delivered nearly 6,000 results as this sentence was being written. The first two results led to the website for his business, Brand Navigation. The third result led to his personal LinkedIn profile, with a snippet describing him as the owner of Brand

Navigation. The rest led to his Amazon author page, Twitter feed, and other pages featuring his expertise. A Google search for Bill's business, "Brand Navigation" (refined by the addition of the word "Oregon" to eliminate results for other references to the term "brand navigation") delivered nearly 13,000 results, with snippets for top results naming Bill as the business owner, and other results linking to case studies and news about branding success stories.

Quick assessment: Based on the online footprints for each brand, the Brand Navigation brand outweighs Bill's personal brand, exactly as he'd wish because clients buy the power of his entire business.

✔ A Google search for "Barbara Findlay Schenck" delivers 250,000 results, led by a link to her business, Bizstrong. A Google search for "Bizstrong" delivers 4,200 results, with nearly every link accompanied by a snippet that includes her personal name.

Quick assessment: Barbara's personal brand outweighs her business brand, which makes sense because her business is a resource for reaching her books, articles, and presentations.

Conduct a similar search and assessment for your brands. Keep an eye on which brand is most visible and adjust brand emphasis if and when the balance becomes out of line with your personal and business goals.

Part II
Building a Brand, Step by Step

Major brands that follow key positioning strategies

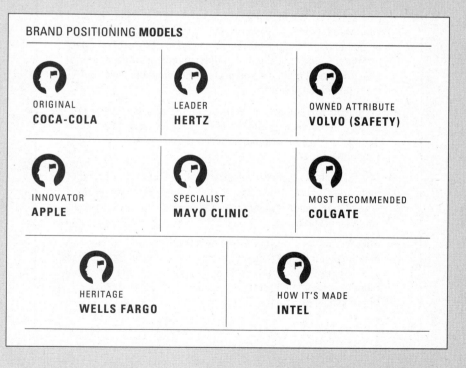

BRAND POSITIONING **MODELS**

ORIGINAL **COCA-COLA**	LEADER **HERTZ**	OWNED ATTRIBUTE **VOLVO (SAFETY)**
INNOVATOR **APPLE**	SPECIALIST **MAYO CLINIC**	MOST RECOMMENDED **COLGATE**
HERITAGE **WELLS FARGO**	HOW IT'S MADE **INTEL**	

In this part . . .

- ✔ Prepare for brand construction by conducting the equivalent of an environmental analysis. Follow steps and tips to research and discover what you need to know about your market conditions, competitive landscape, and customer preferences and buying approaches.

- ✔ Find and stake claim to the position in customer minds where your brand — and only your brand — will live, based on its unique and meaningful attributes and point of difference. Map how your brand is positioned in its competitive landscape and plan how you'll maintain and protect that valuable mind and marketplace position

- ✔ Zero in on words that describe your brand and its style, character, and promise. Create the all-important brand statement that will guide your branding decisions and communications.

- ✔ Drill through the layers involved to pick or invent your brand name, test whether the name is available for your use, grab your domain name, and register and protect the name as your valuable brand asset.

- ✔ Put the right face on your brand by designing a logo that matches your brand style, character and promise. Get familiar with logo design resources, design approaches, and what it takes to create and protect the symbol that represents your brand in its marketplace.

Chapter 5

Profiling and Positioning Your Brand

In This Chapter

▶ Determining your brand's point of distinction

▶ Researching your customers and your competition

▶ Finding the available, meaningful market position only your brand can fill

Depending on who's counting, consumers face up to 5,000 promotional messages every single day. And guess what? They ignore most of them. They tune out anything that doesn't appeal to their interests, wants, and needs. And they brush off messages for products and services they already buy from trusted brands — unless the offering being presented is one that seems to be meaningfully and attractively different and better than their current choice. And that's the whole point of finding and protecting a position for your brand.

It's your job as a brand-builder to figure out who is likely to want or need what you offer, how to reach that person, and what to say to motivate interest, purchases, and loyalty. If you have ESP, you can divine the answers. If you're like everyone else, this chapter helps you take the steps and do the research to learn what you need to know about your customer description, target market, purchase motivations, preferred purchase channels and experiences, competitive alternatives, and why people would choose your brand over all others.

In the process, you'll find your *market niche* — the select group of customers who share unique interests and needs that your offering alone can address. After you find your market niche, *presto!* You've discovered the open position for your brand in the crowded marketplace around you.

Branding expert Walter Landor, the creative and strategic force behind many of the most famous brands you know today, is widely quoted for his assertion that "Products are made in the factory, but brands are created in the mind." This chapter helps you find an available space to create your brand in the minds of your customers.

The Marketing Muscle of Positioning

You can't force a square peg into a round hole. You also can't force a square peg into a space already filled by another square peg, right? From your puzzle-playing days, you know you need to find an open space and fill it with a piece that matches up perfectly. When you do, the piece drops securely in place. The same principle applies to the human mind. You can't fit an idea into a customer's mind unless it matches up with an interest, need, or desire that isn't already fulfilled by another idea or offering.

Positioning involves finding an unaddressed interest, want, or need in customer minds and filling it with your distinctive and ideally suited offering.

Successful positioning approaches

In some ways, branding is like a construction project. Before you can build, you have to select and prepare the site. That's the role positioning plays in the branding process. (Flip back to Chapter 2 for an illustration of the branding process and a description of how positioning paves the way for your brand definition and identity.)

Following are the most common positioning approaches.

Fulfill an unaddressed interest or need

This is the find-an-itch-and-scratch-it approach. You study your customer, see a need or desire that isn't addressed by an existing product or service, and move quickly to beat competitors to the solution. The result? An offering that slides into an available slot in the customer's mind — as long as you seize the position before anyone else stakes claim to it.

WeightWatchers is a great example of fulfilling an unaddressed need. Founder Jean Nidetch turned a conversation about how to lose weight into a brand that's now 50 years old and known around the world for its weekly support group meetings that help customers shed weight and keep it off.

Challenge the status quo

Challengers take on market leaders and business category norms with innovations ranging from new forms of distribution to innovative pricing and promotion approaches. By presenting themselves as torchbearers for the next generation, challengers disrupt norms and win interest and followings that result in marketplace upheaval and, sometimes, market leadership.

EasyJet, now the United Kingdom's largest air carrier, set out to revolutionize air travel by announcing flights priced "as cheap as a pair of jeans" and catering to cost-conscious, plan-it-yourself travelers with self-proclaimed "cheap flights" on "the web's favorite airline." Another example: Airbnb now fills more room nights annually than all Hilton Hotels combined, without owning a single room of their own. Instead, by playing matchmaker between travelers and owners of spare rooms, boats, and even castles, Airbnb has become a prime player in what's called the "sharing economy — and racked up a brand value estimated at $10 billion-plus dollars along the way.

Specialize to serve a new market niche

Rather than trying to compete with the pack, specialty brands serve a narrow segment of the market — winning interest and followings within a *market niche* and sometimes achieving market leadership as a result.

No copycats! Avoiding the fate of a me-too brand

A *me-too brand* is one that offers exactly what another brand offers with no distinctive attributes other than the fact that it's presented by a different marketer.

If you try to slot your brand into a position already taken by a competitor, you face a tough uphill battle. First, you have to convince customers to move away from their current choice. Then you have to convince them to move toward your offering. That's double the marketing work with half the assurance of marketing success. After all, telling customers that what they believe is wrong is a slow way to make friends and influence perceptions.

An equally bad idea is trying to leverage off someone else's brand. By likening your brand to someone else's brand, you cast a spotlight on a competitor while pointing out your own second-string position.

Instead, find your own position by filling an unfilled need, innovating valuable new-generation offerings, specializing to serve a market segment or niche, or creating an all-new solution. (See the section "Successful positioning approaches," for a rundown of these approaches.)

REAL WORLD

DOS For Dummies launched a global phenomenon

In 1990, computerese felt like a foreign language and computer manuals were practically impossible to decode. That's when a frustrated customer was overheard wishing for a simple how-to book that explained the DOS operating system. According to lore, he said, "I need something like DOS For Dummies." In 1991, Dan Gookin's book with that very title hit bookshelves. Booksellers were leery that the title would insult their customers, but they agreed to stock the book after they saw how well it was selling.

Today, more than a quarter billion books later, with nearly 2,000 titles in nearly 30 languages, the *For Dummies* phenomenon is a branding case study. If you want proof that brands emerge with full strength when they address real and unmet needs and when they're propelled by the founder's passion and powerful belief, look no further than the book you're smartly reading.

REAL WORLD

SPANX is a good example of a specialty brand. In owner Sara Blakely's own words, "My footless pantyhose idea evolved into a super niche product category: new-and-improved and comfortable footless pantyhose with super control and body-shaping support."

Transform an established solution

This is the evolutionary approach to positioning. Examples include the transformation of computers into laptops into tablets, cars into electronic or hybrid or self-driving machines, American coffee shops into upscale European-style cafés, and — on the horizon — package deliveries into doorstep-drops by unmanned drones, to name a few.

Creating a transformational solution takes enormous insight into popular culture and plenty of marketing power to get the word out. It also takes plenty of money — both to create innovations and to promote new products with such velocity and strength that you can lay claim to the first position in the category before competitors have time to leap into the arena.

Introduce an all-new solution

Product discoveries come from innovators who see the same problems everyone else sees — or who notice problems no one else notices — and who move on their insights to come up with never-before seen solutions. Some solutions involve altogether new inventions; others transform existing solutions into new product categories.

Recent examples of innovations include fitness bracelets, cloud computing, language-learning apps, and the Segway Human Transporter, introduced to "transform a person into an empowered pedestrian." Older examples include car radios, TV dinners, and Saran wrap.

Gaining awareness and adoption for a brand-new idea requires patience and a massive marketing investment. After all, you're not just introducing a product, you're introducing a whole new paradigm for which the market may or may not be ready. Prepare your nerves — and budget — in advance.

Major positioning strategies

The key to your market position is your *point of difference,* also called your *point of distinction* or your *unique selling proposition* (USP).

The following sections in this chapter guide your assessment of your unique distinctions and the marketplace position you want to hold and defend in your customer's minds. To get your thinking started, take a look at Figure 5-1. It illustrates major brands that follow each of the major positioning strategies.

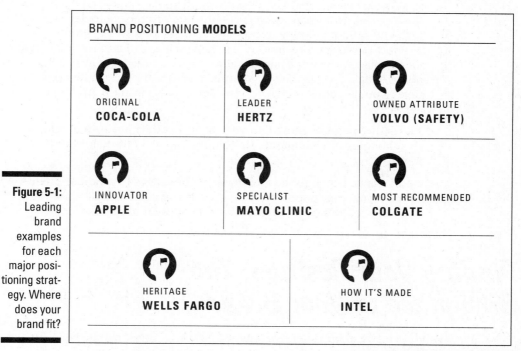

Figure 5-1:
Leading brand examples for each major positioning strategy. Where does your brand fit?

Illustration courtesy of Bill Chiaravalle, Brand Navigation

Positioning around marketplace opportunities

The only way to keep your brand alive and healthy — that is, to maintain its position in consumer minds — is to keep it attuned to the wants, needs, interests, and opportunities that exist in the world not just of today but of tomorrow.

Your brand is a player in pop culture, so the more you tune in to the changing world around you, the more your brand will remain current and relevant.

To keep your brand on top of marketplace opportunities, you don't have to be a seer who forecasts the future. You just have to look beyond the known environments of your business and social arena for new ideas, needs, products, fads, trends, and market frenzies. To put yourself in position to seize opportunities, follow these suggestions:

- **Stay close to your customers.** Only by listening and observing can you know what they want but can't find or what new needs they're dealing with that marketers haven't yet addressed.

- **Get close to noncustomers.** It sounds counterintuitive, but you need to keep an eye on what people who are the polar opposite of your customers are into. Urban youth certainly didn't fit the customer profile of high-end fashion boutiques, but it didn't take long for the grunge look to affect haute couture anyway. To keep your brand current, widen your marketplace view. For example, tune in to what teenager are talking about even if your market is comprised of senior citizens. Read technology publications even if your business arena is in the professional services.

- **Be ready to update and align your brand and its position to adapt to the changing environment.** Check out Chapter 17 for help with this task.

- **At all times, watch for unmet needs and unserved market segments.** A branding success opportunity may await you if you can fill a hole in the market. See the sidebar on *DOS For Dummies* for a prime example.

Finding Your Position: The Birthplace of Your Brand

Without clearly defined and communicated distinctions, people basically view products (or people) as commodities chosen simply for their availability or lowest prices — and easily passed over for any similar offering that seems to fill the same bill with less effort or expense. (See Chapter 2 for plenty of information on commodities.)

By staking your market position based on a unique and valued point of difference, you find the open space in consumer minds where you can build your brand, and you also avoid the one-is-as-good-as-another trap.

The next sections help you find the positive point of difference that you'll reinforce every time people encounter your name, your product, your staff, or any other aspect of your brand experience (which is the topic of Chapter 13).

Zeroing in on the strengths of your brand

Being different isn't enough for an attractive positioning strategy. A car that burns gas at a rate of one gallon every two miles has a point of distinction but no point of attraction.

To position your brand, you need both attraction and distinction:

- ✔ **Attraction** comes from providing values and attributes that customers genuinely want or need.
- ✔ **Distinction** comes from providing values and attributes that customers can only receive by selecting you, your business, or your product.

So what are your most attractive distinctions? To conduct your self-assessment, use the worksheet in Figure 5-2. (If you need help digging up the information you need, check out the research section later in this chapter.) Enter your greatest strengths in the left-hand column. Then use the next columns to enter assessments of how well others feel that your offering distinguishes your business and sets you apart from your competition. When you see a resounding "best" across the board, you know you've landed on an attribute of that give you a compelling point of distinction.

Distinctions only matter if they are meaningful and desirable to those in your target market. As you complete the Figure 5-2 chart, repeatedly ask yourself: Does this attribute truly matter, and to whom?

Defining your point of difference

Your *point of difference* determines your position in your competitive environment. It defines the precise segment of the market that you serve best and how your offering is distinctively unique from that of businesses or products that provide similar but different solutions and experiences.

ASSESSING THE STRENGTH OF YOUR BRAND ATTRIBUTES: WORKSHEET				
✔ How each attribute rates against the attributes of competitive offerings				
Attribute	Your opinion of this attribute	Opinions of top managers	Opinions of front-line staff	Opinions of customers
	Best Good Average	Best Good Average	Best Good Average	Best Good Average
Enter the most outstanding aspect of your best-selling product or service _____	☐ ☐ ☐	☐ ☐ ☐	☐ ☐ ☐	☐ ☐ ☐
Enter the product aspect you've spent the most time or money developing _____	☐ ☐ ☐	☐ ☐ ☐	☐ ☐ ☐	☐ ☐ ☐
Enter the value most customers seek from your offering (such as quality, features, convenience, reliability, expertise, support, service, low price, prestige, or exclusive price) _____	☐ ☐ ☐	☐ ☐ ☐	☐ ☐ ☐	☐ ☐ ☐
If you closed tomorrow, what one attribute would your customers miss most or find hardest to replace? _____	☐ ☐ ☐	☐ ☐ ☐	☐ ☐ ☐	☐ ☐ ☐

Figure 5-2:
Honestly assess the strength of your brand attributes.

Many businesses that want to ramp up sales in a hurry try to make their products attractive to anyone and everyone. They're afraid to pinpoint distinctions or market segments for fear that they'll miss sales opportunities. In fact, the reverse is true. If you can't tell customers what you do best and for whom, you can't give them a credible reason to choose your offering.

Before you begin the process of putting your brand into words (see Chapter 6), define your point of difference in your competitive environment. Use the following template:

> [*Name of your business, product, or service*] is the [*your distinction and the generic term for your type of offering*] to provide [*your unique features or benefits*] to [*your customer profile*] who choose our offering in order to feel [*your customers' emotional outcome*].

In this statement, your distinction may be along the lines of *best, first, only, most-recommended,* or *highest-ranking.* The generic term for your type of offering may be *gluten-free bakery, language-learning mobile app, low-sugar energy bar,* or whatever else describes what you promise to deliver to customers. A few examples of customer profiles include *local residents with global mindsets, upwardly mobile young professionals seeking enhanced status,* or *parents wanting to provide their children with opportunity and enrichment.* Finally, your customers' emotional outcome may be *secure, successful, self-confident,* or *indulged.*

Dealing with brand misperceptions

In a perfect world, what others believe about your offering would match precisely with what you believe to be your brand's distinguishing characteristics and attributes. But you're branding in the real world, not a perfect world. In fact, if you're working on a strategy to strengthen an existing brand, you're probably reading this book because you sense there's a gap between what you think makes your brand different and better and how you think it's perceived by those in your marketplace.

Part of the positioning process involves knowing whether or not people you want to reach and influence already have you slotted into a position — possibly the wrong position — in their minds. If so, you have to move strategically and help them connect the dots from the position your brand currently occupies in their minds to where you want it to be. The upcoming section "Digging Up the Info You Need" guides you through steps to conduct research and collect facts about your customers and their beliefs.

Be aware that moving your brand to a new position isn't like moving furniture. You can't just pick your brand up and slot it into a new space. Your customers — not you — move your brand to a new position. To change your position, you need to build on what people currently believe by conveying messages, making impressions, and delivering experiences that logically move your brand toward your desired competitive position. The chapters in Part III help you get the word out.

Mapping your brand's position

To position your brand, start by looking at how it fits within your competitive landscape. Create a positioning matrix like the one illustrated in Figure 5-3, following these steps:

1. **Choose two attributes that matter most in your competitive environment.** Those will become the axis lines for your positioning matrix. For example, a specialty food products brand might choose food preferences (ranging from traditional to gourmet) and pricing (affordable to premium). A ski resort may choose type of ski experience (one-day recreation to destination resort) and pricing (affordable to premium). In Figure 5-3, you see that the owners of a bakery café chose as their attributes the type of customer experience (global to local) and the café atmosphere (old world to contemporary).

2. **Within the framework of your two sets of attributes, plot where your competitors fit.** In the Figure 5-3 example, Starbucks is the most global and contemporary brand. So that position is taken. Other competitors fill positions ranging from very to somewhat contemporary or old-world, and from somewhat local or global in character. When you find the slot on the map that's unfilled and that aligns with the attributes of your offering, you've located the birthplace of the brand.

Brand Positioning Matrix

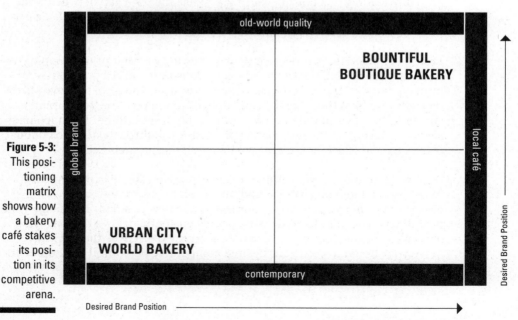

Figure 5-3: This positioning matrix shows how a bakery café stakes its position in its competitive arena.

Illustration courtesy of Bill Chiaravalle, Brand Navigation

Match your position to your brand experience

In nearly every brand category, competitors vie for position in consumer minds, each claiming to be the friendliest, to have the highest quality, to offer the lowest prices, or to excel in any other attribute you can think of. Yet in each position, only one brand prevails. Only one brand wins awareness, credibility, preference, trust, and loyalty, mystifying the competitors who think and perhaps can even prove that their attributes in the area of distinction are better.

So what tips the customer's perception toward the brand leader and away from the others? As in most other things in life, firsthand experience trumps all other forms of communication.

To stake claim to your brand's point of difference and competitive position, make sure every encounter with your brand delivers an experience that reinforces your distinct attributes and brand promise. For example, if you say that your position is economy, create a warehouse environment and experience. If your position is exclusivity, excel at individualized service and second-to-none responsiveness.

To win and hold your precious position in consumer minds, help people constantly experience your attractive, compelling distinctions every time they brush up against any facet of your brand.

When creating a strategy to strengthen an existing brand, doing this exercise twice is worthwhile: once based on the position you want your brand to hold and once based on the position you think it currently holds in consumer minds. The difference between the two positions will guide your efforts as you adjust your offerings, develop communications, and improve your customer experience to support the image you want customers to believe, adopt, and embrace.

Aligning Your Brand's Position with Customer Wants, Needs, and Desires

Branding involves positioning and positioning involves focusing on not just what you do best but also on the market segment you serve best. Instead of trying to please all people in all ways, great brands position themselves to please some people — a defined *market segment* or *market niche* — in an extraordinary way because of the unique and meaningful attributes and experiences the brands offer.

To define the target audience for your brand, complete the Customer Profile Worksheet illustrated in Figure 5-4. If you're not sure of your answers, turn to the later section "Digging Up the Info You Need" for advice on how to conduct research about where your customers are, who they are, what they value, and how they prefer to buy products like the ones you're offering.

CUSTOMER PROFILE WORKSHEET

Location

Define where your customers and prospects live. These facts help target your marketing.

List ZIP codes, neighborhoods, regions, states, countries that include concentrations of buyers or likely buyers.
_____

_____

List where your inquiries, foot traffic, web traffic, social media followers come from. _____

_____

Demographics

List facts about your customers. This information helps aim communications directly at people likely to match your customer profile.

Gender: What is your customer ratio of male to female?_____

Age: What percentages of your customers are age 12 or under, age 13–19, age 20–30, age 30–40, age 50–60, and age 60 or older?_____

Education level: What percentage of your customers are currently in school, high-school grads, college grads, and advanced-degree holders?_____

Household composition: Describe whether most of your customers are single, married, divorced, in partnerships, parents with children at home, couples with no children at home, heads of families, grandparents, recent empty-nesters, and so on._____

Income level: How would you describe the income levels of customers?_____

Home ownership: Do most customers own or rent their homes?_____

Nationality: What is their nationality? Ethnicity? Language?
_____

Occupations: What types of jobs do they hold?_____

Behavioral Patterns

Describe what motivates and interests your customers. This helps you create and deliver messages that inspire their interest and action.

Interests: What are their spare-time activities and hobbies?_____

Information: What magazines, TV shows, types of music, websites, social-media networks, or other media do they use?_____

Beliefs: What opinions do they hold? Do they have strong social, religious, or political affiliations? What do they value?_____

Purchasing patterns: Do they buy on impulse or after careful consideration? Are they loyal customers or do they shop around? Do they base purchase decisions primarily on cost or on other attributes such as quality, convenience, or prestige? Do they have brand allegiances and if so, which? Do they make decisions on their own or based on the advice, recommendations, or reviews from others?_____

_____

Figure 5-4:
Use this worksheet as you create a customer profile to focus your branding strategy on the type of person and the market niche you serve best.

© Barbara Findlay Schenck

What do your customers care about?

When you know a description of the people you're trying to reach and where and how to reach them, you're armed with the knowledge you need to address their values, motivations, and purchasing patterns. The following questions can help uncover useful facts:

✔ **What motivates your customers' purchase decisions?** Put differently, what needs or desires are customers trying to address when they purchase your product? Realize that the answer isn't always obvious. A couple may say that they like the design and quality of a particular new home, for example, when really they're motivated by the prestigious feel of the house or neighborhood.

To get to the root of your customers' purchase motivations, find out how your offering makes them feel. By uncovering the emotions your product evokes, you learn the basis of their motivation and which attributes to highlight in your branding strategy.

✔ **How do your customers approach your business?** Do they buy in-person, or by phone, mail, or online? Do they decide to buy on their own or based on the recommendation or approval of someone else? Does your brand need to make a promise to the product consumer or to the purchase authority or referring agent? Or both? By knowing how customers reach your business and the factors that influence their decision, you can create more effective messages, communications, and experiences.

✔ **How do customers purchase your products?** By studying buying patterns, you discover brand attributes that matter most to customers.

   • Do most customers buy on impulse or after consideration? The answer may indicate a need for trust and reliability assurances.

   • Do they pay cash, charge, or buy on payment plans? Payment plans may indicate a greater sensitivity to price.

   • Do they sign contracts, subscribe, or opt for multipurchase or bulk deals? Long-term commitments indicate high trust.

   • If you offer an add-on warranty or service program, do most customers take the offering or decline it? Acceptance may indicate concern over ease of use or reliability.

   • Are they interested primarily in price, or are their decisions made based on quality, prestige, convenience, or other values?

What sets your ideal customers apart?

Ideal customers are the ones who buy the most from your business, cause the fewest problems, say the nicest things, and recommend you the most often. To determine if your most ideal customers have geographic, demographic, or behavioral traits in common (see worksheet in Figure 5-4 to develop your customer profile), answer these questions:

- Do your most ideal customers tend to buy the same kinds of products or request the same kinds of options, and are those tendencies different from those of other customers?

- Do they buy from your business simply to obtain your product or service, or do they think that your offering fulfills additional needs or interests — such as the ability to socialize, to feel the prestige of joining your exclusive or trendy clientele, to enrich themselves educationally through product samples or seminars, or to enjoy the level of your expertise or the safety of your trustworthiness?

- What attributes of your business do you think your most ideal customers value most highly: product quality, available features, convenience (your location or your purchasing options), reliability, staff expertise, customer support and service, price (high or low — some people are attracted to bargains and others to the highest level of premium offering), or other aspects of doing business with you?

- How do your most ideal customers buy? For example, do they buy on impulse, in bulk, on sale, when shopping with others, when shopping online, on the recommendation of others, and so on?

- Do your most ideal customers share any of the same demographic or lifestyle characteristics, such as gender, age, income, ethnicity, geographic location, beliefs, or values?

Studying the buying patterns and motivations of ideal customers helps determine which attributes and approaches to feature in your marketing.

Why do customers buy from you?

Take all that you know about your customers and answer this final question: *Why do they choose to buy from you?*

Commit your thoughts to words using the template shown in Figure 5-5. Complete the exercise twice: once for your average customer and once for your most ideal customer. Use the information in the average customer form to determine how your brand must appeal to your current clientele. Use the information in the ideal customer form to determine which brand attributes to emphasize in order to shift your clientele to include more customers like those you currently consider the cream of the crop.

Figure 5-5:
Use this
form as you
create two
customer
descrip-
tions:
one that
describes
your current
customer
and one that
describes
your most
ideal
customer.

AT-A-GLANCE CUSTOMER DESCRIPTION
PROFILE: Our customers are predominantly __[gender]__ living in __[region]__ who __[a description of lifestyle facts such as: are married, own their homes, work as professionals, have young children living at home, and are members of business organizations and/or golf clubs]__ .
WANTS AND VALUES: Our customers value __[the attributes your customers value, for example Quality, Features, Convenience, Reliability, Expertise, Support, Service, Low Price, Prestige, or Exclusivity]__ .
MOTIVATIONS: The top reasons our customers buy from our business are: __[we're conveniently located, they get to work directly with the owner/s, they want the best and perceive us to be more exclusive than our competitors, we get things done quickly and on budget, and so on]__ .

© Barbara Findlay Schenck

Digging Up the Info You Need

A few huge companies are responsible for the vast majority of all the time and money spent on market research each year. Hmmm . . . a message is probably in there: Big businesses get bigger by knowing and responding to customer wants and needs.

You can do the same, even without a huge research investment. You can start by looking for telltale signs within your own business and sales records. You can talk directly to customers (something that smaller business owners do on a daily basis anyway), and you can conduct do-it-yourself research.

Putting your brand through a self-exam

A successful brand strategy results in an accurate reflection of what you are and what you promise to those who come into contact with you or your business. That's why it's important to define your brand as it exists right now. Start using your own opinions and knowledge to answer these questions:

✓ **What does your business do best?** What makes you a great choice for customers? If you were to close tomorrow, what attributes that you offer would customers have the hardest time finding elsewhere?

✓ **What do customers buy most from your business?** Customers vote with their pocketbooks, so if most of your revenue comes from a single product or service line, that line probably represents the offering your customers value most highly.

- ✔ **What aspect of your business gets the most internal attention?** Most businesses prioritize efforts in one of the following areas: research and development, operations, marketing, distribution and delivery, management, organization, and customer service. What is the major emphasis in your company? Your answer probably points toward your business strength and a brand attribute.

- ✔ **What services do you offer or promise that your competitors don't?** Does your company make a promise — a promise that may feel like a minimal standard within your organization — that causes customers to choose and stick with your business? Look hard. Something as mundane as consistently putting jewelry in a robin's egg-blue box could be the factor that makes you the Tiffany of your category.

Tuning in to customer insights

If you're working on a brand for an already established offering, conduct research by meeting with customers face-to-face — at the reception desk, at the customer service window, in the complaints or returns line, and on the sales floor. Or place yourself in a position to watch customers in action. What do they like? What attracts them? What confuses them? What causes them to look more closely? What causes them to turn away?

As you tap into customer insights, look for answers to these questions:

- ✔ **What customer requests are you currently not fulfilling?** Do they wish you offered same-day delivery, easier parking, additional product features, streamlined service, or a real person on the other end of the line instead of your voicemail system? Ask everyone in your organization to add every request they hear to a *customer wish list*. You can't fulfill all requests — doing so could cause you to veer away from your brand identity — but you at least need to know what customers want so you can better position your offerings when appropriate.

- ✔ **What complaints do customers register?** Establish a complaint log where employees can list customer complaints they receive or elements they believe lead to customer departures.

- ✔ **What hints of dissatisfaction do your customers give?** According to research, for every complaint you hear, 26 customers have issues they don't mention. Unstated complaints can take the form of compliments that customers share about your competitors, wistful mentions of how things used to be ("Oh, for the good old days when a real person answered the phone"), or an end to the compliments you they used to hear frequently. They also can take the form of questions. If customers consistently ask about prices or bills, be ready to reassess your pricing or billing procedures. If they ask to see samples of your work for other clients, they may have doubts about your offering and need better reassurances than you're currently presenting.

✔ **Which products are on back order? And which frequently get returned?** The answers to these two questions reveal what your customers want and don't want.

✔ **Which displays, web pages, or offers get the most attention from your customers?** There's an old saying in marketing: "Sell what people are buying." Branders might translate the concept to something like this: "Brand the attributes people love." To discover their preferences, watch people move through your business. Watch where they spend time on your website, the promotional offers that win the greatest response, the carpet on your retail floor that's most worn from foot traffic, and, especially, watch to see what's being bought, reordered, and raved about.

✔ **How do they arrive at your business?** Online, use analytics to track the paths they take to and through your website. If they arrive in person, notice what kinds of cars they drive, what kind of clothes they wear, whether they arrive alone or with others, what times of days they arrive. If they arrive via a phone call, monitor how long they remain on hold, how many call directly from your website, how many layers of automated responses they have to go through.

✔ **What do they do upon arrival at your business?** Do they ask about the nature of your business (if so, work to improve brand awareness)? Do they bounce from your home page or seem confused about where to go after physically arriving (if so, enhance your menu options, reception techniques, or directional signage)? Do they wait for slow page loads, on-hold messages, or checkout bottlenecks? Unless you're building a brand image as the busiest business in your category, interpret waits as a reason to seriously improve your customer service.

✔ **What do they do while they wait?** Go to the normal collection points in your business and see what your customers experience during wait times. Are they presented with brand messages? Are they encouraged to make add-on purchases? Are they asked to share their input about your business? If they do nothing but look around for what to do next, you're missing an opportunity to promote your brand or to collect information that allows you to make your brand stronger.

Conducting customer research

This section helps navigate the realm of interviews, surveys, and focus groups.

Just ask! Interviews and surveys

Before you take up your customer's time with an interview or survey, be clear about what you want the research to accomplish. Most research is intended to discover who your customers are and how to reach them, what your customers think of and want from products or services like the ones you offer, and how your customers may react to possible product or marketing innovations or revisions you're considering. As you collect information, follow this advice:

- ✔ **If you're collecting information to clarify your customer profile, you don't need an in-depth interview or survey.** You can collect information through online or in-person customer registration forms, you can host contests that include the requested information on entry forms, or you can issue a customer information update request on a regular basis, perhaps accompanied by a small thank-you gift for those you count among your valuable customer base.

- ✔ **If you're working to assess levels of customer awareness, interest, or satisfaction, customer opinion surveys are a good tool for the task.** You can conduct short surveys in-person at the point of purchase, or you can collect more extensive information through questionnaires delivered via phone, mail, e-mail, or by using the free online survey and polling tools offered by sites such as SurveyMonkey or Zoomerang.

For surveys that involve more than a few questions, don't go it alone. Enlist professionals who can help develop a survey instrument that collects information about your offerings without spotlighting shortcomings or unduly imposing on your customers' time. They'll also help you gain insight without leading customers to the answers you're seeking, a mistake that makes the research basically worthless. To balance your dueling desires for customer input and customer satisfaction, keep this advice in mind:

- • Keep the survey short so it only takes a few minutes of your customers' time unless you're dealing with highly loyal customers who are willing to invest more heavily of their time.

- • Ask specific questions that are more likely to elicit thoughtful and accurate responses. For example, instead of asking, "On a scale of 1 to 10 with 10 being best, how do you rate our service?" ask, "On a scale of 1 to 10 with 10 being best, how satisfied were you with the service you received during your last visit to our business?"

- Ask questions that help you understand how customers relate to your product. For example, you may ask, "How closely did our product live up to your expectations?"

- Ask questions that reveal how you stack up against competitors. For example, ask, "On a scale of 1 to 10, how convenient is our location compared to the location of other businesses where you can purchase similar products or services?

✔ **To see how customers react to a product or marketing idea, or to learn subtleties about what they think or feel, consider talking one-to-one in personal or phone interviews.** When conducting interviews, keep the following points in mind:

- Be open to any customer response to your idea. If you (or those in a leadership position) already know what you're going to do and are simply seeking validation, save your time and money.

- You may not be the best person to conduct the interview. Generally, people don't want to burst bubbles or hurt feelings. If a third-party researcher asks for customer opinions, the answers may be 180 degrees different (and more accurate) than what customers would admit to you directly.

Table 5-1 later in this chapter can help you determine when to seek professional help with your research program and when you can just go it alone.

Just listen! Using focus groups

Focus groups are best left to the professionals. A *focus group* is a gathering of customers, prospective customers, or even customers of competitors who share input about a product or marketing idea with a moderator who guides the conversation, prompts input, and manages the discussion so it isn't dominated by one person or opinion. Hold a focus group when you want to seriously weigh opinions, reactions, and risks before proceeding with an important product or marketing decision. If you're seeking input from a far-flung group rather than meeting in person, participants can meet in an online chat room or web conference. Your social networks are a good place to issue the invitations. Before the focus group session, be clear about the information or idea you're presenting, the kind of impressions you're seeking to collect, and the token of thanks you'll offer in return for participant time and ideas.

Knowing when to get research help

Table 5-1 lays out information-gathering approaches, along with advice regarding when to involve professional assistance.

Table 5-1	Information-Gathering Approaches	
Desired Finding	*Method*	*When to Call in the Pros*
Customer profile	Information capture at point of purchase, website registration, contest entry forms, information requests, intercept interviews	Seek assistance from website developers when creating online registration forms. You can handle the other methods yourself.
Customer awareness, interest, or satisfaction levels	Written or phone surveys	Involve professionals to develop surveys that are clear, concise, and don't lead or skew results, and to analyze findings.
Customer opinions or reactions to product or marketing ideas	In-person or phone interviews	Involve professionals when research involves a sensitive issue. Also, be sure interviews are conducted by an interviewer with whom the customer can be candid.
Customer input on brand, product or marketing perceptions	Focus groups	Use a professional to facilitate and record the discussion.
Customer behaviors	Observation, document review	Professional assistance is usually not required.

Where else to turn for facts and figures

Thanks to the Internet, information-gathering resources are virtually without limit. Following are a few ways to focus your research efforts.

Hit a search engine

Start with these recommendations:

- ✔ **Visit the websites of your competitors.** To see what you're up against, check out how they present themselves, brand attributes they highlight, and new moves they're announcing.

- ✔ **Check out the websites for your industry association and for major media groups that serve your business arena.** They'll probably contain research reports and analyses about customer and business trends.

- ✔ **Use government resources.** Start with www.census.go tion on population and resident characteristics in prac community. Then move on to the websites of business departments that serve your market areas, from your development department to the business resource center at your chamber of commerce.

- ✔ **Search for industry studies and research.** Just enter the name of your business arena plus the word "research" or "statistics," and results should lead to all kinds of industry facts and figures.

Hit the library reference shelves

In addition to reference materials specific to your industry, check out these marketing sourcebooks, available for free use in many library reference areas:

- ✔ **ESRI Community Sourcebook of ZIP Code Demographics:** This source is updated every five years with current demographic, business, consumer spending, and segmentation data for every U.S. ZIP code. The information is valuable as you forecast demand for your products based on market area composition and population trends.

- ✔ **The Lifestyle Market Analyst:** Published by Standard Rate and Data Service (SRDS) and Nielsen, this guide provides demographic and lifestyle data organized by geographic market area, lifestyle interests, and consumer profiles.

Putting Research in Perspective

Use research findings to fine-tune your brand strategy and message. Knowing all you can about who you're trying to reach and what your target customer wants, needs, and currently believes will help as you make essential decisions that align your brand with customer preferences. But beware: People can smell a fabricated fake. You have to *be* what you say you are. If your customers want cool and trendy, you have to *be* cool and trendy before you amplify that message in the marketplace. You have to be able to walk your talk.

Start with passion, and build your brand from there. If your brand doesn't have your heart and soul in it, no amount of research can make it successful.

People with strong personalities, aspirations, and passions create powerful brands. An example is Martha Stewart. On an episode of the show *The Apprentice,* she reprimanded a contestant for relying too heavily on research findings. She said that rather than creating products in response to customer desires, her company created unquestionably great products and *then* created customer desire. The same statement applies to most every other great brand leader, from Steve Jobs to Walt Disney to Oprah Winfrey. All started with strong opinions and clear brand visions. Even when told that their ideas wouldn't fly, they proceeded — and built branding case studies in the process.

Defining and Testing Your Position

As soon as you're clear about your customer profile, your place in your competitive environment, and the point of difference that sets you apart and provides customers a reason to buy from you and you alone, you're ready to write your positioning statement.

Your *positioning statement* defines the niche that only your offering fills in the marketplace. It isn't a public announcement; rather, it's an internal marketing compass. After you establish your positioning statement, use it within your company to guide all your branding and marketing communication efforts.

Before writing your positioning statement, answer these questions:

- Is your point of difference unique and hard for a competitor to duplicate?
- Do your distinctions or differences truly matter to your customers?
- Does your offering sync well with economic and cultural trends?
- Will customers believe your claims about your offering? Can you support or prove your claim?

If you can answer "yes" to these questions, sharpen your pencil or hit your keyboard to write a positioning statement covering the following points:

1. Your customer profile
2. Name of your company or product
3. Your business description
4. A summary of your point of difference

Here's a positioning statement template to get you going:

For [*a description of your target audience or ideal customer*], [*the name of your brand*] is the [*your point of distinction, for example,* the only specialist in, the most recognized, the highest-rated] [*a description of your offering, for example,* café bakery, micro-home builder, hometown brewpub] that provides/delivers/promises [*a description of the value and benefit you promise and deliver to customers*] because only [*the name of your brand*] [*a description of facts that give people a reason to believe your positioning claim*].

After writing your positioning statement, evaluate its accuracy by asking

✔ Is it believable?

✔ Is it consistent with what people who know your business believe to be true about you, the way you operate, and the benefits you deliver?

✔ Can you consistently deliver the distinct attributes as they're stated?

✔ Can you package and deliver your point of difference with such consistency that every single time customers encounter your brand, your distinction is reinforced and the experience reminds customers of why they chose and remain loyal to your brand?

Steer clear of these positioning landmines:

✔ Don't try to claim a position already held by another brand.

✔ Don't base your position on a point of difference you can't protect. For instance, don't base your position on having the lowest price, because a competitor can always best you on that front.

✔ Don't build your position around an attribute you can't control, such as being the "only provider of XYZ service." Unless you establish a barrier to entry by competitors through a license or other protection, you leave yourself vulnerable to having the very attribute you built your brand upon eroded by a quick move by a new player in your game.

When your positioning statement passes these tests, you've found a place to build your brand. Congratulations! Now you can start putting your brand promise and brand definition into words (see Chapter 6).

Chapter 6

Putting Your Brand into Words

- -

- -

*B*uilding a brand and building a home have two things in common: Both need a site to occupy — an available lot in the case of a home and an open marketplace position in the case of a brand — and both require a plan that you can follow in order to achieve the desired outcome.

The process of finding an unoccupied place in your competitive landscape is called *positioning;* it's the first important step in branding and the topic of Chapter 5. Planning the brand you intend to create is what this chapter is all about.

The pages in this chapter help you lay the foundation for a brand that accurately reflects the essence of what you stand for and how you operate. You start by pulling out your mission and vision statements. (If you don't already have them, don't panic but do count on the next section to help you get your statements into words.) Next, you define the promise you make to all who deal with you and your organization. After that, you decide on the brand character that will influence all expressions of your brand — your name, logo, tagline, advertising, website, the products and services you offer, the staff you assemble, the customer experience you deliver, and the reputation you develop as a result. Finally, the chapter ends with steps to follow as you craft the brand statement or brand definition that will steer all your brand-building decisions and efforts.

Building Your Brand on the Strong Back of Your Business Mission and Vision

Your brand is a reflection of what you stand for, so it has to align perfectly with the values and purpose of your business or organization.

If you're unclear about what you want your brand to stand for, the customers it serves, and what it promises, this section is especially for you. It's also a must-read if you have a good sense of your vision and mission but haven't yet committed anything to writing. This is the time to put ideas into words.

Branding starts with two essential statements:

- ✔ **Your vision statement** defines your long-term aspirations. It explains why you're doing what you're doing and the ultimate good you want to achieve through your success. Think of your vision as the picture of where you ultimately want your work to lead you.

- ✔ **Your mission statement** defines the purpose of your work and the effect you intend to have on the world around you. It states what you do for others and the approach you follow as you aim to achieve the aspirations you've set for yourself, your organization, or your business. Think of your mission as the route you'll follow to achieve your vision.

A good historic example of clearly defined vision and mission statements comes from the 19th-century trek across America called the Oregon Trail. The Oregon Trail vision was to find a better life; the mission was to travel by wagon from Missouri to Oregon.

For a far, far more recent example of how a vision and mission relate — and how they translate into a motto or tagline — consider these statements from the business-oriented social-media network LinkedIn:

- ✔ **Vision:** To create economic opportunity for every professional in the world.

- ✔ **Mission:** To connect the world's professionals to make them more productive and successful.

- ✔ **Motto or tagline:** Relationships matter.

Use the information in the following sections to write statements that guide the development of your brand.

Focusing your vision

You probably have a vision of the good that you aim to achieve in your world. Likewise, you probably have a set of principles and values that guide how you operate and what you are and aren't willing to do to achieve success.

If you haven't already done so, commit your vision and values to words. They're fundamental to what you stand for and they guide development of your brand image.

The values you value

Start by clarifying your *values* — your beliefs about your responsibility to others. The worksheet in Figure 6-1 can guide your thinking.

VALUES WORKSHEET

Use the provided values as a point from which to launch your thinking as you list all the values that steer your decision-making and the direction of your organization. After you compile a list of all values you believe play a significant role in your business decisions and plans, put a check mark alongside the few that you feel take precedence over all others.

☐ Satisfied customers	☐ Maximum profits	☐ Long-term success
☐ Enjoyable business atmosphere	☐ Healthy, satisfied, fulfilled employees	☐ Dominant market position
☐ Leading technologies and innovations	☐ Industry and market recognition	☐ Environmental protection
☐ Product quality	☐ Ethical standards	☐ Contribution to community
☐ _____	☐ _____	☐ _____
☐ _____	☐ _____	☐ _____
☐ _____	☐ _____	☐ _____
☐ _____	☐ _____	☐ _____

Figure 6-1: Determine the values that influence your decisions.

© Barbara Findlay Schenck

Your statement of values can take the form of a simple list that declares the principles that steer your strategies and decisions. For example, the Whole Foods website dedicates a page to a list of the company's core values, including the following:

- ✔ Sell the highest quality natural and organic products available.
- ✔ Satisfy, delight, and nourish our customers.
- ✔ Support team member excellence and happiness.
- ✔ Create wealth through profits and growth.
- ✔ Serve and support our local and global communities.

Your highest hopes and aspirations

Your *vision statement* puts into a single sentence the reason your business exists. Regardless of whether you relocate, make operational changes, update your logo, revise your marketing message, or undertake other strategic or tactical changes, the vision of what you're aiming to achieve — the good you intend to do in your world — should remain stable.

Many organizations post their vision statements on their corporate websites. Following are a few examples:

- **TED Global Community:** To make great ideas accessible and to spark conversation.
- **Habitat For Humanity:** A world where everyone has a decent place to live.

As you develop your own vision statement, consider these questions:

- What makes you and those in your organization want to go to work every day? You could earn a living at any number of places, so what is it about the vision and purpose of what you do that keeps you loyal and motivated?
- What change are you aiming to affect in your world? What lasting difference do you want to make?
- What ultimate benefits do your products and services deliver?

Use your answers to compile a vision statement that summarizes what you feel is the highest purpose you (for personal brands) or your business aim for.

Defining your mission

Your vision is your ultimate dream; your mission is how you'll achieve your aspirations. There's no one format to follow in writing your business mission, but it's important to address the following points:

- Who you serve
- How you are unique
- What value, benefits, or greater good you promise

Your statement doesn't have to look just like anyone else's. For instance, the Instagram mission statement is one sentence long:

> *To capture and share the world's moments.*

The Peace Corps mission lists three goals:

1. *Helping the people of interested countries in meeting their needs for trained men and women.*
2. *Helping promote a better understanding of Americans on the part of the people served.*
3. *Helping promote a better understanding of other peoples on the part of all Americans.*

Figure 6-2 includes questions to help focus your thinking, along with a framework for assembling your mission statement.

STATING YOUR MISSION WORKSHEET
In a sentence, how do you describe what your company does?
In a phrase, what product or service do you offer?
In a phrase, what group of people do you serve?
What benefits or positive outcome do you promise to those you serve?
When thinking about your offerings compared to competitive offerings, what words would those who know your business well use to explain how you are different or better?

Figure 6-2:
Use these questions and framework as you assemble your mission statement.

Mission Statement Framework

[*Name of your business*] provides [*description of the product or service your business offers*] for [*describe the group of people you serve*] who seek [*define the positive benefit you deliver*] and who prefer our solution over available alternatives because we [*describe your point of difference as described in Chapter 5*]

© Barbara Findlay Schenck

Describing Your Brand and Its Style

Before you try to put your brand into words, called a *brand statement* (which is the topic of one of the final sections in this chapter), stop to think about what your brand is really all about. If you're working on a personal brand, start by working on your own. If you're developing a brand for a business or product, pull together key team members to do some brainstorming and recon work. Discuss answers to each of these questions:

✔ **What simple idea captures the essence of what your brand stands for?** For example, as we're writing this chapter a hot new service category is emerging around laundry and dry-cleaning services. One major player, Washio, describes itself as the "Uber of laundry," serving "whimsy-embracing millennials" with service ordered via smartphone app, transacted by a "delivery ninja," and concluded with the high-touch gesture of a chocolate chip cookie. Another player, Flycleaners, describes its idea as an app-driven, on-demand premium service without premium prices. A third contender, MintLocker, captures its idea in its brand name: It provides 24/7 lockers for laundry drop-off and pickup, returning clothes with a cupcake to communicate fresh service and a human approach.

✔ **How would you quickly describe your brand as the elevator doors are closing?** We pose this question in Chapter 3 as you self-assess your brand's image in preparation for launching the branding process. We're asking it again because it's such an important question to answer. The minute-long elevator pitch is a relic from the 1990s. We're living in the age of the social-media pitch, which on Twitter takes the form of a 160-character Twitter user bio. That equates to about 20 words to convey your message, cause heads to spin around, and win the chance to tell a fuller story. By asking yourself and your team members to come up with spur-of-the-moment one-sentence description, you collect words that people use conversationally to describe your brand. As a result, you uncover aspects of your brand personality that people relate to — and love. Those words will be invaluable as you define your brand character later in this chapter.

✔ **What one thing, above all others, makes you different from competitors and valuable to customers?** Chapter 5 helps you find your position in your competitive landscape based upon your point of difference and the distinct and meaningful value that you provide to all who come in contact with you or your business. Use your findings to list your competitors and which attributes set each one apart from the others. Then describe how your offerings are different and why that difference matters to people in your target audience. You can't build a strong brand without knowing the answer to this question. It becomes the basis for both the character and promise of your brand.

Polishing Your Business Promise

Your *brand promise* is the pledge upon which you build and stake your reputation. It's what those who come into contact with you or your business can count on you to consistently deliver. It's the expectation that you live up to every time people experience your brand, whether online or in person, or through advertising, promotions, buying experiences, service encounters, or any other form of contact.

Your promise is the essence of your brand. Don't make the common mistake of thinking that your logo is the sum total of your brand identity. When people think of your brand, they may visualize your logo, but your promise is what motivates them in your direction.

When Nordstrom posts that it's "committed to providing our customers with the best possible service — and to improving it every day," it's making a promise. Geico's "15 minutes or less can save you 15 percent" is a promise. Zappo's "The best customer service possible" is a promise. Each one puts a company's reputation on the line by pledging to live up to high expectations, or else. The promise becomes an internal rallying call for excellence and a magnet for new business.

If you're not sure of your brand promise, consider these questions:

- ✔ Why do customers choose your business? What do they seek from you that they can't get elsewhere?

- ✔ What attributes do customers count on that they would find the hardest to replace if your business weren't available to them?

Answer these questions on your own, ask managers and others in your business to answer them, and then go to a few key customers and ask for their input. Explain what you're up to. Tell them that, as part of your branding strategy, you're clarifying the way your business promise is interpreted in the market, and you'd appreciate their responses to the preceding questions.

When you're done with your analysis, take these steps:

1. **List all the reasons customers choose your business and the attributes they count on only your company to deliver.**

2. **Circle all the attributes you're confident that you can deliver consistently and upon which you're willing to stake your reputation.**

3. **Put a check mark next to those attributes that are compelling to customers and to your internal team — the ones you can proudly rally around.**

4. **Take the checked items and make a short list of business attributes that are most assured, most compelling, most believable, and most consistent with the character of your company.**

Your final list of attributes provides the basis upon which to build your business promise. Following are a few more examples of brand promises to get you started:

- ✔ **Samsung:** Taking the world in imaginative new directions.
- ✔ **BMW:** Genuine driving pleasure.

✔ **Walmart:** Saving people money so they can live better.

✔ **Disney:** Only Disney can deliver a fantasy experience for families to share.

You can see from the examples, brand promises often boil down into mottos or declarative statements around which businesses coalesce. They start, however, with internal commitments. Use the following template to write the commitment you'll incorporate into your promise and branding strategy.

> [*Name of your business, product, or service*] is the [*your distinction and the generic term for your type of offering*] to provide [*your unique features or benefits*] to [*your customer profile*] who choose our offering in order to feel [*your customers' emotional outcome*].

> We consistently deliver the unique attributes and benefits our customers count on, and we promise our customers [*the promise customers can absolutely count on from your company*].

Broken promises break brands. As you put your promise into words, make sure it's one you can deliver upon consistently. Staying true to your word and upholding your promise is essential to building brand trust and loyalty.

Considering the Character of Your Brand

Your *brand character* is like the personality of your brand. Some brands are serious or even somber, and some are whimsical, fun, or playful. Some brands are youthful, and some are like silver-haired sages.

As a first step toward defining your brand character, ask yourself these questions:

✔ **What adjectives do those near and dear to your brand use to describe it?** When asked to give a spur-of-the-moment one-sentence description, what do they say?

✔ **How would your brand be described if it were a person who walked into the room?** Sophisticated? Fashionable? Flamboyant? Reserved? Important? Playful? Or one of countless other descriptions? Keep your answer in mind as you go through the rest of this section.

✔ **What words do customers use when they pay compliments, post reviews, or fill out satisfaction surveys? What words do you think they'd use to describe how they feel when they deal with you or your business?** Would they use words like *fun, creative, cool, serious, innovative, sophisticated,* or others? See the following list for words Bill Chiaravalle presents to help brand-builders think about how customers might describe their character of their brands.

Choose Five Words You Feel Best Describe Your Brand:

Cool	Innovative
Gourmet	Irreverent
Hip	Masculine
Fun	Serious
Friendly	Elegant
Fast	Quality
Unique	Youthful
Sophisticated	

The answers are important because the brand character reflected through the look and voice of your brand expressions must be consistent with what your brand actually is and stands for. If not, you'll face two problems:

✔ Your brand expressions will roam all over the map, serious at one time and playful at another depending on the mood and whim of whomever is producing them, and you'll wind up with a schizophrenic brand identity.

✔ The brand identity you project into the marketplace will be inconsistent with the brand experience people actually encounter, leading to a lack of credibility and a poor reputation.

Use the following format to write an accurate brand character statement that guides the development of all expressions of your brand:

Our brand is [*insert a description of the character of your brand*], a trait we reflect through brand expressions that are [*insert a description of the mood and voice that all your marketing will project*].

Mission Possible: Defining Your Brand

Your *brand statement*, also called your *brand definition*, shrinks all your thoughts about your business mission, values, promise, and character into a concise statement that defines what you do, how you differ from all other similar solutions, and what you pledge to consistently deliver.

The brand statement you develop serves as the steering wheel for your branding strategy. It influences every turn you make in presenting your brand — from giving it a name and logo to producing ads and marketing materials to creating the experience that customers will encounter when they come into contact with your brand from any direction.

What to incorporate

As you write your brand statement, be sure that it reflects the following information:

- ✔ The three things you want people to know about your business: What you offer, the audience you serve, and how you're best at what you do.

- ✔ Your point of difference (how you serve your target market differently and better than all other options).

- ✔ Your business promise that will be upheld through all brand experiences.

- ✔ Your brand character or personality that will be communicated through the mood and voice projected in all brand expressions.

The anatomy of a brand statement

Your brand identity is the face of your brand. It includes your name, logo, tagline or motto, advertising, marketing materials, signage, and every other way that you express your brand in your business and in your marketplace.

Your brand statement guides your brand identity. It describes the people your brand must relate to, the attributes it must highlight, and the promise and character it must convey. To write a brand statement that guides your branding strategy, use this format:

> [*Your name*] promises [*your target market*] that they can count on us for [*your unique attribute or benefit*] delivered with [*information about the character, voice, and mood you convey*].

Grading your statement

Before accepting your brand statement as the one that will guide your branding strategy, see if you can answer "yes" to these three questions:

- ✔ **Does the statement illuminate your difference?** Does it make it clear how you differ from other solutions in your business arena?

- ✔ **Is the statement customer-centric?** Does it clarify what valuable benefit or value you provide and promise to others rather than what you aspire for yourself?

✔ **Can you project the statement with a unified voice across all markets and media?** And can you fulfill its promise through every contact with your business and as part of the overall customer experience with your brand?

Putting your brand statement to the test

After you commit to your brand statement, test it internally within your business and with key customer or prospective customer groups.

In personal meetings and focus-group sessions, confirm that the brand statement you've crafted resonates with your target market audience by learning the answers to these questions:

✔ Is the promise you make consistent with the beliefs people currently hold about you? Or if you're branding a new business or product, is the promise one in which you realistically believe you can develop trust?

   • Is the promise one you can live up to through every form of marketplace encounter?

   • Is the promise easy to understand? If one customer were to explain it to another, do you believe they would be able to express it clearly?

✔ Are the unique attributes or benefits highlighted in your brand statement truly meaningful to customers?

✔ Is the character that you've summarized in your brand statement consistent with the character that others believe you exude?

✔ If you uncover slight differences between the promise, benefits, and character defined in your brand identity statement and the attributes others believe to be true about your business, are you clear about what adjustments would align the two mind-sets?

If your brand will serve a concise, easy-to-reach, and relatively small market, you can test your brand statement on your own, using the research advice presented in Chapter 4. For brands that serve larger markets or face major competition from established and recognized brands, invest in professional assistance to test your statement before putting it to work as you name your brand, design its logo and tagline, and create the marketing materials and brand experience that will present it day in and day out in your market.

Chapter 7

Naming Your Brand

*I*f you haven't yet named your brand, you just opened to what may be the most important chapter in this book.

Naming your brand is by far the most challenging, momentous, and necessary phase in the process of branding. Before you can proceed to develop a brand identity, you need a name that's appropriate, available, appealing, and enduring. Truly, naming a brand is as important — and as difficult — as naming a baby.

Other identifiers of your brand — including your logo, tagline, and color scheme — may change over time, but unless you totally rebrand, your name will remain pretty much intact. You may evolve it (Coca-Cola to Coke or Federal Express to FedEx come to mind), but from the day you announce it, your name will likely remain the key that unlocks your brand image in the minds of customers. So you have to get it right the first time around.

This chapter sheds light on the value of your brand name, how to recognize the characteristics of a good name, and how to come up with and protect a name that works well from the start and long into your successful future.

What's in a Name?

The right name distinguishes you from all others, and ideally, it establishes your personality, brand character, market position, and the nature of your offering. The very best name accomplishes the following objectives:

✔ It reflects the brand character you want to project.

✔ It's descriptive of your offering.

✔ It creates an association to the meaning of your brand.

✔ It's easy and pleasant to say.

✔ It's unique and memorable.

Not all great names score a ten in all areas, but nearly every good name scores well on most fronts, and only a rare few successful names strike out completely on any one of the preceding characteristics. Use this section to guide your selection — or creation — of the name for your brand.

What the right name does

The right name establishes your brand from the day you announce it and grows with your vision as you evolve into new market areas, new geographic regions, and even new product areas.

In the same way you wouldn't want to give a baby a name that doesn't transition to adulthood, you don't want to give your brand a name that hinders its future development. For that reason, most forward-thinking marketers avoid names like First Avenue Dry Cleaning, for instance, unless they're absolutely certain that they'll always be on First Avenue and that they'll always focus on dry cleaning as their primary offering.

In choosing your name, the following considerations outweigh all others:

✔ Your name should convey or support your desired brand image.

✔ Your name should convey or be consistent with your brand promise.

✔ Your name should have the capability to grow with your brand and to appreciate as an asset that can be harvested through premium pricing, through licensing, or even through the sale of shares in your business or the outright sale of your brand name to a future owner.

Convey or imply your brand image

If you're at all unclear about your desired brand image, flip back to Chapter 6, which leads you through the process of crafting the statement that steers all decisions regarding the expression of your brand and the image you create in the marketplace.

Your brand statement follows this framework:

> [*Your business*] promises [*your target market*] that they can count on us for [*unique attribute or benefit*] delivered with [*information about the character, voice, and mood you convey*].

REAL WORLD

Bend brand-name rules at a price and with a payoff

Some businesses inherit, live with, or even choose names that go against some or all the textbook criteria for a great brand name — and they end up with great brands anyway. They take the risk because they know unusual names can work (see the later sidebar "The case for an outside-the-box brand name") They also invest marketing time and money to build stories around their names, and in the process they build affection, loyalty, and equity for names that, without significant marketing support, would have probably made it into Chapter 20 of this book as examples of branding mistakes to avoid.

Want an example of a rule-breaking name? Smucker's. In 1897, Jerome Monroe Smucker was pressing fruit from Johnny Appleseed's tree plantings at his Ohio mill and selling the resulting products from the back of a horse-drawn wagon. Before long, Smucker's name became associated with his personal guarantee of

product quality, a promise that evolved over the years into the hallmark of a brand that's distributed worldwide and ranks as North America's market leader in the categories of jams, jellies, preserves, and other specialty items.

Of and by itself, the Smucker's name wouldn't pass brand name tests or research studies. But with time, commitment, and excellent marketing, the name has become a brand success story. To quote from company literature: "We still proudly display our name on every jar because . . . with a name like Smucker's, it has to be good."

Takeaway advice: Before choosing a name that doesn't quickly and clearly convey your brand in a pleasant and easy-to-recall and repeat manner, plan to invest heavily in marketing efforts to create positive associations that don't stem naturally from your name choice.

REMEMBER

A name that doesn't directly or obviously reflect your brand statement — that doesn't obviously convey or imply the nature of your target market, your brand promise, or your brand character — can turn out to be a spectacularly strong brand name if (and this is a big if) you're willing and able to invest the time and marketing budget to win awareness, acceptance, and enthusiasm for what it means. As proof, consider names such as Apple, Google, and Amazon, along with many of today's other best-known brands. The names themselves don't convey promises or differentiate offerings, yet they successfully label megabrands thanks to terrific awareness-building and brand-management programs that have injected the names with meaning in consumers' minds.

At the other end of the spectrum, consider great brand names like Dunkin' Donuts and Southwest Airlines, which instantaneously convey their brand purposes even to those who have never heard the names before.

Either approach works, but the smaller your marketing budget, the wiser you are to settle on a brand name that automatically conveys your brand essence. Doing so lessens the need for extensive and costly education to create meaning for your name.

Advance your brand promise

Your brand name should convey, imply, or support your brand promise. There's no hard-and-fast rule about the degree to which your name must reveal your promise. However, if your name only hints at what you do and offer, then you'd better be prepared to invest marketing time, effort, and money to tell the story not communicated by your name.

Some brands put the brand promise right into the brand name. Well-known examples include

- Jiffy Lube service centers
- DieHard automotive batteries
- Terminix pest control
- Lean Cuisine entrees
- Powerade sports drink
- Coppertone suncare products
- Miracle-Gro plant food
- Ziploc storage bags
- Clear Eyes eye drops

Some brands imply the promise that customers can count on through names that are consistent with the benefits they deliver. Examples include

- NETFLIX: Movie and TV-show subscription service
- Victoria's Secret: Romantic, stylish, and feminine lingerie
- Foot Locker: Athletic footwear and apparel
- Sunkist: Fresh fruit
- The Home Depot: Home improvement retailer
- Legalzoom: Personalized online legal solutions

Other names neither convey nor imply the brand promise. Instead, they support the brand's commitment by being consistent in character and presentation to the brand's offering. Here are a couple of examples:

✔ **Yahoo!:** The name doesn't say or imply *search engine, email, web hosting,* or *news.* Nor does it convey a brand promise. Instead, the name communicates an experience that's fast, fun, and successful.

✔ **Twitter:** The name doesn't say or imply a microblogging social network that "helps you create and share ideas instantly, without barriers," which is what the company promises. Instead, as co-founder Jack Dorsey told the *Los Angeles Times,* the name encapsulates what the product is by conjuring up "a short burst of inconsequential information" and "chirps from birds."

Regardless of whether your promise is directly presented, implied, or simply supported through your brand name, make sure it's pegged to a commitment that's small enough to keep but big enough to grow with your business. You can probably think of a brand that promised to be the "hometown" business only to chase opportunity in a nearby market area where, eventually, the headquarters moved and the hometown promise evaporated.

Become an asset

Good brand names accumulate value that pays off in the following ways:

✔ As a well-managed brand gains awareness, its promise becomes trusted, and that trust carries a value for which consumers are willing to pay a premium, leading to stronger sales and higher profits.

✔ As a well-managed brand gains market recognition, it becomes valued by other marketers who want to cross-promote with or even license the brand name to benefit from its strong and positive image, leading to marketing and business opportunities.

✔ As a well-managed brand grows into a marketplace success story, others want to own part of it, at which time the brand builder can harvest the brand's value through a public offering or a complete or partial sale.

For advice on leveraging your brand's value, see Chapter 15. But first, put yourself in position to build your brand into an asset by following these naming tips:

✔ **Choose a name that can grow with your brand.**

• **Avoid names that limit your product range.** Unless you're certain that you'll never want to sell anything other than lamps, for instance, be careful about calling yourself The Lamp Store.

• **Give your brand some geographic elbow room.** The advantages of not tying your name to a single geographic region are twofold. By avoiding a name like Milwaukee Web Services, you allow your business to expand into new market areas without the burden of an out-of-town name or the need for a new name altogether. You also you keep yourself out of the lineup of all the other business names that start with Milwaukee in business directories.

✔ **Especially if you think you may someday sell your business, choose a name that isn't your own (referred to as *Me, Inc.* in the branding business).** At the time of sale, a good portion of your brand equity resides in *goodwill,* which is the positive value of your name and reputation. If your brand name is *your* name and more closely affiliated with your image than with the image of your business offerings, buyers will probably want rename it, and they'll want to pay less as a result.

✔ **Choose a name that's unique, memorable, and easy to recall.**

When naming happens

Most brands get their names at one of the following three times:

✔ **When a business or product is being introduced for the first time**

This is when most brands are named and is likely the situation you're facing as you read this chapter.

✔ **When an existing business or product name is burdened with a negative connotation**

For example, Kentucky Fried Chicken renamed itself KFC, freeing it to market offerings beyond the range of fried foods and chicken. Another example is Phillip Morris, which became Altria to distance itself from its tobacco heritage.

✔ **When growth opportunities for a business or product are limited by the nature of its existing name**

For example, Federal Express became FedEx, giving itself a shorter name that better exemplifies the company's speed promise while at the same time deemphasizing the word "federal" to better reflect the brand's worldwide market and independent, nongovernment ownership. Likewise, the charge card in your billfold didn't always carry the brand name VISA. It used to be called BankAmericard, a name that was abandoned in the mid-1970s in favor of a name that was shorter, instantly recognizable, pronounceable in any language, and had no country or language affiliations.

Types of names

The brand name selection process usually results in a name that fits into one of the following categories:

✔ **The owner's name or names:** An owner's name can serve as the basis for a business name, such as Joe Smith's Piano Tuning Service. On a far larger scale, an owner's name (or two owners' names, in this case) can serve as the basis for a merged business name, such as ExxonMobil.

Especially for small business sole proprietors, forming a business with the name of the owner is the default naming approach. You simply add words that describe the nature of your business to your own name and just like that Jane Smith becomes Jane Smith Accounting or Jane Smith Portrait Photography. The name is likely to be available and easy to register with government offices (with no need for the search-and-protect steps detailed in "Catch It If You Can: Claiming Your Name" later in this chapter). The name is also capable of advancing the promise that the owner personally stands by the company's products or services.

The downside to using an owner's name is that without significant marketing, personal names rarely develop the kind of widespread awareness and sky-high credibility that translate to premium pricing and future sale value.

✔ **Abbreviation names:** People think of easy-to-recall names like IBM, AOL, or AFLAC and believe that a similarly short abbreviation or acronym will work for them. In each of these examples, though, the businesses started with longer names that only after extensive marketing became the initials that mean something to consumers today. Unless you can invest accordingly, avoid this route. Either you'll end up with a string of initials that mean little to consumers or you'll end up with a generic name like AAA Equipment Rental, which exudes no personality or promise and has only one benefit — it appears first in phone book listings that today's customers rarely consult. That's hardly a brand-building strategy!

✔ **Geographically anchored names:** These are names that work to capitalize on a known local landmark or geographic indicator. Think Central Coast Bank, Pleasantville Grocery, and Cascade Mountain Insurance. Most names of this kind blur into a group of like-named entities. A few stand out as esteemed brands (kudos to Pebble Beach Resorts) but only after significant investments of time and money to market the name into a distinguished brand.

✔ **Descriptive names:** These names describe what the brand offers or promises. U-Haul, Budget Rent A Car, Dropbox, Purex, and Curves are examples of descriptive names.

✔ **Borrowed interest names:** These names use existing words that don't directly reflect the brand's offerings or promise but can be linked to a brand's essence through marketing efforts rather than through direct translation. Good examples include Apple, Nike, Yahoo!, Skechers, and Starbucks.

✔ **Fabricated-word names:** These names combine acronyms, words, or syllables to form previously unknown words and brand names. Google, Verizon, Microsoft, and Mozilla are all are easy to repeat, easy to recall names that have been imbued with meaning thanks to their branding and marketing efforts. Because they're newly invented words, fabricated names are usually available for trademark protection, and the domain names that contain them are likely to be available, too.

Fitting your name to your brand architecture

Before you settle on a brand name, consider how and where the brand will fit within your business, which is known as *brand architecture* (see Chapter 2).

Most brands fit into one of these architecture categories:

- ✔ **Independent brands:** These stand-alone brands represent every offering and activity of the organizations they represent. Most small businesses create independent brands for the simple reason that they're easier to build, manage, and market. At the same time, many very large organizations also present all their offerings under a single brand. The Red Cross is a good example.

- ✔ **Master-brands with parent-driven brands:** Parent-driven brands are closely and very visibly tied to the name and credibility of the top-level master brand. For example, a nonprofit organization that hosts a well-known annual fundraiser probably may treat the yearly event as a parent-driven brand of the organization. On a larger scale, GE is a master brand with an array of parent-driven brands including GE Energy, GE Aviation, and GE Profile, all connected to the parent brand by the brand name GE. Apple is a master brand that connects the brands for iTunes, iPod, iPhone, and iPad to the master brand through consistent use of the Apple logo.

- ✔ **Multiple product-driven brands:** Some businesses introduce each major product as its own brand. The behemoth example is P&G, but smaller businesses also build multiple brands. Think of the chef with three individually named and branded restaurants as an example.

- ✔ **Brand extensions:** These brands piggyback on the recognition of an established parent brand while carrying the brand into a new and different market segment. A few examples are Arm & Hammer Deodorant, Starbucks Coffee Liqueur, and RainX Windshield Wiper Blades. (We tell you more about brand extensions in Chapter 15.)

Most successful smaller businesses build a single, independent brand — for good reason. Building, managing, protecting, and consistently conveying a brand takes time, money, and tremendous dedication. Creating multiple brands doubles or triples the branding work and often results in a lack of focus on the primary brand that drives the company's success.

Rather than create multiple brands, build a single, dominant brand that presides over a number of product lines, events, fundraising campaigns, or other entities. As you name each new offering, be sure that the name you select complements the promise of your top-level brand. If it doesn't, throw it out of the running and move on to other names that fit with the identity and character of the brand under which all other products fit.

Roundabout advice from Mark Twain

Consider this quote from Mark Twain:

Sufficient unto the day is one baby. As long as you are in your right mind, don't ever pray for twins. Twins amount to a permanent riot; and there ain't any real difference between triplets and an insurrection.

Twain could well have been talking about brands rather than babies because one brand is sufficient for most small businesses, and more than one brand is more than most small businesses can handle and manage well.

Unless your marketing expertise is high and your budget large, make all your products, events, or other offerings live under the strong umbrella of your one-and-only brand.

Naming advice to follow

As you brainstorm name ideas, scan Table 7-1 for a list of qualities remarkable names have in common as well as naming mistakes to avoid.

Table 7-1	Naming Advice
Qualities of Remarkable Brand Names	*What to Avoid*
Easy to say, spell, and pronounce	Unusual spellings or pronunciations that consumers won't remember — unless you have the time and funds to invest in developing marketplace awareness
Short enough to present consistently on social media and in marketing materials	A long name that's apt to be abbreviated in ways not consistent with the brand's character
A unique name that you can claim, register, and protect from use by others	A generic name that's hard to distinguish and almost impossible to protect
Reflective of your business offering or promise — either directly, indirectly, or through association	A copycat name that borrows from well-known bigger brands, causing marketplace confusion and risking lawsuits
Capable of expanding to apply to new products or geographic market area	A name that limits the brand's opportunity to expand its offerings or geographic sphere
Consistent with your brand character	Owner names, especially if you plan to sell your business in the foreseeable future
Available to trademark	
Available as a domain name	

The case for an outside-the-box brand name

If you have an offbeat, hard-to-spell, or even controversial brand name, don't ditch it too quickly. Here's advice from Socrates via Plato (we're talking age-old wisdom here): A name should "possess some sort of natural correctness . . . if a letter is added or subtracted, that doesn't matter either so long as the being or essence of the thing is in control and expressed by the name. . . . I myself prefer the view that names should be as much like things as possible, but I fear that defending this view is like hauling a ship up a sticky ramp."

In other words, so long as you can build a name into a good expression of your brand, go for it. In fact, in an age of split-second attention spans, an unusual name can provide the hook that lets you tell your brand story. Here are other advantages of odd names:

✔ They're likely available as domain names.

✔ They're more likely to rise to the top of web searches.

✔ They require explanation and commitment, which forces stronger brand management.

To etch an unusual name into a positive brand asset, consider these approaches:

✔ **Turn a positive to a negative.** Follow the example of Smucker's (see the sidebar, "Bend brand name rules at a price and with a payoff").

✔ **Use humor.** Senator Lisa Murkowski took on those questioning her ability to win a write-in campaign with ads asking, "Alaskans can't fill in an oval and spell M-U-R-K-O-W-S-K-I?"

✔ **Make the name part of your brand platform.** The makeup company Urban Decay defines itself as "feminine, dangerous, and fun," reinforcing its self-declared "crazy name" through product names like Roach, Smog, Rust, Oil Slick, and Acid Rain.

✔ **Stay true to your name.** Consider how Apple didn't run from the name iPad, even when loyal customers initially — and virally — resisted the label.

Picking (or Inventing) Your Brand Name

When it comes time to name your brand, get ready to invest some time and even some money, especially if your brand's going to span a large market area, compete against major brand names, or support a major vision that will take decades to achieve and therefore will live long into the future.

Whether you choose to name your brand with or without professional assistance from a marketing firm or branding group, involve your own team in the process by following these steps:

1. **List the attributes you want to reflect in your brand name.**

   Consider the following:

   - What terms out of your brand statement do you most want your name to convey, reflect, or support?
   - What aspects of your brand promise would you like your name to advance?
   - What words define the character you want your name to convey?

2. **Bring together key business partners, managers, and staff members and ask them to answer the three questions listed in Step 1. Then ask them what kinds of names come to their minds.**

   Before you begin to brainstorm names, or before you involve professional assistance, this initial internal reaction focuses you on the brand essence, attributes, and character that seem true to those who are most involved with your business and its differentiating attributes.

3. **Decide who will actually choose your name.**

   Will the final choice rest with a single person or with the team? Will it require a unanimous vote or will the majority rule? Will one person have veto power?

4. **Involve all who will have a say — especially the key decision maker — in the naming process.**

   You're setting yourself up for trouble if the person who will ultimately approve the name fails to participate in the process and lacks understanding of the reasons behind the name ideas being presented.

Rounding up good ideas

Whether you're naming your brand on your own or involving a branding consultant or marketing firm, begin by giving thought to the kinds of names you think do and don't suit the character and vision of your brand.

Consider holding a retreat to get creative ideas flowing. Not every idea will be a good idea; that's the nature of brainstorming. But the process produces the kinds of names you think fit well with your business. From there, you can narrow down the choices, or you can turn your initial ideas over to a branding consultant or marketing firm for professional advice.

Brainstorming

At the beginning of a brainstorming session, participants usually are shy about getting creative or throwing out what may seem like wild ideas. Ease people into the process by starting the session with a discussion of what kinds of feelings the participants would like people to have when they hear your brand name, whatever it turns out to be.

Have an easel or white board available and write down every emotion you hear. Then group them into categories, such as reputation, expertise, features and benefits, or any other labels that seem to fit over clusters of words that emerged from the discussion.

Then leave the categories in sight as you begin to brainstorm names that may induce the desired responses.

As you brainstorm name ideas, encourage creativity by following these tips:

- ✔ **Give every idea its time and space.** The quickest way to kill creativity is to shut down ideas with comments like, "That's been done before," "That won't work," or "That's not what we're looking for."

- ✔ **When an idea seems to come out of left field, encourage alternatives.** Prompt ideas with comments like, "What other words describe that same concept?" and "How can we say that and fit within our brand character?"

- ✔ **Probe ideas.** Ask participants to describe the underlying meaning of the names they're presenting. Sometimes in their descriptions they'll uncover other names that are even more appropriate.

- ✔ **Encourage alternative perspectives.** Ask participants to stand in the shoes of others and to think of how they'd describe your brand from the point of view of a child, a celebrity, an older consumer, or others who may not be represented by the brainstorming group.

Record the results of your brainstorming session and review them as soon after the session as possible. Circle the ideas that match your brand statement. They make up the short list that you work from as you narrow choices and begin to assemble name ideas (see the section "The hard part: Narrowing your list to the best options" later in this chapter).

Finding inspiration

To find a unique name, reach outside your usual work environment. Give the following ideas a try:

- ✔ **Go to the kinds of places where your target customers spend time.** If they eat in fast-food restaurants, go place an order, take a table, and observe. If they're avid shoppers, go downtown or to the mall. If they commute using mass transit, buy a ticket and take a ride or two.

  As you observe target customers in their surroundings, jot down names of books they're reading, the shopping bags they're carrying, and the labels they're wearing. Your discoveries may unlock ideas for a brand name that fits well with the interests and mind-set of your customer base.

✔ **Scan magazines and websites that you think your customers read.** Note ideas, names, or words that you think fit your brand character.

✔ **Also scan magazines and websites that are well outside the interest area of your customers.** If your customers are interested in fashion, go to a fish and bait shop, for instance. Look around at brand names. You may land on some interesting new concepts.

✔ **Look through dictionaries and a thesaurus.** In the English dictionary, look study the origins of words that describe your brand, seeing if they trace back to Greek, Latin, or other roots that may provide the basis for brand names. In international dictionaries, look for translations of words describing your brand promise or attributes that may make great names. In the thesaurus, find synonyms for words that describe your brand.

As part of your observation, take note of the kinds of names that catch your eye or ear. Are they names that convey or imply promises, names based on borrowed interest, or names that are fabricated from syllables and sounds to create one-of-a-kind new words? Your findings can guide your name decision.

The hard part: Narrowing your list to the best options

Narrowing potential names down to a few best choices is tough and emotional. You know that you're making a lasting decision, and until the name is announced and met with great fanfare, you can't really be certain that it's the ideal name.

When creating your short list of names, follow this advice:

✔ Include only a few top contenders unless you're planning to undertake a trademark search, in which case you need a longer list because many will be knocked out during the legal process.

✔ Keep your top name contenders tightly within your naming committee until you're ready to reveal your name selection. Then (and only then) you may want to show also-ran names as part of the rationale you present to build support for your top choice.

Not even the greatest name contenders can hold up to the scrutiny that follows a leak during water-cooler conversations. For that reason, don't let the names out of your committee until you select one and it's ready for presentation, backed by all the rationale for why it's a great choice and how it will excel in your marketing arena.

Putting your top contenders through a preliminary test

When you arrive at a short list of names you believe fit your brand well, put each one through the following series of questions and investigations.

✔ **Does it accurately depict or support your desired brand image?**

- Does it convey, imply, or accurately reflect your differentiating attributes and brand promise?

- Does it reflect your brand position? For instance, if your position is being the most professional, creative, responsive, efficient, or prestigious in your marketplace, does the name sound adequately professional, creative, responsive, efficient, or prestigious?

- Is it a credible reflection of your business today? For example, if you're a local firm, including the word *global* in your name may be quite a stretch.

- Can it grow with you as you achieve your highest aspiration and the vision of your business?

✔ **Is it easy to say?**

- Write each leading name on a piece of paper and ask a few confidants to read it out loud. Do they pronounce it correctly? Does it sound pleasing to the ear? (To avoid feeding the internal gossip mill, ask people outside your business.)

- Pretend that you're answering the phone and use the name in a greeting. ("Good morning, XYZ Company. May I help you?") Does it roll off the tongue, or is it awkward to say?

- Pretend that you're introducing yourself as the founder or president or chief inventor of the company. How does the name sound in professional conversations?

✔ **Is it easy to spell?**

- Say each name candidate out loud to others and ask them to write it down. Do they spell it correctly?

If the name's misspelled from time to time, you may well select it anyway, deciding that you can market your way around the problem. But make note of and save the various misspellings. As you establish your online identity, you can try to grab domain names for each of the erroneous spellings and automatically redirect them to your official website. (You can find more on the topic of establishing digital presence in Chapter 10.)

✔ **Is it unique?**

- Enter the name in several search engines and scan the results to see if the name is already in use by other businesses — and in which product categories and market areas.

- If your business serves a regional or local market area, search phone and business directories to see if similarly named businesses already exist. Also, conduct the same search in industry directories.

✔ **Does it translate well?** If your business will involve e-commerce or serve international markets, does the name you're considering have a positive connotation in other cultures? If you think you'll be targeting specific international audiences in the future, ask people familiar with the languages and cultures of those groups to react to the name. If you don't know anyone to ask, consider asking a university language professor for input.

✔ **Do you like the name?** If the name feels awkward to say or write, realize that you may simply be resisting a new idea. The fact that it sounds different is good and even necessary to stand out in the crowded market environment. If the name truly rubs you the wrong way, though, back away early and before you build your brand around it.

✔ **Can you protect it?** The final section of this chapter describes how to check availability, stake your claim, obtain your domain name, and protect your brand with a trademark if it will be crossing state and national borders. If the name's not available or protectable in your market area — whether that's your hometown, state, region, country, or the world — the sooner you know, the sooner you can strike it off your list and move on to the next best choice.

Building consensus around your top-choice name

To win support for your name selection, keep your decision makers in the loop throughout the process so that, as a top choice emerges, they're familiar with the name, the rationale for its selection, and the ways that it works on behalf of your business.

As you reach outside your decision-making circle to present the name to your entire company, turn to Chapter 9 for help launching your brand internally.

Checking for domain name availability

Your *domain name* is the string of characters that people type into their web browsers to reach your site. Ideally, you want your domain name to read www.[*yourbrandname*].com, or www.[*yourbrandname*].org if you're branding an organization, but in today's crowded online world, getting the domain name you want is far from guaranteed.

For an initial test of availability, open a web browser and enter the domain name of your dreams in the address line. Based on what you learn, here's what to do next:

✔ **If you get a message that no such page exists, you're in luck.** Open one of the many domain name registrar sites, conduct a free name search, to confirm that the name is available, and then claim it, quickly. Online real estate moves fast. Popular registrars include `NetworkSolutions.com`, `GoDaddy.com`, and `Namecheap.com`, among many others. Even if you end up choosing a different brand name, the low cost of registering and protecting your top contending names just in case is miniscule compared to the value of owning the domain name for what may become your winning brand-name choice.

✔ **If your initial search takes you straight to a web page, the domain name you want is already taken — sorry.** Likewise, if the registrar service reports that the name you want is not available with the top-level domain or suffix of *.com,* you have a couple of choices for what to do next.

• **One option is to bid to buy the name.** It may be owned by someone willing to part with the address — for a price. Be aware, however, that this can be a time-consuming and costly process.

• **Another option is to buy the name with an alternate top-level domain,** such as *.net* or *.info.* We suggest that you avoid this approach, and here's why: Rather than conducting an online search to reach your website, most people searching for your business for the first time will take a shortcut by typing your business name plus `.com` into their browser address lines. If someone already owns the brand name you want, plus .com, many users will reach the .com version by accident. Oops.

• **A third option, but not a good one, is to buy some clever variation of your name by adding hyphens or using alternative spellings.** For instance, if cookiesandcream.com is already taken you could try to buy cookies-and-cream.com or cookiesandcreme.com. But people won't remember how to make the adjustments, and as a result, they'll find your competitor's site while they're looking for yours.

Turn to Chapter 10 for more information on how to establish your brand online.

Catch It If You Can: Claiming Your Name

After you select your name and put it through the wringer to see if people can spell it, say it, remember it, find it online, and relate well to it in your home culture as well as in other cultures, it's time to begin the process of registering and protecting the name to ensure that it will belong to you and only you for as long as it lives in the marketplace.

Conducting a name-availability search

Before taking the final plunge to adopt and start building a brand around a name, jump through some legal hoops to make sure the name isn't too similar to an existing business name or trademark in your market area.

Conducting a name-availability search on your own and without legal help isn't enough to assure that the name you want is available, but it helps you discover which names to rule out because they're definitely already in use. With that knowledge, you can create a Plan B before investing heavily in a name that may not work for your brand.

Follow these steps as you conduct an initial name-availability search:

1. **Conduct an online search for the name.**

   Check to see if the domain name featuring your top-choice brand name is available, following the advice in the preceding section. Also conduct a web search to see if another business already uses the name, even if it doesn't own the domain name.

   If the name already labels another business, you may still be able to use it as your own so long as your market area or industry doesn't overlap with that of the other business. However, proceed with caution and the understanding that you're risking marketplace confusion by giving your brand the same name as another business's brand.

2. **Search your state's database of registered business names.**

   This database is kept by the office of your secretary of state, corporations division, or corporate registry, depending on the state or region in which you're headquartered.

Banks require that you have an approved name before opening a business bank account, and they can usually tell you exactly which government office to call for name registration assistance. If the name's available, you can complete a registration form, pay a fee, and protect the name for your use in your immediate market area.

3. **Screen the name with the United States Patent and Trademark Office, which maintains a massive database of pending, registered, and expired federal trademarks.**

   Go to www.uspto.gov, click on Trademarks, then click Search Trademarks, and enter the name you want. For global and international information, go to www.uspto.gov/main/profiles/international.htm.

Legal mumbo jumbo

Following are definitions for a few of the terms you're bound to hear during the name-protection process. This information comes from the website of the U.S. Patent and Trademark Office. For more information, visit www.uspto.gov or check out *Patents, Copyrights & Trademarks For Dummies* by Henri Charmasson (Wiley).

✔ **Copyright:** Protects works of authorship, such as writings, music, and works of art that have been tangibly expressed. U.S. copyrights are registered by the Library of Congress. They are indicated by the symbol © and last for the life of the author plus 70 years.

✔ **Trademark:** Protects words, names, symbols, sounds, or colors that distinguish goods and services from those manufactured or sold by others and to indicate the source of the goods. Trademarks can be renewed forever as long as they are being used in commerce.

✔ **Registered trademark:** Registered marks are indicated by use of the federal registration symbol of a circled R (®) or by the designation *Reg. TM.* You may use the federal registration symbol only on or in connection with the goods and/or service listed in your federal trademark registration and only after the U.S. Patent and Trademark Office has officially registered your mark (not while your application is pending). Although registration of trademarks is not required to use a trademark, owning a federal trademark registration has several advantages, including notice to the public of the registrant's claim of ownership of the mark, a legal presumption of ownership of the mark, the exclusive right to use the mark in connection with the goods or services set forth in the registration, the ability to bring an action concerning the mark in the federal court, the use of the U.S. registration as a basis to obtain registration in foreign countries, and the ability to file the U.S. registration with the U.S. Customs Service to prevent importation of infringing foreign goods.

✔ **Service mark:** The same as a trademark except that it identifies and distinguishes the source of a service rather than a product.

✔ **Mark:** A term that refers to trademarks or service marks. Anytime you claim rights to a mark, you may alert the public to your claim by inserting the designation *TM* (trademark) or *SM* service mark. You may use these terms regardless of whether you've filed a mark application with the U.S. Patent and Trademark Office.

Treading the trademark ropes

After you register your business name with government offices in your local market area, you're safe to use your name, but your name isn't safe from use by others outside your immediate market areas.

If you plan to do business across state or national borders, a trademark prevents others from infringing on your identity by using a similar name, logo, or other identifying feature of your brand.

Scheduling a root canal for your brand name

Coming up with a name that appeals to consumers and gaining a nod of approval from your trademark attorney is a challenging, frustrating, and even painful process. Part of the dilemma is that consumers generally prefer names comprised of familiar words that create instant connection and understanding, whereas attorneys prefer unusual and coined names — the farther away from any word ever heard before, the better.

If a trademark is important to you (and if your brand will travel nationally or globally, it's not just a matter of importance but of necessity), follow this name-development and trademarking process used by leading brand development specialists:

1. **Establish your strategic objective based on your desired brand position and character.**

2. **Develop anywhere from 500 to 1,000 potential names, using the various approaches cited in this chapter.**

3. **Select your top 50 name choices.**

4. **Send your list to an attorney who specializes in naming and trademarking.**

The attorney will conduct an initial trademark search in your business arena and in related areas of business to determine whether using the name may leave you vulnerable to litigation from other brand holders now or in the future. In most cases, by the time the drilling's over, only two or three of your 50 name entries end up on a "good chance of approval" list. The price for conducting the initial screening for each name usually runs at least $50.

5. **The attorney puts names that make it past the initial screening through an exhaustive availability search.**

This phase generally runs at least $3,000 to $4,000 per name and results in a detailed risk analysis. If your top-choice name is deemed clear to use without risk of an infringement suit from another trademark holder, authorize your attorney to register it as your own. If its use comes with some infringement question marks, work with your attorney (and within the comforts of your own risk tolerance) to determine whether or not to proceed to adopt the name with or without a trademark.

You can obtain extensive information and advice on trademarks from these online resources:

- ✔ **U.S. trademarks:** http://www.uspto.gov
- ✔ **Patent offices throughout Europe:** patlib.european-patent-office.org/directory/overview.pl
- ✔ **Establishing a trademark in a number of countries:** www.uspto.gov/main/profiles/international.htm

Anyone who tells you that the arena of trademarks is an easy one to navigate is wearing rose-colored glasses. We've been through it enough times to strongly advise you to look over the sidebar "Scheduling a root canal for your brand name" and to seek legal assistance from an attorney who specializes in intellectual property and trademark protection.

Your business attorney probably can assist you or refer you to a good legal specialist for help with getting a trademark.

Changing Your Name, If You Must

This short section includes two important pieces of advice:

- ✔ **Don't change your name unless you have to.** If you have to, then follow every single step in this chapter because you're basically starting the brand naming process from scratch.

- ✔ **Do adjust your name, if necessary, to attune it to changing marketplace or business conditions.** Follow the advice in Chapter 16.

Quoting Socrates once again, "The giving of names is no small matter." After you clear the hurdles of name selection, availability search, domain name and government registrations, and establishing legal protections, hold a celebration and then get ready to give the name a face — in the form of a logo, which is what Chapter 8 is all about.

Chapter 8

Designing Your Logo and Tagline

. . . .

In This Chapter

▶ Deciding what kind of logo you want for your brand

▶ Developing and testing your logo design

▶ Using, managing, and protecting your logo

▶ Knowing when, why, and how to create a tagline or slogan

. . . .

ogo design is the point at which the branding process acquires fanfare. The minute people in your organization see your brand emerge in a logo that embodies your name, they get enthusiastic about what may have previously felt like a whole bunch of navel-gazing. To most people, logo creation is the fun part of branding. It's also the part that unduly gets the most attention.

If you opened straight to this chapter with the hope that you could give your brand a face without first wading through the process of researching, positioning, defining your brand identity and protecting a brand name, realize that branding isn't like a game of Monopoly. You can't just jump to "Go." The only way you end up with a logo that accurately reflects the essence of your brand is by defining the essence of your brand *before* you begin the logo design process. If you haven't yet done so, do yourself and your brand a favor by going through the steps presented in Chapter 6. They help you clarify your understanding of your brand's mission, values, vision, culture, and character so that you can create a symbol — a logo — that serves as an accurate presentation of who you are and what you stand for in your marketplace.

If, however, you've taken the necessary steps and are truly ready to create a brand logo, this chapter guides you as you dive right in.

Planning Your Logo: The Face of Your Brand

Your *logo* is the graphic design — in type or symbol form — that conveys your brand name and character in your marketplace.

The best logos are unique, simple, and strong representations of the brands they identify. To those seeing your signage, letterhead, packaging, ads, brochures, website pages, and any other communication that carries a visual representation of your brand, your logo is the face of your organization.

This section is full of advice on how to proceed with your logo design, but above all else, remember these three all-important points:

- ✔ **Keep your logo simple.** Simple logo designs work best for a number of reasons:

    - They stand out in the sea of visual complexity and chaos that exists in today's busy and image-saturated marketplace.

    - They enjoy longer lives than complicated logos that go out of style and require redesign to keep them in step with market tastes.

    - They contribute more significantly to a brand's awareness and recognition than logos that need frequent and significant updates. Look at the long-standing logos of well-known and leading brands, such as Nike, Google, and the Red Cross; they display an amazing amount of visual restraint.

- ✔ **Design a logo that can be presented consistently across all communication channels.** You want your logo to show well on everything from business checks to vehicle signage, web pages, video screens, apparel, and anywhere else you choose to display it. Don't sign off on any design until you know that it will look good large or small, and in color or black and white.

- ✔ **Don't do it yourself unless you're a design professional or you want your logo to look like it represents a hands-on business that, in fact, created its own logo.** Self-made logos are kind of like self-made TV ads; most of them are obvious for their lack of polish.

If you're not sure whether a do-it-yourself logo will present your company adequately, review your business vision (see Chapter 6 if your vision isn't totally clear in your mind). If your vision is to provide the lowest-cost, quickest, bare-bones solution in a low-competition market area, a self-created logo may work just fine. However, if your aspirations for your business involve a long life and a broadly recognized reputation for quality in a competitive field, investing in a professionally designed logo is a moderate down payment on your dreams.

What your logo is and isn't

This short section aims to diffuse the biggest myth in branding: Your logo isn't your brand. We said it in Chapter 1 and it's worth repeating here.

Your brand isn't how you look or what you say or even what you sell. Your brand is what people trust and believe you stand for. Your brand is the set of impressions and beliefs that resides in the minds of others as a result of every encounter and experience with you, your product, your services, and your business. Your name and logo are like keys that unlock that set of beliefs. That's why it's so important to choose identifiers that are apt representations of the brand image you want people to hold and believe.

Matching your logo to your brand image

Whether you do it yourself or hire a professional to develop your logo, you need to think in advance about what image you want your logo to convey.

Any graphic designer can tell you that clients who give no direction, saying that they'll simply know the right logo when they see it, burn through a lot of time and money while they wait for the perfect look to miraculously emerge.

Instead, begin the logo-design process with clear input about the type of image you want to develop. Use the worksheet in Figure 8-1 to assemble your thoughts and give your designer — whether that person is yourself, someone on your staff, or an experienced professional — good directions to work from.

Choosing your logo approach

Most logos take one of the following forms:

- ✔ They feature the name of the business in a unique type presentation called a *wordmark*.

- ✔ They feature the initials of the business in a symbol called a *lettermark*.

- ✔ They feature a symbol that represents the business, called a *brandmark*.

- ✔ They combine the preceding logo elements, for instance using a lettermark or a brandmark accompanied by the full name of the company, and sometimes the company slogan or tagline as well, in a unique configuration that becomes the company's brand symbol.

Take care when combining elements in your logo design. Multiple elements can result in a visually complicated, difficult-to-reproduce logo. If you choose to combine elements, be sure that each component is visually clean and strong. For inspiration, consider the multielement logos of top fashion industry brands. For example, Chanel's wordmark is used in conjunction with the iconic overlapping double Cs to create a strong symbol and fashion icon.

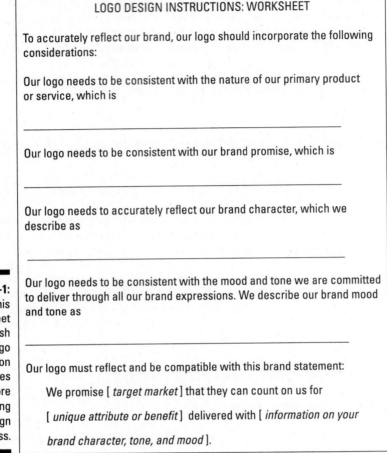

Figure 8-1: Use this worksheet to establish your logo creation guidelines before beginning the design process.

LOGO DESIGN INSTRUCTIONS: WORKSHEET

To accurately reflect our brand, our logo should incorporate the following considerations:

Our logo needs to be consistent with the nature of our primary product or service, which is

_____

Our logo needs to be consistent with our brand promise, which is

_____

Our logo needs to accurately reflect our brand character, which we describe as

_____

Our logo needs to be consistent with the mood and tone we are committed to deliver through all our brand expressions. We describe our brand mood and tone as

_____

Our logo must reflect and be compatible with this brand statement:

We promise [*target market*] that they can count on us for

[*unique attribute or benefit*] delivered with [*information on your*

brand character, tone, and mood].

© Barbara Findlay Schenck

Spelling it out with a wordmark

A wordmark (sometimes called a *logotype* or *typographic symbol*) turns your brand name into your logo by presenting it in a unique typestyle, often with some artistic element that adds flair and memorability. Wordmarks are gaining in popularity among brand builders, as explained in the sidebar "What's in a logo? Increasingly, a name."

The best wordmarks are easy to read and distinctive. A few examples include the logos of FedEx, Google, Kellogg's, and Yahoo!.

Consider a wordmark especially if any of the following circumstances apply to your marketing situation.

- ✔ You want your logo to build recognition for your name.

- ✔ Your marketing budget is lean, and realistically, you aren't able to gain widespread recognition of a symbol, so you're better off gaining recognition of a distinct presentation of your name instead.

- ✔ You intend to develop subbrands under your primary brand, and you want a strong wordmark that can serve as an umbrella over each line.

Using your initials in a lettermark

Lettermarks turn the initials of brand name into a brand symbol. In some logos, the lettermark appears all on its own, as in the IBM logo, which long ago dropped reference to the name International Business Machines. Other stand-alone lettermarks include the logos of GE, CNN, and Louis Vuitton.

In other logos, the lettermark appears along with a wordmark that presents the full name of the brand, such as in the logo of McDonald's, which features the restaurant name along with an oversized "M."

Lettermarks are good logo choices in the following circumstances:

- ✔ You want to make your name the primary emphasis of your logo, but you feel that your name is too long to be a good wordmark.

- ✔ You want to add a stylized monogram to a fairly straightforward presentation of your name in order to convey your brand personality.

- ✔ You have the budget necessary to develop awareness for your lettermark so that, in time, people will see the initials and think of your brand name.

Creating a brandmark or symbol

Brandmarks range from fairly literal to abstract designs that symbolize brand names. The best brandmarks become so associated with brand names that, in time, people automatically think of the brand name when they catch a glimpse of the logo. Think of the Nike Swoosh or the Starbucks or Mercedes symbols as examples of the power of great brandmarks.

Of all the logo approaches, developing a customized, trademarkable brandmark requires the highest level of design expertise and investment. And even the best one-of-a-kind, tailor-made mark requires a strong marketing investment before it becomes a meaningful symbol in consumer minds.

What's in a logo? Increasingly, a name

When you think of logos, you probably think of symbols or brandmarks because that's how logos entered the business world in the 1800s. Back then, manufacturing breakthroughs of the 19th century led to large-scale production of goods for the first time. With mass-production came product supplies that could be sold not just in home market areas but also in far-flung locations.

To succeed in distant markets, though, companies needed to gain consumer awareness and brand recognition in regions where personal sales presence often wasn't possible.

Putting their names on their goods wasn't good enough because many 19th-century consumers were unable to read. So marketers adopted and presented easily understood and meaningful symbols to represent their brands. The bell logo of the Bell Telephone System (known as Ma Bell back in pre-deregulation days) was one of the early symbols to gain widespread prominence.

As literacy rates climbed, reliance on symbols ebbed and companies began to present stylized versions of their names instead of or alongside symbols representing their brands.

Today, new businesses increasingly find brand names by coining new words that are available as Internet domain names. Rather than asking the market to learn both a newly fabricated name *and* a new symbol, the companies turn their names into their logos, designing wordmarks instead of brandmarks. Google and Yahoo! are two globally recognized examples.

Consider a brandmark when these circumstances apply to your business:

- ✔ Your name is too long or cumbersome for a wordmark.
- ✔ A lettermark doesn't fit the character or image of your brand.
- ✔ A symbol will help you communicate the benefit, promise, distinction, or character of your brand.
- ✔ Your market spans the globe, and you seek a symbol that can represent your brand regardless of the language of the consumer.
- ✔ You have the budget required to build your logo into a recognizable, meaningful symbol that communicates with such strength that it can carry meaning even if it doesn't appear with your name.

Most brandmarks fit into one of these categories:

- ✔ **A representation of the business name.** For example, the Target logo is, unmistakably, a target. The Apple logo is an apple, the Red Cross logo is a red cross. The Shell logo is a shell. The Taco Bell logo is a bell. The Dropbox logo is an open box. You get the picture.
- ✔ **A representation of the brand's primary offering.** For instance, the brandmark for YouTube features a video play button. The Best Buy mark features a yellow sale tag. A catering service might use a knife and fork or a wine glass as its mark.

- **A representation of the brand's promise.** For instance, the Morton's brandmark shows a little girl sprinkling salt in the rain. The Amazon logo features an arrow reaching from A to Z. An educational organization might feature a child holding a book, and a yoga studio could feature a body in motion.

- **An abstract symbol that, over time and through marketing, is instilled with meaning for the brand it represents.** Examples of this kind of brandmark include the "good hands" of Allstate Insurance, the rings of the International Olympics, the Nike Swoosh, and the triangle-faced man on the cover of *For Dummies* books. All are highly visible brandmarks that are meaningful to consumers because of diligent use and marketing by the brand holders.

Logo Design Resources

The process of designing your logo begins with a big decision: Will you do it yourself or call on professional resources?

- **Do it yourself** only if you're artistically skilled and have time to commit, or if someone in your business or close circle can lend great design sense to the task. Realize that the logo you're creating will make a lasting impression for your brand, so be sure the skills you can assemble match the image you're aiming to create. If you do proceed on your own, follow the advice in the upcoming sections on logo design and logo taboos.

- **Hire a professional designer** if your design abilities are subpar or your time is better spent developing your business than creating your logo. Turn to Chapter 12 for descriptions of creative resources and advice for hiring and working with a graphic designer, ad agency, or branding firm. The choice will involve a not-insignificant investment that will pay dividends for years to come, especially if you're building a brand in a competitive arena or one that you expect will expand over broad market areas and possibly grow into an asset you'll someday want to sell.

- **Turn to online services** that range from free to hundreds to thousands of dollars if you're short on both time and money.

  - You can enter "do-it-yourself logo creation" into a search engine to reach links to logo-generating websites and logo-development software. For example, Supalogo.com and LogoGarden.com are free services that deliver professional-quality graphics, though without the benefit of personalized or customized design.

  - You can enter "crowdsourced logo design" for links to businesses offering a new approach to customized design services. Sites such as 99designs.com and CrowdSpring.com have enlisted tens of thousands of designers who provide rapid-fire response to logo requests that are treated like design contests. You submit a design brief specifying your requirements and within days you receive ideas to choose from, with the number of responses based on the amount of prize money you offered. The outcome is efficient, relatively inexpensive, fast, and even social, since several services host polls for you to obtain input on your top-choice designs. TaskRabbit and Cloudera are examples of startups that turned to crowdsourcing sites for logo design. This option isn't for everyone, but when time and budget are pinched, it may be a good choice.

Developing Your Logo Design

Whether you do it on your own or call upon professional expertise, start developing your logo design by completing the worksheet shown in Figure 8-1 so that you or your logo-design team members understand the brand your logo must reflect before the creative process begins.

Also, provide the following information to help guide creation of a logo that fits your brand and its market:

- ✔ **A description of your clientele:** For instance, are your customers predominantly male or female, urban or suburban, of a particular age group or income level, and do they share common interests or activities?

- ✔ **Three to six words that you think best describe your brand and offering:** For example, *stylish, high quality, contemporary, classic, casual, professional,* and so on.

- ✔ **Samples of logos you like and don't like, along with some idea of why you feel the way you do about each one:** Designers can't read minds, so the more input you provide, the faster and better the process will go.

- ✔ **Input regarding design, color, and shape considerations:** If you know that your logo will need to work well in horizontal signs, for instance, or if you know that you hate the color brown, say so early on, not after you see the first round of design suggestions. Give creative professionals everything they need to do the job right from the start, when creativity is at its highest. You'll save them the agony of creative death through a thousand little cuts while saving yourself time and money by arriving at a solution that reflects your brand and meets your needs without rounds and rounds of costly revisions.

Design ingredients

As you go through the design process, be aware that typestyle, colors, and shapes have a bearing on the way a logo communicates.

What's your type?

The typestyle you choose — and the way you arrange the type in your logo — has an impact on the impression your logo makes. Follow these tips:

✔ **Choose a typestyle that matches the character of your brand.** If your brand character is buttoned-down and professional, choose a typestyle that looks professional and even formal. If your brand character is casual, choose a typestyle that looks casual, too.

For a quick orientation to the world of typestyles, open your word-processing program and pull down the menu for fonts to see samples of a wide variety of typestyles. Fonts that feature small lines adorning each character are called *serifs;* those devoid of letter enhancements are called *sans serif.* Courier and Times New Roman are examples of serif typestyles; Helvetica and Geneva are examples of sans serif typestyles. In general, serif typestyles convey a more traditional character and sans serif typestyles are more modern.

When choosing your typestyle, opt for a look that can withstand the test of time. For instance, the FedEx wordmark is derived from Helvetica type, which was designed by the typographer Max Miedinger in 1957. How's that for proof that classic styles enjoy long lives?

✔ **Customize the presentation of your name in your logo.** There's a world of difference between a uniquely designed wordmark and type straight off your word processor. Type produced directly from a word processor is evenly spaced so that all letters and words are the same distance apart. Type that's professionally arranged has its spacing adjusted, called *kerning,* so that letters are placed in uniquely pleasing configurations. The difference is almost imperceptible, yet it makes a dramatic difference in the appearance of a wordmark, and it's one of the reasons logo designers earn their fees.

A primer on colors

Your logo's color scheme can become an essential element of your brand identity. Coca-Cola *is* red; IBM *is* blue; John Deere *is* green. For that matter, think of your favorite college or pro team. Put the players in different colors, and fan confusion sets in.

As you choose colors for your brand identity, consider the following:

✔ **Establish a color scheme that differs from the scheme used by your major competitors.** People relate to color so strongly that you'll cause confusion if you adopt colors already associated with another key player in your market arena.

✔ **Choose a color scheme that reflects your brand character.** If your market is comprised of young children, logo colors that resemble decorations on a birthday cake may be ideal. The same colors would hardly work for a respected plastic surgeon or corporate law firm.

Most people perceive neutral tones such as grey, taupe, navy, dark green, or burgundy as subdued, mature, and professional. Pastels convey calmness. Blues and greens are cool. Red, orange, and yellow are warm and energetic.

- ✔ **Choose colors that reflect your brand and the expectations customers have when selecting your offering.** For example, if your brand and your customers' expectations are professional, choose colors that are subdued and cool. If you offer and your customers seek lively entertainment, choose colors that are energetic.

- ✔ **Consider how your colors will be interpreted in other cultures or countries if your brand will be marketed internationally.** If you're not sure, ask for advice from a university professor of the language or culture you aim to target.

- ✔ **If your logo will appear on apparel or specialty items, consider how the colors will look on uniforms, golf shirts, ball caps, coffee mugs, or the dozens of other places it may end up.** If the colors can't be reproduced consistently, alter your color scheme accordingly. Alternatively, decide on an acceptable range of colors in which the logo can be presented without breaking your logo management rules (See the section "Managing Your Logo" later in this chapter for more information.)

- ✔ **The fewer colors you employ, the easier your logo will be to manage.** Logos with full-color illustrations or photos require full-color printing — an expensive and time-consuming process that you should adopt only after serious consideration. Plus, the Internet further restricts color options because the web's color palette is limited.

- ✔ **No matter what color scheme you adopt, be sure your logo works beautifully in plain old black and white.** After all, that's how it will look on business checks, in photocopies, in many ads, and in low-cost communications that will carry your brand identity far and wide.

Logo shapes and sizes

Most logos need to work well in a horizontal configuration that's about half as tall as it is wide. In other words, they need to look good in the return address portion of a business envelope, in the top corner of a web page, and on the shirt pocket of uniforms or logo apparel.

Whatever configuration your logo takes, be sure it can reduce down to the size it will appear on a business card. If it becomes blurry or unrecognizable, simplify the elements so that it reads well even in minute presentations.

Logo design evaluation

When reviewing logo designs, put them through a preliminary test to see if they incorporate the traits of most good symbols.

✓ **Do you think the logo makes a good impression for your business?** Does it reflect the character and standards of your brand?

✓ **Is it easy to see and remember?** Try this test when reviewing a logo design: Look at a proposed design; then set it aside and draw a quick rendition on a scrap of paper. If you come up with a sketch that's close to the design, then you can be pretty sure that the logo is memorable.

✓ **Does it work in a single ink color and at a small size?** If the rendition you're looking at is in color, run it through the photocopier and see if it looks good in black and white and at a size that fits on a business card. If fine lines disappear in the reproduction and reduction, the design and artwork probably won't withstand a broad range of applications.

✓ Is it original? Airbnb is an example of a business that unveiled a logo only to have fans and detractors howl over the symbol's similarity to logos of other brands. Protect yourself: On Google, click to search images. Then click the camera icon and upload an image of your proposed logo. In seconds you'll see whether similar designs already exist.

Logo design taboos

Economy is a virtue — but not in logo design. The biggest mistake that new brand marketers make is saddling themselves with logos that scream home-made. Follow this advice to avoid common logo-design pitfalls:

✓ **Think twice before handing the logo-design task over to your cousin's nephew or undertaking it on your own.** Your logo visually represents your brand and the caliber of your offering. If you want to compete with great brands, hire an expert who specializes in logo design.

✓ **Don't let the design get too fussy.** Keep it simple. The best logos are clean and refined, conveying leadership and longevity.

✓ **Avoid clip art.** The archives of symbols that you can freely drop into your logo are huge, but they're also generic, say little about your brand and its character, and can show up in someone else's logo in the future.

✓ **Don't be a copycat.** Use other logos for inspiration, but invest the time and money necessary to create your own unique mark. For one thing, you end up with a distinctive logo. For another, you avoid the legal land-mines that infringing on another company's brandmark can set off.

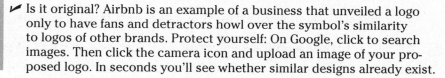

Your logo makes the difference between a strong and a weak first impression for your business. It also makes the difference between a brand of choice and a product purchased simply for its price or availability. Want proof? Take the alligator off the shirt, and what is Izod selling? A shirt like any other shirt you can get anywhere — for less. With the alligator, the shirt becomes an association with the success and stature of the Ivy League.

Preparing your logo artwork

If you feel up to the task of designing your own logo, follow this advice:

- ✔ If you create your logo by using the templates available online or in publishing programs, customize colors, symbols, and typestyles so that you end up with a unique look for your business.

- ✔ Use the same design software that professionals use. Most designers use Adobe Illustrator, known as *vector-based graphic design software,* which means that the final logo design can be enlarged or reduced without design distortion or loss of quality.

If you hire a professional for your logo design, take these steps:

1. **Choose a professional whose expertise, size, and fees fit your needs.**

    Options range from freelance artists to small design studios to local, regional, national or global ad agencies to internationally renowned identity developers. You can spend anywhere from several hundred dollars up to the million-dollar range. If you want a logo that competes well in a local market, set aside a small budget and find a local resource. If you aspire to make the list of the world's top brands, turn to the talents of award-winning brand specialists, and plan to invest accordingly.

2. **Review work samples to be sure that the designer's style matches with your expectations.**

3. **Be clear about your budget and obtain cost estimates before authorizing design work to begin.**

4. **Stipulate that you will own all rights to your logo after you pay in full for its design and production.**

5. **Upon approval of your final logo design, obtain copies of the artwork in EPS format for printing purposes and in JPG and GIF formats for online use.**

Putting Your Logo to Work

After you approve your logo design, apply it consistently to every single communication that carries your name into the marketplace. Use the worksheet in Figure 8-2 to list all the places your logo needs to go. Then aim to get your logo into place on all items just as quickly as possible.

If you apply your logo in a piecemeal fashion, applying it to some brand presentations immediately and others over time, you're setting yourself up for a weak identity and marketplace confusion.

LOGO APPLICATION CHECKLIST	
✔ All items that apply to your business	✔ All items that apply to your business
Advertising ☐ Newspaper ads ☐ Magazine ads ☐ Phone directory ads ☐ Business and industry directory ads ☐ Community publication ads ☐ Online ads ☐ Billboards and outdoor sign ads ☐ Transit ads ☐ Direct mailers ☐ Newsletters ☐ Other:	**Signage** ☐ Exterior building signage ☐ Interior building signage ☐ Entry door and department signage ☐ Vehicle signage ☐ Posters and point-of-sale materials ☐ Product displays ☐ Trade show displays ☐ Other:
Communications ☐ Brochures ☐ Handouts (menus, take-one cards, and so on) ☐ How-to instructions and manuals ☐ Packaging and package enclosures ☐ Website ☐ Social-media pages ☐ Other:	**Stationery and Correspondence Items** ☐ Letterhead ☐ Notepads ☐ Envelopes ☐ Mailing labels ☐ Business cards ☐ Fax cover sheets ☐ E-mail signature files ☐ Forms for estimates, invoices, purchase orders, and so on ☐ Other:
Audio-Visual Materials ☐ Videos, DVDs, CDs ☐ Speaker support materials ☐ Presentation handouts ☐ Other:	**Publicity Materials** ☐ Media kit folder ☐ News release sheets ☐ Company backgrounder and media kit enclosures ☐ Other:
Apparel ☐ Logo-ID gift or sale clothing items ☐ Uniforms ☐ Other:	**Specialty Items** ☐ Shopping bags and packaging ☐ Gift items and giveaways (pens, mousepads, coffee cups, and so on) ☐ Other:

Figure 8-2:
Use this worksheet as a checklist for all the places your logo goes.

© Barbara Findlay Schenck

Saving Face: Giving an Existing Logo a Makeover

In today's world of split-second attention spans, it's easy to assume that change is good and rapid change is even better. Just don't apply that logic if you're thinking about updating an already-established logo.

People form a relationship with your brand, and your logo is the visual link to the positive images they hold in their minds. Unless you believe that changing your logo will strengthen your identity and deepen the customer relationship, and unless the story of your business has changed, leave your logo alone.

Chapter 16 is your guide to assessing the current strength of your logo and other brand assets and deciding whether evolutionary to revolutionary changes are necessary.

Making evolutionary logo changes

Evolutionary logo changes accompany evolutionary changes to your business and brand strategies. They retain the essence of your logo but modernize the design to make it visually stronger and more in step with your business and market.

Sometimes a logo gets tired. Perhaps it's been used inconsistently and, as a result, it loses the ability to represent your brand. Maybe it's failed to keep pace with changes to your brand's offerings, character, and target market. Or maybe it's just plain gone out of style.

If you think that the time has come to update your logo, begin by evaluating your needs. Consider whether you seek a quick nip and tuck or a more extreme logo makeover.

To come to this conclusion, answer the following questions:

- ✔ What image do you want to project, and how does your logo fall short?

- ✔ What about your business has changed since your logo was created? Is your target market different? Has your product offering changed? Do you still make the same brand promise? Has your brand character changed?

- ✔ Can you update your current logo to reflect your updated situation, or do you need an altogether new symbol even though the complete change may result in short-term market confusion?

✔ What elements of your logo are most important to your identity? The symbol? The colors? The wordmark? If you could keep only one portion of your logo, which would it be?

✔ Do you have the budget required to change your logo throughout all brand communications?

Look back at Figure 8-2 for a list of all the places your brand logo goes. In addition to the cost of redesigning your logo, you need to be prepared to update every single place your logo appears, and the sooner the better.

Making revolutionary logo changes

Revolutionary logo changes are necessary when you want to signal a major change of strategic direction, when you want to raise a new flag and say, essentially, "This is what we now stand for."

The high cost of underestimating brand love

Brands thrive on love, and yet brand owners act surprised when brand loyalists feel cheated by radical brand changes. Before replacing your logo, keep these two cautionary examples in mind:

✔ **Gap:** You likely recall the disastrous 2010 Gap logo redesign that resulted in one of the quickest retrenchments in logo history. So what went wrong? Gap introduced a logo signifying the brand's transition from "classic, American design to modern, sexy, cool" without first tuning into customer affection levels. It turns out, people had a good feeling about Gap and felt the logo was a good reflection of the brand. The new logo wasn't better, didn't signal anything different, and, to customers, communicated a shift to a lower-price position. They took it personally — and not quietly. Within a week, the logo was retracted.

✔ **University of California:** In 2012, a new university mark was withdrawn after 54,000 students, alumni, and others signed a petition and voiced "significant negative response" to a brand symbol they felt showed disregard for a heritage they thought was well represented by the university's 144-year-old symbol. Termed a "university logo fail," the new logo was as much a failure of communication as of design. After-the-fact, university spokespeople said the new symbol was never meant to replace the venerable and beloved historic seal, but to go places where the seal couldn't reproduce clearly, adding that the controversy was a reminder that "people strongly identify with the symbols and icons that represent their school." The lesson is counterintuitive for educators: Test first, and teach second — by clearly communicating the new logo before and after its adoption.

Before designing an altogether new logo, assess the level of recognition, understanding, and loyalty your customers have for your current mark. If value for your current logo is high, think long and hard about changing the symbol people fondly link to your brand image. (See the sidebar, "The high cost of underestimating brand love," for case histories summarizing what can go wrong.) On the other hand, if the value customers place on your current logo is low or severely damaged, start the redesign process following every step in this chapter, including and especially planning a budget to get your new symbol into your marketplace.

Managing Your Logo

To ensure that your logo is presented consistently, create a set of usage guidelines to be followed by everyone who produces marketing materials for your business. This section provides a logo-management outline to follow.

Creating standards and usage rules

As a first step toward controlling the presentation of your logo, create high-quality artwork and stipulate that your logo must be reproduced only from approved files.

Beyond requiring use of approved artwork, also control how your logo can appear by establishing usage guidelines in each of the following areas.

Presentation of your logo as a single unit

Too often, those with creative urges want to take liberties with your logo by increasing the size of one element and decreasing the size of another, or by moving elements into different positions to alter the shape of the logo in order to fit it into a space it otherwise doesn't fit. Ban individualized treatments by providing artwork for your logo in several allowable shape variations — horizontal and vertical treatments — along with the stipulation that any alternative configuration must be approved prior to usage.

Placement of your logo

Define how your logo can appear in printed materials.

✔ **Clarify how much open space must exist between your logo and surrounding design elements.** For instance, if a wordmark begins with the letter *T*, instructions may require that the logo be surrounded by open space at least equal to the size that the *T* appears on the page. This rule ensures the logo won't be crowded by surrounding artwork.

✔ **Define how your logo can be positioned.** Indicate whether it can appear on its side or in a diagonal placement or whether it must always run parallel to the bottom of the page or screen.

✔ **Define the smallest size in which your logo can appear.** Especially if your logo involves type or fine lines, it may become illegible at small sizes, which reflects poorly on your brand image.

Color treatments

In your guidelines, define the colors in which your logo may appear.

✔ Stipulate whether or not you allow the logo art to appear in white on a black or colored background (called a *reverse treatment*).

✔ Clarify whether you allow your logo to appear on colored paper or in colored backgrounds and, if so, whether background colors are limited to a range of allowable colors.

✔ Spell out the colors in which your logo can be reproduced. If your logo is to appear in green, for example, take the guidelines a step further by telling exactly which shade of green, giving the ink number from the Pantone Matching System (PMS) used by most printers. Also stipulate how to build the approved color through the four-color printing process (called CMYK for cyan-magenta-yellow-black) by defining what percentage of each of the four inks a printer should use to create the desired tone. Further, define how to arrive at the color through the RGB (red-green-blue) process for computer screen display.

Naming a brand cop

People don't fiddle with your logo to be mischievous; they think they're being creative on your behalf without realizing that their help is apt to harm the strength of your brand identity. That's why you need to create and circulate usage guidelines and name a person who must approve any variations from the approved usage of your logo.

Chapter 17 includes detailed information on writing and enforcing your brand usage guidelines.

Creating a Tagline

A *tagline,* also called a slogan or motto, is a phrase that accompanies your brand name to quickly translate your positioning and brand statements into a few memorable words that provide an indication of your brand offerings, promise, and market position.

Discovering what makes a great tagline

Great taglines have a number of common attributes. When writing your tagline, see that it meets these criteria:

- **It's memorable.** You hear it, remember it, and repeat it with ease.

- **It's short.** Great taglines have as few as ten syllables so that they're quick to recite, easy to tuck in alongside logos, and short enough to include in the briefest of communications.

- **It conveys a brand's point of difference.** A good example of this element is Zipcar: "Wheels when you want them."

- **It differentiates a business from all others.** In fact, a great tagline is so unique that it doesn't work when linked to a competitor's brand name.

- **It reflects the brand's identity, character, promise, and personality.**

- **It's believable and original.**

A great tagline excels on most or all of these fronts while also avoiding a couple of major tagline mistakes:

- It invokes positive feelings without running the risk of triggering sarcastic retorts.

- It appeals to consumers. In other words, the tagline doesn't get bogged down with the input of executives who inadvertently turn the slogan into a corporate rallying call rather than a consumer magnet.

- It adds to the meaning of the brand name without repeating any of the same words or concepts.

Deciding whether you need a tagline

Taglines carry your brand identity and promise where your logo can't go, like your e-mail messages, word ads, voicemail greetings, and other nonvisual communication channels.

Some brand names tell a pretty complete brand story (for example, Coppertone, Jiffy Lube, U-Haul). Other brand names benefit from some quick explanation, which is where taglines come to the rescue. Plus, even seemingly self-sufficient brand names gain dimension through their slogans.

To determine whether you need a tagline, answer these questions:

✔ Does your business offer consumers distinct advantages that aren't conveyed in your name?

✔ Would your brand character be more clearly presented with a line that travels with your brand name?

✔ Is your company best at something that you want consumers to know about but that isn't conveyed by your name?

If you answered "yes" to any of these questions, a tagline may well be a strong addition to your brand name, logo, and marketing program.

Tag (line), you're it! Coming up with your slogan

In crafting your tagline, follow this advice:

✔ Know your positioning statement. What meaningful and available niche in your market do you fill better than any other brand? (Turn to Chapter 5 if you're not sure.)

✔ Based on your unique position, come up with a list of quick, memorable one-liners that convey your special distinction.

✔ Put each of your tagline contenders to the test by seeing if they live up to the qualities listed in the section "What makes a great tagline?" For further evaluation, seek input from branding experts and take advantage of the free tagline test tool offered at `TaglineGuru.com`, identified by the great tagline, "It's your brand on the line."

Part III
Winning Brand Fans and Followers

Website Search-Engine Optimization Tips

Do	Don't
DO develop website content around keywords that people are likely to use to find information on you, your business, and your offerings.	DON'T cram your content with keywords to manipulate your search ranking. Search engines warn against keyword stuffing and placing hidden text or links
DO build each page of your site around specific keywords that define the page focus so users are linked straight to the web page that fulfills their interest.	DON'T forget that keyword searches may send users to internal pages of your website, so include your brand ID and a link to your home page on every page.
DO place keywords into each page's <meta> tags, code commands, titles, navigation links, photo or graphics labels or tags, and also in imbedded text links.	DON'T use default photo file names, non-descript captions (like, "Buy Now"), non-descriptive labels for in-content hot links, or navigation icons that feature only graphics, which search engines don't read.
DO devote a page to site map with page links if your site has more than 50 pages.	DON'T use splash pages that feature a graphic while the site loads. Search engines index content and keywords from your site's first page, and splash pages usually contain neither.
DO choose and register domain names with words that describe your site's business and brand.	DON'T forget that site visitors will leave if they don't think your site will solve their problem or address their interests quickly on an easy-to-see, easy-to-scan screen.
DO build a network of incoming links from high-traffic sites.	DON'T miss the opportunity to develop links to your website from online business and industry registers, publicity featuring your business, mentions on review and rating sites, referrals from other sites, and, especially from your social-media profiles, online content, and blog posts and comments.

Check out www.dummies.com/extras/branding for advice on developing brand communications that are targeted, consistent, and effective.

In this part . . .

- Launch your brand, following the right rules and sequence: Script a great brand story, develop knowledge and support inside your business, preview your brand with priority customers, and, finally, move your brand into the spotlight with a public launch capable of achieving awareness, affection, distinction, and success.

- Leverage digital communication to level the playing field between your brand and its big-budget competitors. Seize your online opportunity and reach your branding objectives by staking claim to one name across all online channels; developing and optimizing a fast-loading, great-looking, findable, usable website; and attracting brand attention that pulls interest to your business and its online home base.

- Build brand engagement and interaction by accelerating your social-media activity on the major networks where your customers hang out and expect to meet up with the brands they love. Use online comments, posts, video, blogging, news, and brand-generated content to spark clicks, sharing, lead generation, and valuable expansion of your brand's online footprint and reputation.

- Follow best principles to capitalize on every brand communication opportunity, including print and broadcast ads, packaging, promotions and co-promotions and — the triple-win of brand communicators — publicity that spreads news, builds credibility, and provides trustworthy content to share far and wide through digital and other communication channels.

Chapter 9

Countdown to Takeoff: Launching or Relaunching Your Brand

*W*hether you're branding a new business or product, revitalizing an established brand, or rebranding with an all-new name, logo, and brand promise, when you're ready to lift the curtain on your new brand, give the moment the fanfare it deserves.

That's what this chapter is all about. It helps you launch your brand from the inside out, making sure you bring every aspect of your business into alignment with your brand promise, personality, and character before you raise the curtain and introduce your brand in your marketplace.

The upcoming pages lead you through the key phases of your brand launch: preparing for your brand debut, writing your brand-launch marketing plan, launching your brand internally, and moving your brand into the public eye.

Carpe Diem! Seizing the Opportunity to Put Your New Brand in the Limelight

When it comes to brand launches, we've seen extreme successes and real flops, and the difference, almost without variation, comes down to whether or not the launch took place within the organization before it traveled to the outside world. If an internal launch doesn't occur first, a brand fails to win the kind of organization-wide buy-in necessary to imbed the brand message into the entire brand experience.

Your brand is conveyed through everything people see, hear, and encounter. How you answer your phones, how you treat your employees, how your employees treat your customers, how it feels to deal with your business, the look of your workspace or website, the music that plays in the background, the nature and quality of your logo and marketing communications — these are all expressions that make your brand message and promise a reality. To create the experience that accurately reflects your brand, your internal team needs to embrace your brand before it sees the light of the world outside your doors. That's why pre-launch planning is essential.

Preparing for Your Brand Launch

After you've decided on and approved your brand name, logo, and tagline (see Chapters 7 and 8), hold that information close to your vest while you put your brand through final tests and prepare it for unveiling.

Whether you're launching a new brand or revitalizing an existing brand, you need to announce a complete brand story. If your new brand identity leaks out in bits and pieces — your name one day, your logo another day — people within your organization are likely to think one of two things:

- So what?
- They spent all that time and money on *that?*

Especially if you're relaunching an established brand, brand changes can be difficult for those in your organization to embrace until you share the reasons and reasoning behind the changes you're unveiling, following the steps in the upcoming sections.

Knowing your story, chapter and verse

Before you enlist the understanding, interest, and support of others, be sure you're 100 percent ready for your internal launch by assembling short statements that summarize each of the following brand elements:

- **Your market position:** Chapter 5 helps you arrive at a statement that tells what you offer, who you serve, and the unique benefits you offer in your competitive market arena.

- **Your brand promise:** If your brand promise isn't already clearly established, turn to Chapter 6 to define the benefits customers can count on and the value and experience they can expect to receive without fail.

- **Your brand character:** Chapter 6 also helps you arrive at a one-sentence brand character statement that defines the personality of your brand

and the mood and tone that will be reflected through all brand expressions, including every contact and experience with your brand.

✔ **Your brand definition:** Also called your *brand statement,* this short definition wraps your target market, market position, point of difference, brand promise, and brand character into a statement that directs all your branding efforts. Your brand definition is an internal steering device, not an external marketing message. It guides your brand's development, following this format: [*Your name*] promises [*your target market*] that they can count on us for [*your unique attribute or benefit*] delivered with [*information about the character, tone, and mood you convey*].

Putting your brand launch into context

You're probably reading this book because you're in the midst of creating a new brand or revising an existing brand, either through a brand identity facelift or through a complete rebranding effort — which we liken to a golfer's mulligan, because rebranding involves basically walking away from your established brand and starting the brand-building process all over again.

Either way, before you unveil your brand, all employees, shareholders, and customers need to understand what you're doing and how the effort will contribute to the value of your organization.

To prepare for your brand launch, know your answers to the questions in the following sections.

Why are you undertaking this branding effort?

Most branding programs aim to achieve one or more of the following outcomes:

✔ **Build awareness:** Awareness leads to marketplace dominance and easier sales efforts, so awareness is usually a top objective in any brand launch.

✔ **Create an emotional connection:** Brands need to build emotional connections with those they serve, and that's especially true for brands with offerings that contribute to a sense of personal satisfaction or security. Additionally, brands aiming to enhance customer loyalty often aim to deepen emotional connection, realizing that customers remain true to brands they love.

✔ **Differentiate your offering:** For brands in crowded market categories — where many competitors offer similar products, services, and promises — differentiation is usually a key brand launch objective.

✔ **Create or enhance credibility and trust:** Every service or online business needs to make credibility and trust a branding priority because service and online purchases are, essentially, made based on nothing but trust. Customers can't see, touch, or try out a service or online offering before saying "yes" or clicking to buy. Instead, they select based purely on the belief that the company will deliver on its promise.

✔ **Motivate purchases:** Rapid sales growth is a primary objective especially for those introducing product brands, largely because retailers offer such a small window of opportunity before booting new products off the shelf to make room for those with greater sales potential.

For help determining your branding priorities, turn to Chapter 3. It includes a worksheet to help you determine the strategic importance of various brand functions to your branding success, while also helping you assess the pre-launch strengths of your current brand if you're undergoing a brand revitalization or rebranding program.

What do you expect your brand launch to achieve?

After you set your branding priorities (drawing from the list in the preceding section), you need to set objectives for the quantifiable outcomes you want your brand launch to achieve. The more clearly you state your objectives, the more quickly you'll win buy-in from shareholders, funding partners, your management team, and the staff who will help make your brand a success.

✔ **If you're launching a new business or brand,** you're starting from zero, with no brand awareness, emotional connection, credibility, brand differentiation, or sales momentum. Therefore, setting objectives is a matter of determining how quickly you intend to reach certain levels of success in each priority area.

✔ **If you're rebranding or revitalizing an existing brand,** begin by assessing the pre-launch strength of your brand to establish the benchmark against which you'll measure the success of your brand launch or relaunch.

Chapter 3 can help as you analyze your current brand strength. For help conducting research or enlisting professional assistance, turn to the research sections in Chapter 5. After you know your starting points, you can set your brand launch objectives by defining the increases you intend to achieve above the pre-launch level in each priority area.

Be realistic about how much change you can effect over the brand-launch period and how much it will cost in terms of marketing investment to reach your objectives. The market adopts change incrementally, which is a nice way to say *slowly,* so be prepared to invest in the effort and to set objectives with your eyes wide open about the momentum you're likely to achieve.

Plan to assess your brand's performance pre-launch, at the completion of your brand launch, and several times over the next year. Doing so allows you to monitor increases in sales, distribution, market share, and pricing, and also to gauge changes in consumer awareness, preference, perceived value, perceived point of difference, satisfaction, reviews, ratings, social-media following, and customer word-of-mouth, referrals, and sharing.

Depending on the size of your organization, you can conduct this research on your own following the survey and interview advice in Chapter 5, or you can enlist the assistance of a research firm. You can find research firms through business directories or by requesting referrals from advertising agencies and branding firms.

Do you need to launch your brand on or by a certain date?

If you plan to have your brand launch gain momentum with a tie-in to a major conference, trade show, or industry event, or if it will benefit from introduction at a certain date for some other reason, make that date clear when you launch the brand internally.

People in your company can easily be complacent about something that seems like an aesthetic change. But if you make it clear that, on a certain date, the curtain needs to rise and the brand needs to be ready to go in order to achieve awareness, momentum, and important objectives, they'll step on board with a greater sense of mission.

What's your message?

Before unveiling your brand internally or externally, be certain about the message you want to convey during your brand launch. By clarifying your message in advance, all brand-launch communications — formal and informal, from the CEO to the front-line staff — align, contributing to a strong, clear impression. Use the following guidance for creating a message for new brands or revitalized brands:

- ✔ **When launching an altogether new brand:** Your message should convey your brand's unique position, point of difference, promise, and value. (Turn to Chapter 5 for information on determining your brand's competitive position and point of difference. Chapter 6 is your guide to putting your brand promise and your brand definition into words.)

- ✔ **When launching a revitalized brand or a announcing a rebrand:** Your message needs to convey your unique position, point of difference, promise, and value, just as in any other brand launch, but you also want to convey the reason behind the changes you're unveiling. Count on Chapter 17 for help as you make and announce minor-to-major changes to your brand.

Producing introductory brand prototypes

As you prepare to introduce your brand, be ready to show how your brand will appear in the marketplace over the coming weeks and months. Do this by creating *prototypes,* also called *mock-ups,* of everything from signs to ads to web pages to uniforms, apparel, specialty items, and product packages. By showing samples of how the brand will look in actual applications, you allow people on your team to engage and interact with the brand identity. By seeing how the identity works, they begin to lose their attachments to previous brand identity representations. The also begin to release doubts, if any, about the new brand identity representations you're unveiling.

Don't skimp on the production of your prototypes. If the samples you show aren't impressive, the reaction to your brand won't be impressive either. Invest in prototypes that look as much like the real thing as possible. If you've hired designers, an ad agency, or brand consultants to help develop your branding program, they can help you create these prototypes.

Checking your internal readiness

In branding, what you say pales in comparison to what you do. The experience your customers have with your brand trumps your logo presentation, advertising, and marketing efforts in a heartbeat. In fact, given the choice between a beautifully presented brand identity that's backed by an uneven brand experience and a marginally presented brand identity that's backed by a brand experience that's impeccably reinforced at every touch point, we and most other brand consultants would vote for experience over identity any day.

To prepare your organization to consistently deliver a superb brand experience following the brand launch, create an inventory of all the ways people encounter your business. Evaluate each contact point to see that it accurately reflects the mood, tone, and promise of your brand. Chapter 13 provides a complete guide for testing, auditing, and strengthening your brand experience. Before your brand launch, be sure the following points of contact are ready to reflect your brand and strengthen your brand promise:

- ✔ **Telephone:** Are you prepared to answer phones promptly and with a message that reinforces your brand, including your new brand name? Do voicemail recordings convey your brand name, tone, and message?

- ✔ **In-person arrival:** If customers reach you at a physical location, will signage reflect your new brand? Upon arrival, will the entry area make a good impression for your brand? Are people who greet visitors prepared to reinforce your brand promise?

- ✔ **Online arrival:** Is your website ready to present the new brand identity and message on pages that are quick to load and easy to view on all screens — especially on mobile devices? Have you reserved your brand name on social-media networks, and are you ready to develop and interact with a following? Turn to Chapters 10 and 11 for advice on launching your brand's digital and social-media presence and interactions.

- ✔ **Within your business:** Does the look, sound, and even the smell of your business convey your brand character? Do your employees reflect your brand identity by the way they look and act, the clothes they wear, and the way they interact with customers?

✔ **Correspondence:** Have you standardized mail and e-mail correspondence so that communications, whether they come from a salesperson, an invoice clerk, or a service representative, create an echo chamber for the quality and caliber of the brand you're launching?

✔ **Service:** Are you ready to project your new brand at each of the following eight service points?

- Initial contact

- Establishment of rapport

- Product presentation

- Sale negotiation and transaction

- Payment

- Delivery

- Follow-up to confirm customer satisfaction

- Ongoing customer service and communication

If any of these service points fails to convey the brand well, you run the risk of an uneven customer experience with your brand, which is a fast track to breaking your brand promise and eroding brand strength.

The minute you're sure that everyone in your organization understands your brand message and is prepared to contribute to an experience that conveys and strengthens your brand at every customer touch point, you're ready to take your brand public, beginning with your highest-priority audiences: your investors and most-loyal customers.

Previewing your brand with priority audiences

Prior to the widespread public launch of your brand and again on at least an annual basis, tell your brand story to your most important outside audiences: your investors and your best customers.

Taking your brand story to key partners, investors, and analysts

The financial world watches the Interbrand and *BusinessWeek* annual surveys on power brands for a reason: Investors realize that a good way to monitor a firm's earning potential is to monitor the strength of its branding program.

In addition to watching how a brand stacks up against others, investors watch how well brands are managed. When presenting to those who invest in your business — whether with money or with partnership decisions — convey information that assures them of positive answers to the following questions in most investor minds:

- ✔ Does the brand convey the same identity, message, and promise when dealing with all stakeholder groups, from investors to consumers to employees?

- ✔ Does the brand express itself through an integrated marketing program that projects a consistent look, tone, message, and promise online and offline, within and outside the business, in advertising, in fulfillment materials, to all audiences, and at all points of contact?

- ✔ Does the brand retain its customers — an indication that it delivers well on its brand promise?

- ✔ Does the brand have coordinated internal management, as evidenced by a brand experience that's without variation whether it's encountered as a prospect, a customer, a job applicant, a supplier, or an investor?

If you're seeking investor support, first build a branding program that assures a strong "yes" response to each of the preceding questions. Then, at the time of brand launch and periodically thereafter, deliver your brand story to the investor and analyst community by

- ✔ Creating an investor/analyst presentation that features your brand story and success indicators (for examples of brand presentations, search online for "investor analyst brand presentations" to find corporate sites that allow you to click on investor podcasts, webcasts, presentations, news releases, and fact sheets)

- ✔ Hosting online or conveniently located events to present and discuss your brand story

- ✔ Following presentations with news recaps released to investment firms and financial media

- ✔ Posting investor/analyst information in your website's news center

Treating your best customers to an insiders' preview

If you're rebranding, revitalizing your brand, or introducing a subbrand or brand extension, don't let your best and most loyal customers hear the news through the grapevine. Instead, treat them like the insiders they are by reaching out with invitations to in-person or online brand-preview events. Share your enthusiasm, help them understand and embrace your brand changes and message, and reward their interest with meaningful brand offers or gifts. Chapter 14 gives you advice to follow as you cultivate brand loyalty and turn customers into raving fans and brand ambassadors.

Ten, Nine, Eight . . . Writing Your Brand-Launch Marketing Plan

Don't leave your brand launch to chance. By putting a plan in writing, you force yourself to clarify your launch objectives, the strategy and tactics you'll follow, the timeline you'll meet, and the budget you'll live within.

You can launch your brand with a plan that exists only in your head, but you shouldn't. To keep yourself and everyone on your team on track for a successful launch, take these steps, which the following sections explain in greater detail.

1. **State your brand-launch message, following the tips and advice in earlier sections of this chapter.**

2. **Benchmark your pre-launch situation by determining your brand's current levels of awareness, emotional connection, distinction, credibility and trust, and sales.**

3. **Set your brand-launch objectives by prioritizing what you want to accomplish and by pinning each priority to a measurable outcome, such as a percentage increase in brand awareness, emotional connection, distinction, credibility and trust, and sales.**

4. **Define your target market so that you can direct communications specifically toward this group.**

5. **Define the brand promise and brand character to be conveyed in all brand communications and experiences.**

6. **Establish your brand introduction strategies.**

7. **Detail your marketing tactics, including how you'll use advertising, publicity, social media, promotions, online marketing, sales efforts, packaging, and point-of-sale efforts to introduce your brand.**

8. **Establish your budget.**

9. **Create your action plan and timeline.**

10. **Measure and monitor your success.**

Benchmarking your pre-launch situation

Chapters 3 and 5 include information on assessing your market situation and conducting research to find out more about your brand's awareness, distinction, and preference in your market. Use the form in Figure 9-1 to benchmark your pre-launch situation and to monitor shifts in brand presence and performance during the post-launch period.

MEASURING THE IMPACT OF YOUR BRAND INTRODUCTION				
	Pre-launch benchmark	Results at launch conclusion	Results 2–3 months post-launch	Results 6–12 months post-launch
Sales: Revenue; units sold; other sales indicators				
Market share: Percentage of sales of like-offerings in your market area captured by your brand				
Price: Price per item sold or other pricing indicator				
Awareness: Percentage of market that knows your brand name				
Emotional Connection: Percentage of market that prefers your brand over competitors or that places your brand in the Top 3 or Top 5 in your category				
Distinction: Percentage of market that understands how your offering is uniquely different				
Credibility and Trust: Percentage of market that understands and believes your brand promise				
Purchase Motivation: Percentage of market that intends to purchase, repurchase, or recommend a purchase of your offering				

Figure 9-1:
Benchmark and monitor the impact of your brand introduction by using this worksheet.

© Barbara Findlay Schenck

Setting your launch goal and objectives

Your *goal* is what you want your brand launch to achieve; your *objectives* define how you'll achieve your goal. For example:

- ✔ **If your goal is to win awareness for your brand and its distinctions,** your objectives may include gaining name recognition, knowledge of your unique point of difference, social-media followers, and favorable publicity within a certain length of time from the conclusion of your brand launch.

- ✔ **If your goal is to enhance credibility and trust,** your objectives may be to win industry recognition and awards; to receive endorsements from those who influence prospective customers; to obtain favorable ratings, reviews, and recommendations; and to achieve online sharing and interaction within a certain length of time from the conclusion of your brand launch.

- ✔ **If your goal is to motivate sales,** your objectives may be to add new distribution channels, to generate and use an opt-in mail list, and to realize a sales increase without sacrificing unit sale price within a certain length of time from the conclusion of your brand launch.

Commit your goals and objectives to writing in order to keep your efforts focused only on marketing strategies and tactics that contribute to your success. Then each time a new marketing opportunity arises, you can put it to this easy litmus test: *Will this opportunity help us meet our goal? Does it support one or more of our objectives?* If the answer is "no," you can quickly decline the offer and turn your attention back to your plan.

Defining your target market

In defining the target market for your brand launch, answer these questions:

- ✔ Are you targeting new customers?

- ✔ Are you targeting existing customers?

- ✔ Are you targeting those in a position to refer customers to your business or to speak on your behalf?

- ✔ Will your introduction be confined geographically to a city or region, will it target specific social-media or online audiences, or will it aim to communicate with broadly dispersed consumers who fit a defined prospect profile?

Targeting your market puts you in a position to reach prospects effectively with well-chosen media and messages. It also helps you plan staffing and distribution to meet the market demand your communications generate.

Nearly all successful brand introductions start with narrowly focused target markets for these reasons:

- ✔ **A brand introduction requires intensive communication in order to rapidly achieve a necessary level of awareness.** It's far easier and vastly more affordable to achieve intensive communication when prospects all live in a limited geographic area that can be reached with regional media, or when they share lifestyle or interest similarities that allow you to reach them with social media, special-interest media, or one-to-one communications.

- ✔ **Most brand introductions come from small businesses that work with relatively small budgets.** Huge corporations either buy and reintroduce existing brands or introduce parent-dominant brands that slide into the market under the strong umbrella identity of the well-known parent brand. Nearly all other brands start with budget, distribution, and staffing constraints that are best managed by introduction in highly focused target markets.

- ✔ **Even major brands benefit from target marketing at the time of introduction.** By introducing a brand in a single geographic market or through a single distribution channel or even a single retail chain, the brand can achieve a high level of awareness while building a success story that creates publicity, word-of-mouth, and other forms of viral marketing.

Setting your strategies

Marketing plans include strategies for the *4Ps:* product, pricing, promotion, and place (or distribution channels). When creating your brand launch marketing, establish the strategy you'll follow in each of these four areas:

- ✔ **Product:** Most brand launches revolve around the announcement of an altogether new offering or the announcement of changes to an existing offering. Be aware that new brands or products require a higher level of introduction, explanation, and purchase motivation than are required by product or brand revisions, which are often introduced to an already committed audience.

- ✔ **Pricing:** If one of your brand-introduction priorities is to achieve new sales, particularly from new customers, your pricing strategy is an essential element in your brand introduction. To motivate decisions, consider limited-term introductory pricing or payment options, rebates, trial offers, or other purchase incentives.

- ✔ **Promotion:** Your promotion strategy describes how you'll get the word out about your brand. Most brand-launch promotions involve public relations, advertising, and online communications, each described in detail in Chapters 10, 11, and 12.

- ✔ **Place or distribution:** Your brand introduction needs to be backed by a distribution strategy that allows consumers to access your offering as soon as interest is ignited. To a business-to-business brand marketer, the distribution strategy may take the form of a new location, new website, or some other new means of access. To a consumer brand marketer, the distribution strategy must lead to an easy-to-access purchase point, whether online, via mail, or at a bricks-and-mortar location.

Often, businesses introduce consumer brands first through a single distribution point or chain. This approach allows the marketer to maximize in-store visibility while minimizing the requirements of distributor discounts and slotting fees that can erode profits to the point of killing a consumer brand before it has time to get off the ground.

Selecting your brand-introduction tactics

To achieve cost-effective visibility while also generating awareness and building credibility, most brand launches rely heavily on publicity, public relations, one-to-one communications, and social media, rather than on advertising, which often is used as a follow-up to news stories and personally delivered announcements of the new brand. The following list describes various communication approaches:

- ✔ **Public relations activities:** These communications are the backbone of most brand introductions. The field of public relations includes employee relations, member relations, community relations, industry relations, government relations, and blogger and media relations that result in news coverage. Events, meetings, newsletters, exhibitions, and publicity all fall under the category of public relations. All spread news and generate understanding without involving paid advertising. Turn to Chapter 12 as you plan your public-relations game plan.

- ✔ **Promotions:** Special offers trigger a desired consumer action over a short period of time. Marketers introducing products or launching consumer brands use promotions to win support from distributors and retailers and to prompt customers to a first-time trial of the new product. See Chapter 12 for guidelines on promotions.

- ✔ **Advertisements:** Ads in newspapers and magazines and on radio, television, social-media networks, and targeted web pages transmit messages over large yet targeted market areas to reach broadly dispersed markets. Chapter 12 offers advice for scheduling, creating, and placing your ads.

   When using advertising as a brand-launch tactic, time your schedules so that ads break *after* your brand is released via news stories. After your message runs in ad form, editorial contacts may not view it as news, and you miss the chance to gain the credible third-party voice of a reporter, blogger, or newscaster.

- ✔ **Mailings:** Direct mail reaches a highly targeted audience on a one-to-one basis through mail boxes or email in-boxes rather than through mass media. If you're delivering your brand announcements or event invitations via email, be sure to turn to Chapter 13 for information on how to follow online direct-mail rules and how to deliver email that gets opened and read.

- ✔ **Personal presentations:** Presentations to key audiences are especially important if the success of your brand launch depends on support from established contacts and customers. Most business and service brands host launch events and consider personal presentations as essential introduction tactics. Turn to Chapter 13 for information on building brand trust during presentations and at the point of sale.

- ✔ **Sales materials, packaging, and point-of-sale displays:** These visuals are essential for consumer brands and for brands with offerings that involve complex features, high prices, or considerable deliberation prior to the purchase decision. If your brand launch involves a new or re-introduced product, review the section on packaging in Chapter 12 and then hire a designer, ad agency, or branding or packaging specialist to create packaging that represents your brand well, because your package becomes your brand representative at the point of purchase decision.

- ✔ **Online or digital communications:** These messages play an essential role in brand introduction tactical plans, as described in Chapters 10 and 11.

Brand-introduction budget worksheet

After you've selected your brand-launch tactics (see the preceding section), you're ready to plan and set your budget. The worksheet in Figure 9-2 helps you estimate costs involved to implement each tactic.

BRAND-LAUNCH BUDGET WORKSHEET		
Tactic	Cost Estimate	Included in existing marketing budget?
Mass media ads in newspapers, magazines, radio, TV, and out-of-home		☐ Yes ☐ No
Public relations		
Events and functions for employees, customers, community groups, industry groups, and other VIP groups		☐ Yes ☐ No
Publicity generation including media kit development, news release generation, and professional assistance		☐ Yes ☐ No
Direct mail including list development/ purchase, mailer production, mailing costs		☐ Yes ☐ No
Marketing materials including brochures, packaging, displays, videos, and ad specialties		☐ Yes ☐ No
Website development		☐ Yes ☐ No
Online ads including site ads, search ads, social media ads, promoted posts		☐ Yes ☐ No
		☐ Yes ☐ No
		☐ Yes ☐ No
Other:		☐ Yes ☐ No

Figure 9-2: Prepare your brand-launch budget by estimating costs for each tactic you intend to employ.

© Barbara Findlay Schenck

Takeoff! Launching Your Brand

Your brand launch needs to happen in two phases: first an internal phase and then an external phase. Only after your internal team is on board and every customer touch point is in alignment and ready to deliver on your brand promise are you ready to take your brand outside your organization and to your target market.

Launching internally

Even your internal launch needs to occur in two phases: the first one for senior management and the second one for your full employee team. This sequence is important because you need to get all executives firmly on board before you start rallying the troops. Otherwise, you risk gaining enthusiasm from employees only to have some vice president (also known as someone's boss) say something like, "I don't know why we're spending so much time and money on this." Just like that, internal support for your branding program can take a giant backslide.

If your company is small to medium in size, your two-phase internal launch can happen over a short time period. If you're dealing with multiple locations or divisions, however, it will take longer. Either way, by involving executives in the brand planning and development phase, you cut down the time needed to bring top-level leaders on board because they're part of the planning team from the beginning.

Starting with the bigwigs: Launching with upper management

Your top-level executive team was involved in the brand-development process (right?), so you don't need to unveil your new or revitalized brand to this group. Instead, use the launch as your chance to bring the whole brand picture into focus, following these steps:

1. **Review and win unanimous consent for your brand position, promise, character, definition, and launch message.**

   Address any questions or doubts so that all leaders are reading from the same page when your brand message moves into your organization.

2. **Gain agreement regarding your brand-launch objectives and timing.**

   This is the last chance to learn about timing conflicts between the brand launch and other business activities so you can iron out kinks by altering the schedule, shifting launch responsibilities, or hiring employees or outside professionals to handle the tasks involved. Deal with any issues at this stage of the launch so they don't become a barrier to success as you implement your broader launch.

3. **Preview your brand-launch materials and presentation.**

   The tasks covered in the section "Preparing for Your Brand Launch" earlier in this chapter help you prepare your presentation materials. Now is the time to preview them with your top-level team so there won't be any surprises (or resistance) at the company-wide presentation.

4. **Discuss and win agreement regarding how each executive's department can tangibly integrate the brand promise into every aspect of the organization's products and services.**

   Chapter 13 includes a form for conducting a brand experience audit. Consider asking your executive team to use the form as they assess any brand contact points in need of repair and as they take responsibility for implementing change in their individual management arenas.

Launching company-wide

By taking the time to explain why you're branding, rebranding, or revitalizing your brand and how your efforts link to your business mission and goals, you preempt internal resistance and kick-start the process of creating a team of champions for your brand. (Turn to Chapter 13 for information on turning your staff and business partners into your best brand champions.)

Your internal brand launch should be both an education process and a company rally. For a successful launch, follow these steps:

1. **Make a case about the value of branding.**

   If you can't connect the idea of branding to your business vision, mission, values, and goals, you're setting yourself up to hear murmurs of, "They paid how much for *that?*" Turn to the section "Putting your brand launch into context" earlier in this chapter for advice on developing a meaningful and inspiring brand story.

2. **Present your brand strategy, putting special emphasis on the brand promise and the importance of a brand experience that's reflected through every point of encounter with your business.**

   Refer to the section "Checking your internal readiness" earlier in this chapter as you prepare for this step.

3. **Unveil your brand identity.**

   Show the logo, preview the slogan, and present prototypes of how the brand identity will appear throughout your business and marketing materials over coming weeks and months.

4. **Give each employee a quality gift featuring the new logo.**

   The nicer the item, the better the impression, so avoid anything cheap or cheesy unless that's the image you want your employees to take away with them. Instead, accompany your internal brand launch with distribution of quality items that employees will like and want to keep. Please, no click-top pens with flaky metallic imprints up the side.

Remind employees of the external launch date and ask them to keep your identity under wraps until that day arrives. If your staff is too large to control, consider distributing gifts or copies of the new identity until after the external launch occurs.

5. **Ask each member of your team to personally embrace the brand and become an ambassador who delivers the brand experience to customers.**

   Count on Chapter 13 to cover this step in detail.

Launching externally

Only when your company is ready to walk the talk is it time to take your brand message to the world outside your business by following these steps:

1. **Time your external launch to coincide with public interest in your story.**

   If you serve a particular industry, consider timing your launch around a major conference or trade show. If you serve a local market, coincide your launch with an annual economic development conference, regional business fair, or some other event that brings regional leaders and media together in one place.

2. **Launch a public-relations program to carry your brand message into your community, market area, and industry arena.**

3. **Place ads presenting your brand and the promise it makes.**

4. **Unveil your brand promise and message on the home page of your website and social-media pages.**

As you announce your brand outside your organization, use the information in Chapters 10, 11, and 12 to leverage publicity to launch your brand, advertise to put your stake in the ground, and put the power of digital communications to work to spread your brand message far and wide.

Chapter 10

Branding in the Digital Age

In This Chapter

▶ Planning and activating your brand's online presence

▶ Building site that looks great on any size screen

▶ Getting found online by search engines and customers

The Internet is the most-traveled route to your business offerings. It's the starting point for finding directions to and information about your business and for evaluating and considering your products and services. It's where many if not most people form their first impression of your brand. It's also where small-scale brands can level the playing field when competing with the best-funded big-brand marketers. Online, no one knows how big your office or budget is, because your business fills the same screen as that filled by the pages of your biggest competitor. This chapter helps you make the most of your online opportunity.

Pulling People to Your Brand Online

Your brand has to be online. That's all there is to it. To anyone with a website, that first sentence sounds like a no-brainer, and yet small-business owners lead the list of people who think they can develop brands with no or only haphazard web presence. If you're among the great many freelancers or super-small businesses without web pages you own and control, flip back to Chapter 4 for a tutorial on building personal and one-person business brands and where web presence fits into the success strategy.

Online, a strong, well-managed brand tips the balance between success and failure for two very different reasons.

> ✔ **If you use the web as a sales channel, strong brand management is necessary for sales success.** Unlike in a bricks-and-mortar outlet, web users can't touch or try your product, and no one's there to personally explain and reinforce your promise. More than in any other distribution channel, when customers reach you online they need to either arrive confident in your brand's quality and promise or they need to develop

confidence practically at a glance. Whether they're on your site, on a review site, on a page where you're featured, or on the first page of search results, if your brand doesn't show up quickly and well, you're out of luck. The branding process helps you do the advance work that results in the confidence and trust necessary to prompt positive customer decisions online.

✔ **If you use the web to provide customers with information, service, or interaction, strong brand management is necessary to make your page and posts familiar and recognizable while also making a visit to your site a seamless extension of your overall brand experience.** Whether people meet up with your brand online or offline, you must always deliver a consistent message, tone, look, character, and promise. This consistency leads to a single, positive experience regardless of where or how customers reach you.

To a good portion of your target audience, online contact is the first and most frequently visited approach to your brand. What they see on your website or when they see your name mentioned online becomes your brand image in their minds. Brand management ups the odds that the impression they get is the one you want them to have.

The open-and-shut case for building your brand's online presence

The stats tell the story. Web activity influences half of all retail sales. At least a billion people search for names of people, products, and businesses online daily. American homes have more Internet-connected devices than they have people. And, according to Google research, worldwide more people have access to a mobile phone than have access to a toothbrush.

All that digital connection comes with some high expectations:

✔ **People expect to find you online.** They expect to find you through searches, on social-media networks, on review and rating sites, and at your own website, which they expect will give them quick access to information and one-click directions and connection to your business from any sized screen. Count on this chapter for site-building advice.

✔ **People expect prompt interaction.** The days of waiting for responses to questions, concerns, or even compliments are history. If people mention you in a Tweet, post, or review, they expect you'll see their comments and that you'll react — quickly. With this chapter you get your social-media presence started, and Chapter 11 gets your social-media involvement kicked into high gear.

✔ **People expect to control what they see and when they see it.** They don't want to be bugged and bothered by ads. They want to access information when they're ready for it by using web searches, social-media networks, favorite sites or apps, and links provided by trusted friends or resources. That's part of the value of branding. It builds an emotional connection that turns your brand into a trusted friend whose posts and links get noticed, followed, and shared far and wide.

Today's customers block, ignore, or are annoyed by most marketing messages that are pushed at them. They want to be pulled to your brand and to access your information on their terms rather than on your terms.

Capitalizing on the difference between push marketing and pull marketing

Pre-Internet, marketers successfully pushed messages to their target audiences using ads and other one-way communications in an effort to, quoting from the very useful marketing site Hubspot.com, "buy, beg, or bug their way in" to customer minds.

Digital communication changed everything. It empowered people and gave them control over how and when they receive information. Today, *pull marketing* reigns over *push marketing* because customers prefer it by a mile and also because it costs two-thirds less per lead generated than the old tried-and-no-longer-true approach of push marketing. Here's what the terms mean:

✔ **Push marketing** interrupts customers with one-way communications that involve the marketer talking and the customer (hopefully) reading or listening and (ideally) taking whatever action the message is intended to inspire. Push marketing usually involves mass-media ads, direct mail, online banner ads, and cold calls to prospective customers. Fact is, people actually pay extra or take extra steps to avoid push marketing when they can. Online, push marketing is called *outbound marketing*.

✔ **Pull marketing** engages customers with two-way communication. It begins when the marketer delivers nonintrusive and useful, entertaining, or educational information, called *content,* which customers encounter primarily through web searches, social media, blogs, or online sharing. Upon finding and taking interest in the content, the customer initiates contact with the marketer by using embedded links or contact directions that pull to the marketer's business or website where the leads are captured, information is delivered, and sales are made. Online, pull marketing is called *inbound marketing*.

Pull marketing isn't new. Half-off promotions pull customer interest, as do promotional events. The difference is that digital communication makes pull marketing inexpensive, customizable, interactive, and sharable from customer-to-customer at a level that can climb to viral proportions. What's not to like?

Ego-Surfing to Benchmark Your Brand's Online Footprint

If you've already established a brand — a personal, business, or product brand — when was the last time you opened a search engine, typed in your name, and studied the results? If you're among the rare few who have never gone ego-surfing, as self-searching is sometimes called, or if it's been awhile, do it now. See what others learn about you and your brand when you're nowhere in sight. Check out the sidebar "Self-sleuth to see how your brand looks online" for advice on avoiding skewed results by closing out of your Google account or by entering an incognito or private search to obtain results that aren't influenced by your location or search history.

Then study the results. Here's what to look for:

✔ **Do you own the all-important first result?** When you enter your brand name the way you think others will search for it, does the first result lead to your website, blog, major social-media page, or to another page you control and keep updated with current, positive, accurate information?

✔ **Do you dominate the entire first page of results, with links to positive content all the way down the page?** This is the mark of a great online brand. You get it by building your own website (with a domain name featuring your brand name plus .com or .org), brand pages on all the major, high-ranking social-media networks, a blog (WordPress ranks highest of all blogging platforms), and a broad array of positive publicity or mentions on major sites that help optimize your presence in search results.

✔ **Does an accurate, positive link to information about your brand appear at least once on the first-screen of results?** The first page is as far as nine of ten web users go, so that's the very least you're aiming to achieve.

✔ **Have you managed to avoid a single negative or brand-damaging result on the first screen of results?** Also, go deeper in search results to check for embarrassing entries in the top results for your brand in news, video, and photo results. If what you see doesn't match the brand image you want to develop, you have double your resolve to set online branding objectives that force you to accelerate your efforts in an effort to bury the offending results under a heap of positive, findable brand pages.

Self-sleuth to see how your brand looks online

It's referred to as *ego-surfing, Googling yourself,* or *vanity searching* — but we call it good brand management. Check out your brand's online presence early and often. Here's how:

✔ **Go incognito and use multiple browsers.** Most search engines personalize the results they give you, basing results on your location and stored search history. For your self-search, though, you don't want personalized results. You want to see what others see, so you want to hide your location, IP address, past search results, and other identifiers. If you're using Google, sign out of your Google account if you have one. Or better yet, go to the right edge of the Google top-of-screen menu, pull down the menu, and click "New Incognito Window." In Safari, select "Private Browsing" from the menu bar. In Bing or Internet Explorer, click "In Private Browsing" under the Safety tab. In Firefox, select "New Private Window" from the File menu.

✔ **Search for your name the way (or ways) you think those looking for you or your business will enter it.** A good starting point is to type your name the way it appears on your business card. Then, if you use other treatments of your name on social media or in signage, search for those versions as well. Don't worry about punctuation or capitalization, though, because search engines overlook those details.

✔ **Put quotation marks around your name.** This limits search results only to pages that include your exact name with the words presented exactly as you specify them. Be aware, though, it can also exclude results. On its help page, Google explains that "a search for 'Alexander Bell' will miss pages that refer to 'Alexander G Bell.'"

✔ **Use descriptions that others might use to when trying to find you among those with sound-alike names.** If a search for your brand name delivers a great many not-you results, study the results anyway, because they show what people searching for you are apt to find online. Particularly if another brand owns your name with a .com URL, realize you'll probably never own the first slot in search results, which may encourage some thinking about a different brand name altogether (see Chapter 16 for help, if that's the case). Next, refine your search by adding qualifying terms you think your customers might use. Add a word designating your location or your business arena or type. For instance, instead of searching for "Main Street Cleaners," search for "Main Street Cleaners" plus "Tulsa." Or instead of searching for "Smith and Associates," search for "Smith and Associates" plus "accounting," or "design," or whatever.

✔ **Look beyond the first set of results.** Use search filters to study results for News, Images, and Videos to get a clearer idea of your online footprint.

✔ **Search online directories customers might use to find you.** Also, search for your business address in Google Maps. If you can prove the information is wrong, you can report a problem to get the results updated. (For help, see the sidebar "Get your business on Google for free.")

Study how prominent and dominant your brand appears in the results, how many results show up for your brand, and whether the results lead to current and positive information. The section in this chapter on ego-surfing gives advice on what to look for. Your findings provide the basis for setting objectives for improving your online presence and strengthening your brand as a result.

Use your ego-surfing findings as the benchmark for how your brand appears to online users today. Also, use it as the starting point for boosting your brand's online presence, engagement, and interaction, which are the keys to sales, loyalty, and valuable customer-to-customer sharing.

Paving the Way for Your Online Presence

Few brand owners question the need for broader online presence, but many question where to start, what to do, and how to best invest their efforts. Recommendation: Take the following four steps, in order, once and for all. After that, it'll be a matter of staying active online, which is the topic of Chapter 11.

Set your online branding objectives

Based on what you learn through an online self-search for your brand name, match your findings to one or more of these online branding objectives:

✔ **Increase awareness:** If you're launching a brand or if your established brand is practically invisible in search results, set an objective to develop online presence and awareness by launching a website or blog and creating profiles on major social-media networks. At the very least, establish a Google presence for your business, for free, at www.google.com/business (see the sidebar, "Get your business on Google for free").

✔ **Enhance credibility:** If search results for your brand name are weak, inaccurate, irrelevant, or inconsistent with the brand image you want to establish (for example, bad reviews, bad photos, or bad publicity), improve credibility by generating new links to favorable information about your brand including publicity, referrals from other sites, blog posts, useful brand-generated content, and social-media profiles and pages that you can keep updated with current, positive information. The new links, especially if they're on high-traffic sites, will dilute the impact of unfavorable links by pushing them from first-page results to subsequent, less-visited screens.

✔ **Develop engagement and interaction:** After your brand presence is broad and accurate, set an objective to build on your strength by developing connections and communication with your online audience, realizing that interaction leads to preference and loyalty for your brand and its offerings. Turn to Chapter 11 for steps to follow.

✔ **Generate sales:** Before setting an online objective to increase sales, flip back to the section in this chapter on push versus pull marketing. Online, more than anywhere else, people detest intrusive and pushy sales pitches. Sales occur as a result of your brand's success at developing online awareness, credibility, and interaction that pulls people to the point of purchase through useful, interesting content and easy-to-follow directions and links. Online, make friends, and then make sales. In that order.

Establish your brand name across your digital channels

In the same way that your brand name is the key that unlocks your brand image in the mind of consumers, your *domain name* (the string of characters web users type into a browser to reach your site, such as www.yourbrandname. com), and your social-media handles or monikers are the keys that unlock your brand online.

Ideally, your domain name is comprised of your brand name plus .com or .org, depending on whether your brand represents a commercial business or a nonprofit organization. When it comes to establishing a domain name, though, the Internet isn't an ideal world. For one thing, it's populated with millions of websites accessed by domain names that tie up most of the words in the English language. Beyond that, it's a world where cyber-squatters camp on attractive unclaimed domain names, registering and tying them up until someone pays what can feel like a ransom to free them for use.

If you have or can claim the domain name featuring your brand name, hold a celebration and move on to Step 3 in this list. Otherwise, get ready to jump through some hoops. This section can help you get through relatively unscathed.

Landing on your website's domain name

By a mile, making your brand name the centerpiece of your domain name is the quickest route to establishing your online identity, and here's why: A good portion of web traffic takes the form of *type-in traffic,* a term that describes users who bypass search engines and simply type the name of the company they're looking for, followed by .com, in the address bar of the web browser. By making your brand name the basis of your domain name, you capture visits from this group of web users.

✔ **If you're developing a new brand,** don't settle on a brand name until you've checked it out at a domain name registry to confirm it's available as a domain name. Research availability on registry sites like www. GoDaddy.com, www.NameCheap.com, or www.NetworkSolutions. com. The advance effort will help eliminate the grief of settling on a brand name that you later discover isn't available for online use. Plus, it will help you end up with the same name on your physical establishment and on your website, a vital first step in creating a strong brand identity.

To shortcut the process, avoid choosing a brand name that's straight out of the dictionary. Nearly every entry in the English dictionary is already part of a registered domain name and therefore likely unavailable for your online use. You can preempt a ton of frustration by coining a word that you can use in both your brand and domain names. Chapter 7 is packed with advice on creating brand names, including how to fabricate syllables or words into great brand and domain names. Microsoft, DreamWorks, Netflix, and Firefox are just a few examples.

✔ **If your brand name isn't available as a domain name,** try these Plan B approaches:

- Come up with a tagline or slogan that becomes a major part of your brand identity and the basis for your domain name. For example, if you type in www.wetryharder.com, you're taken to the Avis website. Type in www.justdoit.com and you land on the Nike site.

- Look into purchasing your top-choice domain name from its current owner. This process can be costly and time-consuming, but if you plan to build a valuable brand, it can be worth the investment. Many domain name registrars offer assistance with this step; go to www.internic.net/regist.html for a complete list of registrars.

Following is a lineup of domain-name selection advice, including a few things *not* to do when you resort to a Plan B brand name:

Domain name advice

As you plan your domain name, consider the following points:

✔ **Keep your domain name short and easy to remember.** Some of the best-known web addresses provide good examples: www.aol.com, www.ebay.com, www.google.com, www.yahoo.com, www.amazon.com. Each one is short and just about impossible to forget or misspell.

✔ **If your brand name plus .com or .org is taken, don't try to end-run the system by using your brand name plus .net.** If web users instinctively type .com, they'll go straight to someone else's site.

✔ **Don't get clever by adding hyphens or making unusual alterations to your brand name.** For instance, a domain name like www.cookeezncream.com may be available, but the chances that most users will remember and instinctively type it correctly are slim.

✔ **Don't invent an abbreviation for a long brand name unless you're sure it will be easy to memorize and recall.** For example, the Hawaii Visitors and Convention Bureau can be reached by typing www.hvcb.org, but they don't ask you to remember the lineup of initials. Instead, they market the domain name www.gohawaii.com, which offers an easy-to-recall address and a desirable remedy to the mid-winter blues.

✔ **Think globally.** If your business plan calls for international presence, register your name with international codes to specify your global offices. For example, `www.microsoft.com/en-gb` is the address for information about Microsoft in the United Kingdom.

Registering your domain name

When you find the domain name you want, register it immediately. Most registration services charge somewhere between $25 and $75 for a three-year period of domain name ownership.

When registering your name, consider this advice:

✔ The first domain name you need to register is your site name, as in `www.yourbrandname.com`.

✔ Consider also registering your site with various extensions, such as `.net`, `.org`, `.info`, or `.biz` so others can't later grab the alternative addresses. Should online users type in one of the alternates, you can redirect the traffic to your main address, following information in the sidebar, "Redirecting online traffic."

✔ Consider registering versions of your domain name that people are likely to type when trying to find your brand online. For example:

• Register your tagline as a domain name so people who forget your brand name but remember your slogan can reach your site.

• Register your brand name with misspellings. For instance, if you type `www.googel.com`, you're redirected to `www.google.com`. Or if you type `www.fordummies.com`, you arrive at `www.dummies.com`. Use a similar error-capture program in your strategy by thinking of ways people may mistype your domain name and registering each version.

• Register additional domain names as you discover new user-error tendencies. After your website is up and running, regularly check error logs to see what kinds of mistakes people are making when trying to reach your site. And ask those who deal with customers to pass along pronunciation or spelling mistakes that they see or hear so that you can work the errors into your URL-forwarding strategy.

Creating a multiple-domain-name strategy costs very little. The registration fee on each name is nominal, and you can use a process called *URL redirection* to point all traffic to the website that carries your primary domain name, incurring no additional site building or hosting fees. (See the sidebar "Redirecting online traffic" for more information.)

Redirecting online traffic

If your branding effort involves a name change and a new domain name, or if you're buying versions of your domain name to protect it from use by others and from typos by customers, you need to know about something called a *301 redirect*. It's the web's version of a post office change of address card.

A 301 redirect tells browsers and search engines to permanently send people trying to reach Domain Name A to Domain Name B instead. Setting up a redirect isn't difficult, but it does require access to your server, your Apache Configuration file, and certain access files. The preceding sentence alone should be enough to convince you to contact your web host or call on tech assistance to be sure you get it right. And getting it right is especially important when you're changing an established domain name because you'll want to transfer your old domain name's *search engine authority* — its search ranking based on a mysterious blend of site age, traffic trends, history, content, and incoming links — to the new domain. With a 301 redirect, your established domain name's ranking power transfers to the new address. Without a 301 redirect, you have to start the search-engine optimization effort all over again, and we've yet to find anyone who wants to volunteer for that opportunity.

Registering your social-media name

Chapter 11 is all about social media, but right now, while you're choosing and registering your domain name, register your name across social-media networks as well. We've said it before and we'll say it again, online real estate moves fast.

When deciding how to present your name, follow this advice:

- ✔ **Decide on a social-media moniker that's short and memorable.** Twitter limits names to 15 characters, and even shorter names are better because they take up fewer characters in online mentions and retweets. To achieve brand continuity, apply Twitter's 15-character limit to the name you use on all networks.

- ✔ **If your brand name is available, use it as both your domain name and your social-media handle.** For example, if your domain name is www.ourbrandname.com, aim to use "ourbrandname" as your name across social media. For free and in seconds you go to a social-media name registration site to see if the social-media name you want is available. Sites such as knowem.com, checkusernames.com, or namechk.com will tell you on-the-spot whether the name you want is taken on various networks. If it's available, click to claim and protect it.

- ✔ **If your brand name isn't available on the social-media networks you want to use, consider this advice:**

- **Avoid adding odd hyphenation or characters** that people are apt to forget or mistype. While adding your area code, Zip code, or, for a personal brand, your birth year, may make sense to you, it's likely to lack meaning and recall for others.

- **Invent a version of your name** by combining your name with a word that describes or reflects your brand promise, business arena, or niche. For example, Johnson & Johnson is too long for Twitter's name-length limits. Instead, the brand uses a lineup of well-branded monikers for different audiences, including J&JCares, J&JNews, J&JStories, to name a few.

- **Use one name on all networks to build brand awareness.** Reserve your name on the networks you plan to use immediately or in the future for across-the-board continuity in how you present your-self in online. The only exception is on sites such as LinkedIn that require use of your personal rather than your business name. In those cases, settle on a single presentation of your own name and always include your business brand name in your personal description. Chapter 4 has more information on cross-promoting your business and personal brands.

Establish your brand's digital home base

Here are three words of advice for anyone trying to build a brand without a website: *Get a website.* This section is especially aimed at freelancers and solo-preneurs, who comprise the surprisingly large percentage of businesses with no controllable online presence. In today's screen-obsessed world, building a brand and building a website go hand-in-hand. Here's what you need:

✔ **A site you control:** A listing in regional or industry directories isn't enough. You need a place where people can learn current business facts and news, a sense of your reputation and brand promise, and how to access your business, preferably with a single click. The gold standard is a website with a domain name featuring your brand name. A blog is a good alternative, and Facebook and LinkedIn business pages are neces-sary complements that can also serve as surrogate sites so long as keep them current and use them for ongoing interaction. For personal brands, consider establishing a free page on About.me, from where you can link people to all your content on the web.

✔ **A site findable by a search for your brand name:** People may search for your business name, your product name, your personal name if you're building a personal brand, or both your personal and business names if you're the primary force in a very small business (in which case, flip to Chapter 4 for information on cross-promoting the two). In any case, their search needs to lead to a page you control and keep updated.

✔ **A site you can easily update:** Commit to keeping it current and interesting.

✔ **A site that loads quickly and looks great on any size screen:** Insist on what's called a *responsive site* that shows well whether on the smallest phone or a wall-sized monitor.

The following sections guide your website-building plans.

Planning your website

Give early thought to the kind of people who will want to reach you online, the kind of information they'll be seeking, and what you want to achieve through your online presence. Answer the following questions:

✔ **Who is likely to visit your site?** Will it be visited primarily by current customers? By those doing price or product comparisons? By job seekers, suppliers, reporters, bloggers, editors, or other people seeking information about your business?

✔ **How will people use your site?** Will they want information about your location, open hours, and products? Will they want answers to frequently asked questions about your offerings? Will they want to learn about your background, experience, or product details? Will they want to request quotes or to study customization options? Will they want to buy online? Will job seekers want to search open positions or apply online? By knowing what people will want from your site, you can design its features and functions accordingly.

✔ **What do you want your site to do for your brand?** Every site should advance the brand image. Beyond that, do you want to generate leads, capture online sales, develop relationships, develop credibility, provide customer support, showcase work, deliver information about your business, or stay in frequent contact with customers and brand followers? Your answers help you weigh site development approaches and costs.

✔ **What do you want people to do on your site?** Buy a single product? Review and choose from an array of products? Join a mailing list or become part of your following? Request an appointment or estimate? Learn more as part of the decision-making and purchase process? As part of your answer to this question, also consider how you'll measure success, so you're prepared to establish a site that leads to the results you seek.

✔ **What information does your site need to convey?** It needs to present your brand identity, for sure. Beyond that, you need to plan content to support your site's objectives. Biographies, testimonials, and announcements of awards and recognition develop credibility and trust. A news center with publicity, backgrounders, photos, graphics, and quotable material supports publicity goals. Pricing, scheduling, and delivery information, along with secure payment options, encourage sales. A schedule of events, video clips, and FAQs enhance interaction goals. One-click arrival directions, phone contact, and mailing-list invitations develop customers.

Settling on the right type of site

Most websites fall into one of the following categories:

- **Contact sites:** Easy and economical to build and maintain, these sites are like online business cards that present your brand name and image, descriptions of products, services, open hours, and information for reaching you by email and at your physical location, preferably with access to a single-click map or phone contact.

- **Brochure sites:** These sites are online cousins to print brochures. Your site needs to advance your brand image while inspiring interest and confidence in your brand, background, products, and services.

- **Support sites:** This category of site deepens customer relationships by providing customer service and communication, including information about product usage, installation, troubleshooting, updates, and news. They're useful when many web-connected customers have similar questions or service needs that you're prepared to address and promptly respond to.

- **Ecommerce sites:** Exactly as you'd think, these sites sell goods online. They let customers view products, make choices, place orders, submit secure payments, and, often, track delivery. Because of the complexity of the functions required, these are the most expensive sites to build and maintain.

- **Mobile sites:** Designed specifically for viewing on smartphones and tablets, these sites are quickly being replaced by *responsive sites* that display effectively on screens from tiny to huge. Going the responsive-site approach makes a ton of sense for two reasons. One, it saves you site-building effort. Two, and even more important, it improves your search-engine optimization. Mobile sites require their own domain names, with a subdomain of .m, creating a second URL for you to manage and optimize. That's why Bing and Google recommend one URL, one site, everywhere your brand goes.

One way or the other, you absolutely, positively have to be sure your site looks great on a small screen, which is where most people will view it. Whether you decide on a mobile site or a responsive site, remember that especially online, people want to save precious time, spend idle time, or make quick connections. Plan accordingly and make your site suitable for small-screen viewing with:

- A clean and simple design

- Large, easy-to-read type

- Important information high on the screen — especially your brand identification, click-to-access phone number, arrival directions, and information your customers are most likely to be seeking, such as open hours, prices, product descriptions, and links to additional information

- Useful links with buttons that are easy to see and large enough for fat fingers to use

Test your site on various phones to be sure it loads quickly, is easy to view and navigate, and is free of details or functions that intrude on the mobile customer's interest in immediate gratification.

Site-building tools and tips

You can create your website from scratch or with a website-building template.

- ✔ **From-scratch website:** Unless you have great design and technical expertise, plan to hire a pro and invest time and money to end up with a site that presents your unique brand image and supports your brand and business growth goals.

- ✔ **Site from a template:** To create this kind of site, either work with a web designer or turn to one of the many do-it-yourself site-building resources, which keep growing in number and getting better in terms of functions, themes, and ease-of-use. A search for "Build your own website" will lead to plenty of options, with Web.com, WordPress.org, Weebly.com, Wix.com, GoDaddy.com, and Yola.com among the frequently cited services. As you study the options, keep these tips and cautions in mind:

  - Most site-building services offer free and paid levels (as well as free trial periods). The free levels usually include site-builder logos or ads that only go away if you upgrade to a premium service level. Check out the visibility and placement of the ads and the price of upgrading before making your choice.

  - Services with drag-and-drop designs are easiest to use on your own to create a site within days. Other services offer a greater range of complex functions but also require more time and either a greater investment of your own time or the expertise of a site-building professional.

  - Some services allow you to change templates if you want to overhaul your design in the future; others require you to basically start your site building from scratch if you want a new look.

  - Most services offer website hosting, but not all allow you to later export your site to a different host. Before committing, look into whether you can back up and basically take your site with you at some point in the future. Also, be aware that your site will share the service's hosting servers, possibly resulting in slower load speeds for pages with large image files.

Conduct an online search for the term "Compare DIY website builders" to reach and study analyses of various services, options, and benefits. For expert help, turn to these two books: *Do-It-Yourself Websites For Dummies* by Janine Warner (Wiley) and *WordPress For Dummies* by Lisa Sabin-Wilson and Matt Mullenweg (Wiley).

Optimize your site

Announcing a new website is a lot like opening the doors to a new business location or getting a new phone number. It only matters if you promote the news, gain interest in the offering, give people a reason to be in touch, and prompt them to take action.

The process of building your brand's online visibility starts by showing up in search-engine results, but it can't stop there. It also includes a heavy dose of self-promotion to develop awareness of and engagement with your brand within your target audience so they'll type your domain name or click on links to reach your site directly.

As you develop your traffic-generation strategy, here are terms to know. They also happen to be the terms used by Google Analytics when it reports on your site's user acquisition statistics:

✔ **Organic traffic:** Users who reach your site by clicking on an unpaid link (not an ad) that shows up in search-engine results. You generate organic traffic by building a website full of quality content that matches the interests of those conducting web searches (including good use of *keywords* that match terms people are apt to use when searching for you, your business, or your offerings) and by developing unpaid placements of your URL link in high-traffic sites that help *optimize* or improve your site's visibility with search engine crawlers.

✔ **Direct traffic:** Users who reach your website by typing its domain name into a browser address bar or by clicking on a link to your site in an email, newsletter, or some other document you've provided.

✔ **Referral traffic:** People who reach your website by clicking on a link in another website, whether the link was included in an unpaid mention of your site address, left by you in a blog post, comment, or online profile, or included in a pay-per-click ad (for more on ads, see Chapter 13).

✔ **Social traffic:** People who reach your site from links on social networks.

Generating organic traffic through search engines

Improving the chances that your website gets discovered by people using search engines is a never-ending process. Success results when search-engine crawlers find your site on their own or by following links to your site on other high-traffic sites. Any website owner knows the term *search-engine optimization* because every website owner wants to rank high in search-engine and directory results. Here are key terms:

✔ **Search engines** like Google or Bing collect information by using a program called a *crawler* or *spider* to read and index websites, sending keywords from the sites back to the search engine index. Each time a user searches for keywords, the engine goes to its database, finds sites with words that match the request, and provides a list of results.

✔ **Directories** like BOTW (Best of the Web) and DMOZ (the Open Directory Project) include lists that are categorized and indexed information for access by users.

To get your site found by search engines and directories, follow these steps:

1. **Register your site at Open Directory (www.dmoz.org/add.html).**

   The Open Directory Project is the web's largest, most comprehensive human-edited directory. It powers the core searches of the largest and most popular search engines. As soon as you're on this free directory, you're likely to be listed by the other major search engines as well. Submit your site address for free, wait three weeks, check to see if your site is in the directory, and resubmit it if it hasn't been picked up.

2. **Build a site that search engines can find.**

   Search engines crawl the web looking for content. Speed the process of getting found by following the tips in Table 10-1.

Table 10-1	Website Search-Engine Optimization Tips
Do	**Don't**
DO develop website content around *keywords* that people are likely to use to find information on you, your business, and your offerings.	DON'T cram your content with keywords to manipulate your search ranking. Search engines warn against *keyword stuffing* and placing hidden text or links.
DO build each page of your site around specific keywords that define the page focus so users are linked straight to the web page that fulfills their interest.	DON'T forget that keyword searches may send users to internal pages of your website, so include your brand ID and a link to your home page on every page.
DO place keywords into each page's <meta> tags, code commands, titles, navigation links, photo or graphics labels or tags, and also in embedded text links.	DON'T use default photo file names, non-descript captions (like, "Buy Now"), non-descriptive labels for in-content hot links, or navigation icons that feature only graphics, which search engines don't read.
DO devote a page to site map with page links if your site has more than 50 pages.	DON'T use *splash pages* that feature a graphic while the site loads. Search engines index content and keywords from your site's first page, and splash pages usually contain neither.
DO choose and register domain names with words that describe your site's business and brand.	DON'T forget that site visitors will leave if they don't think your site will solve their problem or address their interests quickly on an easy-to-see, easy-to-scan screen.

Do	Don't
DO build a network of incoming links from high-traffic sites.	DON'T miss the opportunity to develop links to your website from online business and industry registers, publicity featuring your business, mentions on review and rating sites, referrals from other sites, and, especially from your social-media profiles, online content, and blog posts and comments.

Finding your keywords

What words are people going use when searching for information that matches the content on your site? Using those words in your titles and in the photo tags, link descriptions, navigation icons, and site text is how you give your site a fighting chance of appearing in the search results.

Choosing the right keywords is a necessity and an art. Follow these tips to get it right:

- ✔ **Match the interests of your target audience.** If your target is someone getting ready to remodel a kitchen, the word "kitchen" is necessary, but alone it probably casts too wide a net. Get specific by using phrases, called *long-tail keywords,* such as "kitchen remodeling ideas," "kitchen remodel estimator," or "kitchen remodel on a budget." You'll better target decision-ready customers and your site will land higher results, because fewer sites compete for more precise and highly relevant search terms.

- ✔ **Include your location.** Obviously, someone wanting to remodel a kitchen isn't seeking a contractor who is a plane ride or long drive away. If your business serves a geographic area, feature your location as a keyword. For example, "kitchen remodel on a budget in Seattle."

- ✔ **Get specific about your product or service.** Instead of building your site around a term like "car repair," build it around "Toyota car repair" to pull your target audience.

Luckily, free online tools help you out — especially these two from Google:

- ✔ **Google Analytics:** This free service through `google.com/analytics` provides an extensive look at your website traffic and traffic sources, including which terms are driving traffic to your site. Apply the findings as you plan site revisions and expansions.

- ✔ **The Google Adwords Keyword Planner:** This free tool shows the search popularity of keywords you're considering. Just create a Google AdWords account at `adwords.google.com` (you don't have to buy ads, just create an account), select "Tools and Analysis," click "Keyword Planner," click "Search for keyword and ad group ideas," and follow the prompts to receive suggestions for key terms and phrases based on the word or term you entered. In a Google-provided example, a keyword search for "low-carb diet plan" leads to the terms "carb-free foods," "low-carb diets," low-calorie recipes," Mediterranean diet plans," and "low-carbohydrate dietary program." This information is useful whether the site owner is creating content or selecting keywords for pay-per-click ads. (A web search for "using keyword planner" leads to all kinds of tips and advice.)

Self-promote your site

Don't sit around waiting for people to find your website through search. Use every resource available to lead people to your site, beginning with the following approaches:

- Include your web address on business cards, letterhead, envelopes, note cards, invoices, order forms, estimates, and all other printed products.

- Include an invitation (and a reason) to visit your website in all your ads, brochures, news releases, presentations, displays, and also in your voicemail recording, on-hold messages, and email signature file.

- Feature your web address on your packaging and products.

- Post your website address on your business vehicles and signage.

- Link to your web address in all digital newsletters and content and include it in all news releases and contacts.

- Add a sharing function to your website to encourage visitor referrals.

The best way to self-promote your site is to get your site name, invitation, and reason to visit in front of those in your target audience. Chapter 11 is full of advice for interacting via social media, blogs, video, and content sharing. Chapter 12 is packed with information on getting the word out with advertising, direct mail and email, new and publicity, packaging, and promotions.

Get your business on Google for free

The headline for this sidebar comes right off the website for Google My Business (google.com/business). If you have a local business, brand, organization, or service, Google My Business lets you create a free page with information that can show up in Google Search, Google Maps, and Google+. You can add photos, virtual tours, respond to reviews or comments, and add, correct, or update your address, phone, store hours, and more.

Face it: Everyone wants to be found by Google. Free is a good price. Getting found by Google is a good thing.

Chapter 11

Engaging Your Brand Audience Online with Social Media

In This Chapter

▶ Mapping and navigating the social-media landscape

▶ Developing and sharing content that pulls people to your brand

▶ Leveraging blogs, video, and presentations into online engagement and interaction

S ocial media is where your brand goes to interact with its online audience. It's also where your customers and fans introduce your brand to their friends and followers through their comments, likes, posts, retweets, and more. Their actions make transmission of your brand message a customer-generated action that builds both your reach and credibility.

On social media you can share information, make friends, generate leads, develop followings, and post content that pulls people to your point of purchase, whether that place opens from a front door or a home page.

The downside is that social media is also where your brand can get beat up. When brand builders forget that social media is, first and above all, social — when they jump over the sharing and interacting steps to start pitching and selling — they lose not only their audience but also their likeability. Worse, when brands lose a grip on their brand message, promise, personality, character, and common sense, the backlash can be brutal

This chapter helps you manage the balancing act as you get social, stay social, and mind your online manners. If you have a brand and it has a good and positive social-media presence, we tip our hats and suggest you scan this chapter for steps and advice to help as you strengthen your good start. If your brand isn't already active on social media, for the strength of your brand please make each one of the upcoming sections required reading.

Getting Organized before Getting Social

With three out of four screen-connected adults spending time on social-media networks, it's no wonder that nearly all marketers consider social media important for brand exposure. Yet in marketing and branding meetings, social media is still the elephant in the room: Everyone knows it's important, but most aren't sure how to get in on the act.

The most frequently asked question usually has to do with how much time it takes to "do" social media right. Here's the answer: Social media can take as much time as you have — and a whole lot less if you lay the foundation by taking the steps outlined in the following three sections, one time only.

Define your social-media objectives

Like any other part of your marketing plan, your social-media plan needs to start with your aim in mind. What do you want to achieve? Here are examples of some possible answers to the "what's your social-media objective" question:

- ✔ To achieve brand awareness and trust as a leader in your field or community
- ✔ To attract the attention of prospects and generate leads
- ✔ To gain awareness, credibility, and trust with those who influence the opinions and decisions of your customers
- ✔ To engage and interact with customers
- ✔ To tune into conversations about your business, products, or business sector
- ✔ To create interest that leads to positive decisions and transactions ranging from sales of products or services, speaking engagements, news coverage, mailing list opt-ins, subscriptions, or other desired outcomes

Don't confuse social media with a call-to-action sales channel. If you try to use it primarily for placing brand or sales messages your efforts are almost sure to backfire. Instead, aim to develop an engaged following by posting useful, interesting content that isn't always about you or your brand. After you develop a following that might appreciate special offers, post promotional offers only rarely. Never forget: Social media is social. Participate to develop relationships and trust above all else.

Reserve your social-media name

By a mile, the best name to use across social media is your brand name. Check out the brands whose names you know best and you'll find that nearly all use only one name — their brand name — everywhere. For example, Starbucks has the domain name `Starbucks.com`, the Twitter name @Starbucks, and the Facebook name Starbucks. Perfect! One name, everywhere.

If you're developing a brand-new brand, turn to Chapter 7 for advice on researching and selecting a name that's available across all channels, and then turn to Chapter 10 for help reserving your brand name as your social-media username.

But if you're working to strengthen an established brand with a name that's not available for use across social media, you'll need to get creative. The following tips will help:

✔ **If your brand name is long:** If your brand name has more than 15 characters, it exceeds Twitter's name limitation. If that's the case, devise an alternative that conveys your brand identity. For example, National Geographic, uses @NatGeo on Twitter, with accounts under the name @NatGeoChannel, @NatGeoPhotos, @NatGeoTravel, and others. Hamburger Helper goes by the friendly name @helper. Luxor Las Vegas goes by @LuxorLV. Southwest Airlines goes by @SouthwestAir.

✔ **If your brand name is already in use:** You have two choices:

   • Go to the account and see if the name is used by an egg. Don't laugh. On Twitter, an account with only one tweet, no or very few followers, and an egg instead of a photo or other avatar, is likely a dormant account. If your brand name is trademarked, and if your trademark is in use by an inactive or dormant account, you can look into Twitter's trademark policy to see if you can get the name released for your use, but don't count on a positive outcome.

   • Come up with an alternative username. Twitter suggests that you add hyphens or letters or develop an abbreviation. YoungDesign could become Young_Design or YoungDesignUSA, for example. Or PhilsBookstore could become PhilsBooks.

When you find a name you want to make yours across social media, go to a username directory such as `NameChk.com`, `KnowEm.com`, or `CheckUserNames.com`. For free and in seconds, see if the name you want is available, and reserve it if it is. Then protect it with a strong password and by setting up *two-step authentication* on any network that offers the option. Two-step authentication requires an additional passcode should your account be logged into from a new machine or location.

Turn your brand's elevator pitch into a 160-character social-media introduction

Online, more than anywhere else, you have only seconds to introduce yourself and convince people that they want to follow you or note what you have to say. While Twitter allows you 140 characters per tweet, the character allocation for your Twitter bio is slightly (only slightly) more generous. You get 160 characters — about 20 words — to introduce your brand in a way that turns heads and creates interest. In those few letters (and spaces), include some or all of the following information:

- What you or your business does and for whom

- Keywords or terms people are likely to use when searching for people or businesses like yours

- A sense of the kind of information people following your social-media posts can expect to receive

- A sense of the tone of your brand, whether humorous, serious, controversial, authoritative, academic, newsy, whatever

- A thought-provoking, interesting, likeable indication of why you're credible, trustworthy, and worth following

- Fun facts about who you are, what you're into, and what you've done that's cool and brag-worthy — without actually bragging

Visit the social pages of competitors, friends, and brands and people you admire. Read their introductions. Great and likeable bios can be friendly, funny, or factual. But none are self-aggrandizing. Strike terms like premier, expert, or guru in favor of facts that convey your point of difference while making people want to know more. Here are examples from some widely applauded business and personal brands using social media:

- @Oreo: Your favorite cookie. Filling your world with Wonder 140 characters at a time.

- @GoPro: Official GoPro Twitter. We make the World's Most Versatile Camera. Wear it. Mount it. Love it.

- @Netflix: Official Netflix US Twitter page. Tweeting about movies, TV, docs, comedies and Netflix original series anytime, on any device. Customer service: @Netflixhelps.

Mapping the Social-Media Landscape

Want to know where to dive into the ever-expanding world of social media? The answer is really pretty easy: Go where those you want to reach hang out.

Start by reviewing your social-media objectives. If you aim to reach industry and business leaders, business-oriented social networks fill the bill. If you want to generate customer or client leads, learn where customers and clients spend time online and make those networks your jumping-off point. If you're working to develop credibility that draws customers from competitors, watch what your competitors are doing online. Go to their websites, learn which social networks they use, and click to study their pages, posts, and followings. You'll gain insight into what others are doing on social media and how their activity syncs with or differs from the aims you want to achieve.

The most prominent social networks fall into these categories:

- ✔ **The major, dominant social networks:** Facebook leads the pack with the most active monthly users, trailed closely by LinkedIn, Twitter, Instagram, Pinterest, and Google+, which gets indexed by Google and is a hub for Google properties including Picasa, Blogger, and YouTube.

- ✔ **Location-based, geosocial check-in sites:** Foursquare and Google are the major networks for on-the-go, screen-connected customers seeking storefront locations, user reviews, and check-in or purchase incentives.

- ✔ **Review and rating sites:** Yelp and TripAdvisor are the best-known review and rating sites, but other sites serve regional, special-interest, and industry-specific audiences.

The dominant social networks

This section comes with a caveat: The social-media landscape is growing and changing so quickly that no published list stays accurate for long. To stay on top of breaking news, follow the same blogs or social-media feeds that social-media pros follow, including Social Media Examiner (www.socialmediaexaminer.com), Tech Crunch (www.techcrunch.com), Mashable (www.mashable.com), Social Media Today (www.socialmediatoday.com), and Small Business Trends (www.smallbiztrends.com).

Facebook

Unlike Facebook Profiles, Facebook Pages are for businesses and brands. They're discoverable through Facebook and browser searches, they help you develop a community, and they let you share updates, video, and links that brand followers can reshare within their social circles. Other advantages:

✔ Because Facebook Pages are public (unlike Facebook Profiles), Page updates and posts help boost your brand's search results.

✔ If you have a physical storefront, customers can use the Facebook app to check in and alert friends to their whereabouts.

✔ You can post questions and interact with responses and comments.

✔ You can promote events for free by clicking the Event tab in the Status section of your page.

✔ Posts are free. That's the great news. The not-so-great news is that thanks to Facebook's algorithms, the average Facebook Page post reaches as little as 7 percent of your page followers. For greater reach, you have three choices: Develop a history of sky-high sharing and interaction, pay to promote your posts, or buy ads at low prices that have made Facebook a top selling platform for brand owners. See Chapter 11 for information on how to tread carefully into the arena of social-media advertising.

Especially if you serve customers rather than other businesses, if you haven't already done so, set up a free Facebook Page. Follow these steps:

1. **Log into your Facebook Profile, hover over "Pages" in the menu, click "More," and then click to "Create a Page."** Only someone with a Facebook Profile can create and administer a Facebook Page.

2. **Select the classification category for your business.** Be careful about your selection, because it can't be changed later. And when Facebook invites you to share your page, wait until it's completed and ready to represent your brand well.

3. **Quickly acquire 25 fans so you can customize your URL.** After your Facebook Page is up, invite friends, family, employees, and customers to become followers. When you have 25 fans you can change your page URL from the default string of characters to a more findable URL featuring your social-media user name. Go to www.facebook.com/username and follow the prompts.

4. **Develop your community by following brands, customers, media outlets, and others who affect your success and influence your customers.** Following other pages lets you benefit from their posts, plus liking begets liking and is a quick route to growing your own Facebook following.

5. **Participate regularly by commenting on relevant posts by others and, especially by posting interesting, useful updates accompanied by photos, video, and graphics, because images drive 50 percent more engagement from followers.** See the upcoming section "Getting and Staying Active and Engaged" for more tips on content creation.

Monitor your Facebook activity to see what's working by clicking Page Insights from the top-of-page menu. You'll be able to track which mentions result in Page likes and which posts achieve high reach and engagement.

Twitter

For just about everything you'd want to know about using Twitter effectively, check out the page titled "Getting started with Twitter" in Twitter's own help center. Keep this advice in mind:

✔ Become findable in Twitter Search by creating a Twitter bio that presents what your brand offers, why it's credible, and how your brand's Twitter stream is interesting, valuable, and worth following. Use keywords (no hashtags necessary) to show up in user searches.

✔ Maintain your brand message and voice in all tweets, whether you're creating, replying to, or sharing the content of others. (Chapter 18 is a guide to crisis management if your brand seriously goes off brand message, but we hope you'll never need it.)

✔ Choose a couple of *hashtagged keywords* — topic categories noted by the symbol # — that you want associated with your brand. Develop authority in your topic areas by keeping your Twitter interactions on message and by using hashtags (but only a few per tweet) to attract the attention of topic followers.

✔ Keep tweets short. Twitter allows 140 characters, but don't use them all. Leave at least 20 characters for followers to use when they retweet your posts. Less is often even better: Example "Click for five Twitter don'ts," followed by a link to great content. (The word "click" is proven to increase engagement and retweets.)

✔ Share content, photos, and video to make your tweets more interesting and sharable.

✔ Include a call to action that conveys urgency (for example, *right now*) and invites engagement and interaction (for example, *watch, discover, do* or *don't,* or a good reason to click to reach the content you're sharing).

The key to success on Twitter is to use it frequently. Tweet, retweet, reply, and mention others by using their Twitter handle (for example @ForDummies). The Twitter app or one of many other free third-part apps including HootSuite and TweetDeck let you organize followers into groups, schedule messages, and study interaction analytics.

LinkedIn

LinkedIn is the 21st century version of the Rolodex file — and a whole lot more. It's where people turn to find people they want to work with. It's also where LinkedIn members increasingly turn for business content and news.

Take these steps to get started:

1. **Set up a free personal LinkedIn Profile.** Your profile allows you to be found by LinkedIn users, plus LinkedIn profiles rise to the top of online search results for your personal name. Think of your profile as a second or stand-in personal website.

   • Place keywords for your area of expertise in your headline, titles, and descriptions of your specialties, interests and education, and ask those writing recommendations to use your keywords as well.

   • Use a close-up photo that presents you as a professional, preferably with a smile.

   • Personalize your public profile URL by clicking Profile, scrolling down to Public Profile, clicking Edit, and changing the default address to read http://linkedin.com/in/[yourname].

   • Give people reasons to connect and to consider your offerings. Include testimonials, success stories, and easy-to-scan descriptions.

2. **Set up a free Company Page.** This business profile presents your brand, keeps people in touch and engaged with brand news and job openings, and links to your brand website and other digital marketing channels. From your personal LinkedIn profile (or from the profile of the person who will serve as your company page administrator), click "Interests" from the top-of-page menu, click "Companies" from the drop-down menu, and click "Create" to make your page. Use personal outreach or LinkedIn targeted ads to attract followers.

3. **Create Spotlight Pages to showcase individual products or business units.** Just click the Company Page edit menu and select "Create a Showcase Page."

Get active by joining groups, starting groups, participating in groups, and asking and answering questions relevant to your brand and its topic areas. Post status updates to share news, valuable information, and useful links, taking care to avoid a slew of sales-oriented self-congratulatory messages.

Google+

The name says it all. Google+ is a Google network, and Google+ posts are indexed by Google. Who doesn't want their content to be indexed by Google?

Go to `www.google.com/+/brands` to take five steps, each accompanied by instructions that lead you through the easy process:

1. **Create a Google+ page.**

2. **Complete your profile.**

3. **Verify your page and claim your customized or vanity URL.**

4. **Add the Google+ badge to your website and other brand pages.**

5. **Link your Google+ account with your YouTube account, if you have one.** This link gives you added YouTube management capabilities and the ability to run live broadcasts via Hangouts on Air, which stream worldwide and are automatically saved on your YouTube channel.

To use Google+, establish circles for various customer segments and influencer groups so you can target your posts to those with specific interests. Then post regularly, using a keyword-rich headline for search optimization.

Pinterest

Pinterest is the corkboard of social media, where people and brands pin and repin images and videos that drive more referral traffic to websites than any network except Facebook.

Pinterest isn't a showcase for your brand so much as a portrayal of the culture of your brand and the interests of your brand followers.

- ✓ Share bold, attention-grabbing behind-the-scenes images and videos of the origins of your products, the activities of your customers, infographics of your findings, and inspiration behind your innovations.

- ✓ Create boards for various topic areas, each named with keywords that make them findable.

- ✓ Post content to your own website or blog first, and then pin it to Pinterest. That way the image will link back to your site, increasing your traffic and search rankings.

To open a brand page on Pinterest, go to `business.pinterest.com`. When you're asked to sign up from your Facebook or Twitter account, choose your business Twitter account unless you want to tie your brand's Pinterest presence to your personal Facebook profile.

Instagram

Sixty million photos — and climbing — are uploaded daily on Instagram, and they aren't all selfies. Instagram users are young (most are under 35), mostly female (60 percent), and highly engaged, clicking more than a billion "likes" daily and commenting at a rate of more than a thousand times a second. No wonder brands are signing on in ever-growing numbers. Following are some examples:

- ✔ Virgin America invites followers to "tag travel pics with #virginamerica."

- ✔ American Express offers followers "insta-access to exclusive experiences news, and rewards through our lens."

- ✔ Warby-Parker used Instagram to celebrate the brand's fourth birthday by posting photos employees when they were four years old.

On Instagram, you can't schedule posts, embed links, or use a third-party tool for analytics or insights. What you can do is publish images on-the-spot, using the free Instagram mobile app, to reach followers known for sky-high levels of user engagement and customer conversion.

For help, check out `business.instagram.com` and follow the Instagram For Business Blog at `blog.business.instagram.com`.

Location-based and check-in sites

If you have a physical location, two major sites help you lead mobile customers to your door and reward them with check-in offers and perks:

- ✔ **Google My Business** (`google.com/business`) is the most recent version of Google Places, providing a free opportunity for businesses to show up in Google Search, Google Maps, and Google+. Establishing a Google My Business page lets you post your address, phone number, store hours, contact information, photos, virtual tours, and updates. The result: Customers can find you, reach you, and interact with you. They can also read and add reviews.

- ✔ **Foursquare** split itself into two apps in 2014: Foursquare and Swarm by Foursquare. Foursquare focuses on location-based recommendations and suggestions. Swarm is how customers check in and broadcast their locations to friends and family. Go to `business.foursquare.com/listing` for information on adding your business, rewarding your customers with check-in perks, placing ads, and interacting with followers.

Review and rating sites

We've yet to meet a brand owner who doesn't care about customer reviews and ratings, because what people say can make or break brand reputations.

Take the following three steps to manage your presence on review sites and improve the odds that people say good things often enough to overshadow the occasional and likely inevitable one-star rating someone lobs your way.

Claim your presence on review sites

If you aren't sure which review sites are important to your business, ask your customers. In person or through surveys (Chapter 5 can help as you conduct research), learn which sites they turn to when making business or product choices. Likely your findings will lead you to some of the following review collection points:

- Almost any consumer-serving brand can benefit by claiming presence on Yelp (biz.yelp.com), Google Places for Business (www.google.com/business), and CitySearch (www.citysearch.com).

- If you're in the travel business, your customers or those who influence them most likely use TripAdvisor (www.tripadvisor.com).

- Restaurant-goers count on sites like UrbanSpoon (www.urbanspoon.com), OpenTable (www.opentable.com), Zagat (www.zagat.com), ChowHound (www.chowhound.com), and others that reign in regional areas.

- Depending on your business sector — legal, medical, consumer electronics, and so on — there's likely a set of review sites where customers and clients weigh in, and where you need to keep your ear to the grapevine.

Encourage reviews

Here's your goal: Get your customers to say great things so that when some malcontented customer (or the friend of a competitor, or someone who wandered in on the one day your brand experience was sub-par), the praise will drown out the pan. Take these steps:

- Display review site logos in your business and on your web pages so people know where to go to share their experiences.

- Personally invite best customers to share their opinions. Make it easy by providing links or handing them cards with your review URLs. You can give them a next-visit discount or offer with the request, but you can't reward or try to bias the review. Google warns about paying for reviews, writing negative reviews of competitors, posting reviews on behalf of others, or misrepresenting your identity or affiliation when posting reviews. The warning is stern and worth heeding across all review sites.

- Cultivate a steady stream of reviews rather than a slew of reviews over a short period. When review sites see a burst of good reviews, they look into whether incentivizing is going on.

Don't lose your cool over an occasional bad review

Sooner or later, someone will write a review you don't like. When the inevitable happens, take these two steps:

✔ **Look for any truth you can find in the complaint or criticism.** Even if the transgression was minor, fix it. Then use your blog, the review comment box, your Facebook page, and — best of all — direct contact with the reviewer to describe the changes you've made. Telling a disgruntled customer, and all who read about that person's experience, that you care is often more valuable than the rant is damaging.

✔ **Don't get defensive and don't try to tell the customer they're wrong.** You'll escalate the argument and give it even more online attention. Instead, double your efforts to overshadow the rant by generating good reviews, with full knowledge that people reading review sites expect a bad rating from the occasional can't-be-pleased customer.

Getting and Staying Active and Engaged

Reaching brand goals on social media engagement results from three activities:

✔ Create and post relevant, interesting content or information.

✔ Share relevant, interesting content created and shared by others. Think of it as re-gifting.

✔ Interact with thanks, praise, expertise, and input by posting comments on your own pages and by engaging on the pages of others.

This section helps you get organized, visible, and active.

Setting your social-media strategy

Flip back to the start of this chapter to review your social-media objectives. They'll be the basis of your social-media strategy.

✔ **If you're aiming to heighten brand awareness and credibility:** Plan to develop and post content that establishes your value and reputation, including publicity, reviews, research findings, white papers, presentations, and other interesting, useful, sharable information.

✔ **If you're aiming to increase interaction with customers and influencers:** Plan to create and post surveys, ask questions, host forums, announce events that prompt engagement, and engage in two-way conversations and discussions that deepen relationships and loyalty.

✔ **If you're aiming to gain customers or increase sales:** Plan to share content that pulls people to your business, perhaps by offering free samples, estimates, e-books, survey results, white papers, or other information customers and prospective customers find valuable. Be sure offers are social and useful — not just sales pitches — and that they link directly to the page on your website that fulfills the interest you generate, because most people won't bother to click twice.

If you think those in your audience will see your post on a mobile device, keep your message super-short to win attention and interest. Then, especially if you're aiming to develop credibility or a position of thought-leadership in your field, link to longer content, including traditional reports and white papers, but also videos, infographics, and landing pages on your website.

Creating and posting content

Grab a stopwatch. The key to getting recognized online is to seize interest immediately because nearly everyone has a short attention span and people sweeping their eyes down social-media screens are the most elusive of all. You have seconds to win attention.

✔ **Each online post needs to make a single point — fast.** Studies show that 80-character posts win a quarter more engagement than longer posts, and short questions or fill-in-the-blank requests do even better. When you can, include a link, photo, video, or graphic to dramatically boost how well your post is shared.

✔ **If posts link to your website, be sure web pages load at lightning speed.** Realize that a third of web users abandon slow-loading sites within five seconds, with each one-second delay further reducing page views. On average, those who do stick around stay less than 30 seconds, with half of all visits lasting less than four seconds.

Here are some tips for increasing speeds:

- Reduce web page size to speed loading.

- Use headlines and visuals.

- Keep text spare and scannable by using bullet points and short copy blocks.

- Use clickable hyperlinks to site sections and secondary pages with more information.

For more information on creating websites, turn to Chapter 10.

✔ **If your posts link to video, realize that video viewers won't tolerate slow loads or long introductions.** One of ten online video viewers clicks away in the first 10 seconds, and three more are gone after 30 seconds — and that's without buffering problems, which cause viewer abandonment following a two-second wait.

Make opening seconds captivating and relevant to viewer interests. YouTube advice is to keep brand introductions to less than five seconds "unless it's hilarious." Instead, front-load content, because the average view lasts less than three minutes. If your video content runs longer, consider dripping it out in a series of segments.

For more information, see the section on creating and sharing video later in this chapter.

Before approving brand content, make sure it passes this three-question test:

✔ Is it consistent with our brand message and tone and does it strengthen our brand image?

✔ Will those in our target audience be convinced that it's worth reading, watching, or hearing?

✔ Is it easy to share, and, at-first-glance, will those we're targeting think it's worth passing along to others?

Making blog posts the backbone of your content strategy

Inbound, or *pull,* marketing (there's more on these terms in Chapter 10) involves sharing useful, relevant content that attracts people to your store-front or website.

If you have one of the Internet's 200 million-plus blogs, your social-media content strategy is already underway, because maintaining a blog forces you to create useful information that you can repurpose and feed into your social-media streams.

Blog topics run the gamut, but most blogs share the following features:

✔ They're graphically simple and full of short *posts* or entries that are added frequently and arranged so that newest items appear first.

- They focus on a single point of view or interest area and reflect the opinions of the blog owner. They contain news, but they're also a lot like the newspaper's op-ed page.

- They present an informal version of your brand voice.

- They feature content using keywords those in your target audience are likely to search for and topics they'll want to find, read, and share.

- They allow users to search story archives.

- They use RSS (Rich Site Summary or Really Simple Syndication) or a similar format that allows blog posts to be distributed and shared on other sites with a link back to the originating site.

Blog publishing platforms

Most blogs are published using one of three platforms:

- **WordPress** is the most popular blog-hosting service. It gives you the options of free hosting through the site or self-hosting on your own website:

  - **If you create a free hosted blog through wordpress.com,** your design choices and features are limited and your blog will have a name like `yourbrandname.wordpress.com` unless you pay extra to use your own domain name.

  - **If you create a self-hosted site through wordpress.org**, you can upload and install the blog on your own website. Benefits include greater design customization and features, the opportunity to accept advertising, and the ability to add a shopping cart, membership forms, or other extensions. Also, self-hosted blogs use your own domain name as an address, driving site traffic and improving your site's search ranking.

- **Blogger** (`www.blogger.com`) is owned by Google. It's free and easy to use but doesn't offer a self-hosting option.

- **Tumblr** (`www.tumblr.com`) is a microblog site that's free, cool to view, and easiest of all the platforms to use. What you can't do is self-host your Tumblr blog with your own domain name, archive your Tumblr contents for user searches, or expect much success if you aren't an active user.

Anatomy of a blog post

Good blogging follows a consistent posting schedule and a recognizable blog-post format that includes the components shown in Table 11-1.

Table 11-1	Blog Post Components
Necessary elements	**Description**
Headline	A title that grabs attention and interest, featuring keywords that make it findable in searches
Subheads	Keyword-rich titles that convey section contents at-a-glance
Meta-description	A keyword-rich summary that appears as the snippet in search results; without a description, search engines display the first 160 characters of the post
In-text links	Links that lead readers to landing pages where they can take action or access the information mentioned in the post
Call for engagement	Requests that prompt interactions such as newsletter or mail-list signups, RSS subscriptions, social sharing, comments, poll or survey participation
Credit due	Provide citations for quotes or shared content, including accurate names, links, and thanks
Byline	The blog post author's name, title, and contact information
Accuracy	No typos or misrepresentation of facts

Announcing, repurposing, and republishing blog posts

Automated plug-ins like Twitterfeed (twitterfeed.com) and Jetpack by WordPress (wordpress.org/plugins/jetpack) let you schedule and automatically post your content to selected social-media networks.

Whether you use auto-posting services or not, as soon as your content is online, boost the chances of it being seen by taking these actions:

✓ Announce and link to the post on your social-media pages by sharing a summary, quote, or key point, and by tagging those you've mentioned.

✓ Use subsequent updates to link to the post by presenting different key points, subheads, or interesting sentences.

✓ Offer your post as a guest post on another blog. Or turn it into an ezine article (check out ezinearticles.com). Or publish past posts into an e-book you offer as an incentive for blog or newsletter subscribers

✓ Update and retitle blog posts to give them new relevance. Take a new angle, use new examples, or offer updated advice. By revising and republishing, you'll extend the post's life and reach those who may have missed it the first time. Just be sure the update is significant enough that Google won't view it as a duplicate, which can work against you as you try to build search authority on key terms.

Before finalizing and publishing blog posts, be clear about what you want readers to think or do after reading the content. Whether you want them to laugh, learn, click, complete a lead form, subscribe, buy, or share (almost certainly, you want them to share), develop your content accordingly.

If you're aiming for conversions, tell people the benefit of taking action, give them clear instructions for easy steps to follow, and watch your site analytics like a hawk to see what's working.

Creating and sharing video

The quickest way to humanize your brand, short of meeting people face-to-face, is to share interesting, entertaining video featuring your brand leaders, staff, customers, experts, products, and behind-the-scene views that let others get to know your brand and the value it provides in your marketplace.

Videos also help improve your brand's online visibility, because they provide content to post on YouTube, which is the second-largest search engine. They're also easier than ever to create, with Vine and Instagram 6- to 15-second microvideos (the topic of an upcoming section) quickly eclipsing all other forms of sharable content.

Shooting, editing, and posting video

Whether you opt for broadcast-quality studio-produced video, video produced from an in-home, in-office, or in-garage studio, or video produced using a mobile app, the price tags vary (hugely) but the requirements are the same:

- ✔ **Create video that matches the quality, image and voice of your brand and the interests of your target audience.** Make sure that every segment offers what you think people — particularly customers, prospective customers, and customer influencers — want to see.

- ✔ **Open with a strong introduction.** Research shows that viewership plummets after the first few seconds if the introduction doesn't immediately grab attention.

- ✔ **Edit your video with viewer retention in mind.** Videos of five minutes or longer outperform all others in YouTube rankings, but first you have to hook and hold viewer interest. From the opening seconds include content that's surprising, unusual, funny, new, different, entertaining, or especially useful and valuable — and clip out everything else.

- ✔ **Include a call to action.** Invite viewers to visit your website, subscribe, like your brand on Facebook, or take some other action.

- ✔ **Choose a video filename using keywords that targeted viewers are likely to use in searches.** For example, "brand_keyword_tips_video. mp4" and a video title that begins with keywords, such as "Choosing Brand Keywords in Five Steps."

✔ **Create a keyword-rich summary.** Include the link to the video and a summary of about 250 words that tell what it's about.

✔ **Share the video.** You can upload your video directly to your blog, Facebook page, or other sites, but you're smart to upload it first to YouTube, for no cost, and then embed it from YouTube onto your other online locations so that all viewer engagement is captured on your YouTube channel.

YouTube ranks video based how many people view it, how long they watch, how many comments they leave, how many subscribe after viewing, how many share the video or click to "Watch Later," and how many incoming links point to it. By pointing all traffic to YouTube, you improve your ranking. Just don't try to pump up your numbers with fake views, because YouTube deletes videos with suspicious activity.

With just a Google account, you can watch, like, and subscribe on YouTube. But without a free YouTube channel your business or brand won't have any public presence on YouTube. To create a YouTube channel for your brand, Google Help provides these instructions:

- Make sure you're signed into YouTube.

- Go to "All My Channels."

- If you want to make a YouTube channel for a Google+ page you manage, you can choose it here. Otherwise, click "Create a new channel."

- Fill out the details to create your new channel.

After your channel is created, click "Upload" to add content to your brand channel. Then as you share links to your video on your social-media pages, alert followers that the post includes a video by using a headline like "(VIDEO) How to Post Video," Or "WATCH: Five SEO Tips from the Pros."

Brand-building with microvideo

With video on track to account for two-thirds of consumer Internet traffic by 2017 and with 6- to 15-second microvideos more likely to be shared than any other form of online video, it's no wonder that brands of all types and sizes are adding quick-clip video to their social-media pages. Following are the top microvideo options:

✔ **Vine** (vine.co) is the Twitter-owned mobile app that makes creation of looping, replaying video easy and inexpensive. Just download and install the free Vine app and sign in with your Twitter account or email address. From that point, it's a matter of coming up with ideas for super-short video content that can inspire, entertain, impress, tell a story, and contribute to your brand image in six-second increments.

You can face the camera toward or away from you before clicking the app's camera icon to record. You can save videos for later consideration. You can use low-tech editing features to slice out bits and pare the video down to a quick, smoothly flowing piece.

When it's ready, click "Share," add a caption with hashtagged keywords, your location, and your channel tag, post it on your Facebook and Twitter accounts, and embed it on your website or blog to encourage the kind of viral sharing that microvideo often generates.

✔ **Instagram** lets you share 3- to 15-second video that you've recorded using the Instagram app. In addition to length, Instagram microvideos differ from Vine's 6-second videos in several ways. They don't loop and replay. They appear on Twitter as links and on Facebooks as videos — the exact opposite of how Vine videos display. They can be customized with filters and edited with features not available to Vine producers.

With either platform, use great lighting, quality production and editing, a clear visual cue that establishes your brand identity in the first seconds, and an amazing, entertaining concept capable of winning attention, recognition, and, best of all, viral transmission of your brand's micromessage.

Giving slide presentations long life through social media

If your brand goals include developing credibility as a thought leader, move SlideShare (`slideshare.net`), the world's largest online community for sharing presentations and professional content, onto your list of social-media tools. Take these steps:

✔ Create a set of PowerPoint or Keynote slides to support a new presentation or to compile and repurpose content from your blog or from a recent webinar, conference, report, or other material.

✔ Give your slide presentation (often called a *slide deck*) a title, description, and individual slide labels that use long-tail keywords, which are more specific than single words and more apt to be searched by those seeking detailed information. (Flip back to Chapter 10 for more information on keywords.)

✔ Be sure your first slide uses bold graphics and colors, an interesting and legible type font, and a title conveying a strong and interesting topic that will attract attention from those glancing at thumbnails of your slides.

✔ Use as little text as possible to convey information that's highly informative, interesting, and capable of building into a story that viewers feel you're narrating. On average, SlideShare presentations have 19 slides and 24 words per slide. Develop a look and use a template throughout the presentation and, ideally, for all brand presentations so you save time and build awareness for your brand look at the same time.

✔ Feature hyperlinks on slides to drive traffic to your website landing pages and social-media brand pages, along with a call to action that inspires people to click the link. (Be careful, though: SlideShare doesn't allow hyperlinks in the first three slides, to other slides within the deck, or within infographics.)

✔ Upload your slide deck to SlideShare and enable the share function to allow and encourage others to share or embed your presentation.

✔ Click the "Embed" icon to add the slide deck to own website or blog. Then share the link on your social-media brand pages and in other online communities or comments.

Whether you create slides for a new presentation or to repurpose content from your blog, webinar, conference, or other presentation, by uploading it to your free SlideShare account you expand the reach of your material, extend the life of your message, and improve search ranking in one fell swoop.

Chapter 12

Advertising, Promoting, and Publicizing Your Brand

*B*rands need awareness like plants need water. If people don't know about your brand or if they don't have a clear idea about what your brand is and stands for, it will never take root in their minds, which is where brands thrive.

Chapters 10 and 11 are all about achieving awareness through digital communications by driving traffic to your website and getting active on social-media networks. This chapter guides your development of more traditional communications, including ads, direct mailers, packaging, promotions, and publicity capable of carrying your brand message into target market homes, offices, cars, mailboxes, and mobile screens.

The Power of a Strong Brand Image

When marketers talk about *integrated marketing communications,* they're talking about communications that project one look, voice, and *core message* or brand promise across all communication channels, whether through personal presentations, web pages, social media, promotions, advertising, direct mail, or public-relations efforts.

Brands benefit from integrated marketing communications for a number of reasons, including the following:

- **People gain confidence in brands that present themselves consistently.** If communications sound or look elegant one day and whimsical or irreverent the next, customers won't know which expression accurately reflects the brand character and what experience they can count on.

- **People expect your brand voice to reflect your brand's character and personality.** Then after you establish your brand voice, you can alter the tone of your voice depending on the audience and communication channel in the same way you'd use a different tone of your voice at the dining room table versus the conference table. For example, the operators of a preschool may adopt a voice that's caring and playful rather than clinical or professional, which is the voice you might expect from a hospital or bank. When their voice is established, they might use a soothing, friendly tone when addressing children, a more confident tone when presenting to parents, and a more authoritative tone when presenting at a childcare-providers conference. Likewise, they'd probably use a personal tone in customer emails and a casual, conversational tone on social media and in broadcast ads. At all times, though, they'd want to their voice to come through as caring and playful, which is the personality of their brand.

  Here's an example of a brand voice description: *Our brand voice is friendly and confident. We want to sound expert but not uppity; casual but not complacent. We want our customers to know through our communications that we're the kind of people they'd like to visit with in their own backyards and that they can count on us as partners who provide expert, efficient, earth-sensitive landscape services.*

- **People trust companies more when the core message of communications is in line with the brand image.** Your core message is the promise of your brand. It defines the meaningful value customers can count on your brand to deliver and the claim you'll make and prove — directly or indirectly — in all communications and brand experiences.

  For example, *Our core message is that we deliver the best solution for ecologically sound, affordable landscape solutions in the Pacific Northwest, proven by before-and-after photos and an environmental savings guarantee.*

By presenting your brand consistently, projecting the same core message and voice in all communications and through all brand experiences, you develop an integrated marketing campaign that conveys a strong, clear image and builds a strong, clear brand. Turn to Chapter 6 if you haven't yet put your brand promise and voice into words.

A Clear Purpose: Don't Communicate without One!

When it comes time to start communicating your brand message, you may be tempted to race to the creative part of the process. Resist the temptation.

Start by taking time to figure out what you want to accomplish. Go beyond a vague idea, like "We want to introduce our brand." Instead, get specific with instructions such as, "We want to announce our brand to our 40-something, predominantly male, regionally based audience with an ad that conveys our brand promise to offer the most natural oceanside golf experience on the West Coast by extending an invitation to take a club tour and enter a lottery for a limited number of inaugural memberships."

In other words, detail what you want to accomplish. _Then_ get creative.

Whether you're producing an ad, display, brochure, presentation, blog post, or any other brand communication, begin by defining the purpose of your communication and what you want the communication to achieve. Marketing pros call the creative directions that result from this pre-planning effort your _creative brief._ To keep yourself and those producing your communication on the right track, write a creative brief for each communication project by answering these seven questions:

- **Who is your target audience?** In a sentence or two, describe who this communication aims to reach, where they can be reached, who they are in factual terms, and how and why they buy products like the one you're offering.

- **What do people in your target audience know or think about your brand, product, or service?** Do they lack knowledge about you? In that case, your communication needs to establish awareness. Do they hold positive perceptions you want to reinforce, or inaccurate perceptions you want to change?

- **What do you want people in your target audience to think — and do?** Do you them to call for appointments, ask for estimates, visit a website, attend an event, make a purchase, or simply increase awareness?

- **Why should people believe you and take the recommended action?** Summarize the unique benefits you promise and the reason to act now.

- **What information do you need to convey in this communication?** List what the communication absolutely has to include, including your core marketing message and voice, proper presentation of your brand identity, and other necessities.

✔ **How will you measure success?** What do you want people to do following this communication? What will you say or do to prompt the action? How will you measure success?

✔ **What is your timeline and budget?** Set and share your timeline and a budget. If you don't, the date will slide and costs will mount.

Creating and Placing Ads

Advertising, by definition, aims to inform and persuade through paid announcements in mass-media outlets. Advertising pays its freight when it reaches the people you're aiming to influence at the right time, with the right message, and with enough frequency to change their perceptions and actions. As you schedule media buys to introduce your brand, remember these terms:

✔ **Reach:** The number of individuals or homes exposed to your ad.

✔ **Frequency:** The number of times that an average person is exposed to your message.

If you have to choose between achieving reach or frequency (and unless your budget is massive, trust us, you *have* to choose) follow this advice: Limit your reach and then spend as much as you can to achieve frequency through multiple ad placements in carefully selected media outlets that reach your targeted audience.

Reach creates awareness; but frequency changes minds.

Deciding on your media channels

Good advertising schedules deliver messages people want to see through media channels that get your message in front of exactly the audiences you want to reach. For example:

✔ **If the objective of your advertising is to reach and influence prospects and customers:** Place ads in media with audiences that match your customer profile (complete the Customer Profile Worksheet in Chapter 5 if you're not sure how to define your customer).

✔ **If the objective of your advertising is to reach and influence those who influence the success of your brand:** Create a definition of the person whose referral, advice, or recommendation tilts your customer's opinion and then find media outlets that reach people who match that description.

For example, if you're branding a senior citizen assisted-living housing community, you may decide that your success depends on referrals and recommendations from the attorneys, physicians, and adult children of your prospects. Therefore, in addition to advertising in media outlets that reach adults 75 and older, you'd also want to announce open houses and deliver information in media outlets that reach physicians, attorneys, and middle-aged adults in your market area.

In most cases, a number of media channels fill the bill in terms of reaching your audience. When that's the case, you can make media selections based on which best reach your market within the cost and timing realities you face. See the sidebar "The media menu" for a quick look the costs, placement considerations, and advantages of various media channels.

Print ads

In great print ads, the headline, copy, and design work together to grab attention, inspire interest, promote a brand promise, prompt the desired action, and advance the brand image. That's a lot, but it's not too much to ask. In fact, it's what you need to demand out of *every* print ad you place.

To achieve success, each print ad must include three powerful components:

- ✔ **Headline:** The ad's stop-'em-in-their tracks introductory statement.

- ✔ **Copy:** Adspeak for the text of your ad. Good copy talks directly to the reader, conveying information that tells the benefits of your offering, the promise of your brand, and what to do next to obtain information, take advantage of an offer, or make a purchase.

- ✔ **Design:** The way your ad looks — how it uses type, art, open space, borders, and placement of elements to guide a reader's eyes through the message while also presenting the brand identity of the advertiser.

Punching up headline power

Four out of every five print ad readers read *only* the headline, so write one that's capable of targeting your prospects, grabbing attention, and making people want to read the rest of your story.

Plenty of great ads have no headlines, but instead they feature an amazing photo or illustration that seizes reader attention. Unless you can afford a graphic element with sure stopping power, use a headline every time.

Headlines can be long or short. They can sit at the top, in the middle, or at the bottom of the ad. They can feature a single word, a phrase, a sentence, or a question. It isn't the headline form that matters. It's the function. See Table 12-1 for headline advice to follow and traps to avoid.

Table 12-1		Headline Advice
Do	**Don't**	**General Advice**
Feature your most powerful point.	Feature a clever statement that requires people to read on to learn what you're talking about.	Use your headline to convey your primary message, and use copy to back up your claim.
Feature benefits rather than features.	List the bells and whistles you offer without telling what they mean to the customer.	*Twice as fast* is a feature. *Get the job done in half the time* is a benefit.
Convey a positive message.	Focus on the problem you solve.	*Get a great night's sleep* presents the solution. *Eliminate insomnia* presents the problem.
Use powerful, compelling language.	Use technical terms, blah-language, or words people won't understand.	Power words include *free, new, save, better, how, now, easy, guarantee, health, love, save, safety*, and, most important of all, *you*.
Involve the reader.	Talk to yourself.	*Save 20% during our 20th anniversary celebration* beats *We're celebrating our 20th anniversary*.
Be clear and credible.	Be outrageous or clever to the point of being incoherent.	At a glance, seize attention, make a point, and advance your brand promise.

Convincing copy

Effective image ads sometimes contain no copy at all. They rely on the strength of the brand name and logo, along with a captivating photo or other image, to advance the brand and expand awareness, credibility, and loyalty. Look at fashion ads for good examples.

Most advertisers need their ads to ignite measurable action, though, and for that reason, most ads count on copy to play a pretty important role. If you expect your ad to generate consumer response — in the form of changed opinions, enhanced interest, requests for more information, inquiries about price or options, business visits, or other actions that move consumers toward a buying decision — include ad copy that's up to the task.

The media menu

Mass-media channels each offer unique advertising requirements and advantages and each offer a number of media choices — from highly targeted vehicles that reach narrowly defined audiences to widely distributed vehicles that reach diverse audiences.

Media Audience	*Cost Realities*	*Placement Facts*	*Advantages*
Newspapers reach broad cross-sections of local, regional, or national populations	Reasonable placement cost to reach readers; reasonable ad production	Deadlines allow for quick placement decisions; ads are seen shortly after publication	Immediately delivers messages to market-area adults; less effective if only a minor percentage of readership matches your customer profile
Magazines reach targeted audiences that share unique characteristics and interests	High cost to reach highly targeted audiences; high production costs to create visually competitive ads	Ad commitments are due long before the publication date; ads are read over a long time period from date of issue	Establishes credibility and builds a competitive reputation over time; less effective for immediate or short-term campaigns
Out-of-home media reaches audiences in target geographic areas on a repeated basis	Costs are based on traffic counts and audience exposure	Prime locations are reserved far in advance; ad commitments usually span multimonth periods	Builds name awareness and conveys single-sentence messages; less useful for conveying messages with more than seven words
Radio reaches audiences with defined interests, often in concise geographic areas	Costs for non-prime time often negotiable; quality ad production enhances image and impact	Ads must run repeatedly to catch listeners; stations welcome last-minute ads except during peak periods	Builds immediate interest and prompts responses; less effective if schedule lacks necessary level of frequency
Television reaches audiences with defined interests via network or local-station ad buys	Costs soar when audience counts are high; quality ad production requires a significant budget	Ads must run repeatedly to catch viewers; prime-time ads are expensive and in high demand	Builds credibility, good for showing or demonstrating products; less effective if ad lacks creativity and high production value
Online or digital ads include banner and other online display ads, search engine ads, pay-per-click ads, AdWord ads, social-media ads and promoted posts	Costs based on ad views or clicks; ad testing is easy and effectiveness is highly measurable; production costs are low	Ads on major sites book far in advance; pay-per-click ads can be placed on short notice and can be quickly replaced if they aren't drawing results	Reaches targeted online users with call-to-action messages that prompt lead generation though click-through responses; less effective if ads fail to engage or spur interaction

When writing copy (or when reviewing copy written by ad professionals), keep these points in mind:

- ✔ **Be sure the first sentence is capable of capturing interest and enticing the reader to want to know more.**

- ✔ **Be sure the second sentence lures the reader into the third sentence, with each additional sentence advancing your brand promise and building more credibility and trust.**

- ✔ **Include an invitation to take action.**

- ✔ **Inspire action with an incentive.** To persuade people to request information, view demonstrations, ask for cost estimates, sample the product, join your brand community, or in some other way interact with your brand, stimulate action with limited-time special buying terms, promotional pricing, trial offers, guarantees, or other offers that lower the risk or heighten the ease of taking the desired action.

- ✔ **Call for action.** Don't assume people will know where to find you, how to reach you, or whether or not you have a website, give free estimates, or welcome drop-in business. Make responding easy (*Call us toll-free, Go to our website to request a free estimate, Visit our business seven days a week, Like us on Facebook,* and so on). Then tell how to take action by providing your phone number, arrival directions, your web address, and other information that makes responding easy.

Designing for impact

Graphic artists and art directors earn their fees for many reasons, but high on the list is the simplicity of their designs. Flip through the pages of any newspaper or magazine. The ads that catch your eye are likely those with few elements, most striking visuals, and clean, attention-grabbing looks.

If you're investing a significant amount of money in ad buys, seriously consider investing in the creation of professionally designed ads. The section "Where to turn for creative help" later in this chapter guides you through the resource selection process.

As you create or review ad designs, consider this advice:

- ✔ **Use art.** Readers flip through publications at rapid-fire speed, stopping only when a headline or visual grabs their attention.

  In some ads, the art shows the product being advertised. In other cases, it shows the product in use or represents the benefits the product delivers. In yet other cases, the art relies on what's called *borrowed interest* by featuring a photo or illustration that indirectly relates to the ad message. For example, a company featuring Tuscan vacations may feature a photo of Florence (the product), it may show a photo of people sitting near a villa overlooking a Chianti landscape (the product in use), or it may feature an illustration of wine glasses or grape vines (borrowed interest).

✔ **Keep it simple.** Print media is a cluttered environment packed full of news articles, feature stories, facts and figures, and ads large and small. On a crowded page, the clean ad with open space wins attention for the simple reason that it gives the reader's eyes a place to find a moment's refuge from the visual overwhelm. To streamline your ad design:

> • **Frame your ad.** Rather than running copy or design elements to the edge of your ad space (where they run into adjacent ads or stories), isolate your ad with unfilled space or a strong border.

> • **Eliminate unnecessary elements.** Ads that win awards for their effectiveness almost always feature design restraint as opposed to design overload. Readers' eyes sweep across ads, usually from upper left to lower right. In a matter of moments they note the message, the advertiser logo, and whether or not they want to take a closer look. If your ad lacks a focal point or fails to convey a message at a glance, it doesn't get a second chance.

✔ **Size your ad to match your message.** If you're promoting a $1.99 offer, a small-space ad may work just fine. But if you're launching a brand and want to say, in essence, "Hello, world. We're going to be a big deal, and here's why," size your ad accordingly.

✔ **Project a single look and voice in your brand's ads.** For example, use the same typestyle in all headlines, the same border design, the same style of illustrations, the same personality, and the same placement of your logo. To establish your guidelines, see Chapter 17.

Broadcast ads

In the same way that print advertisers benefit from a recognizable brand look, broadcast advertisers leverage the power of a consistent look and/or sound that people can immediately link to the brand's name when they see or hear the ad. Use these tips to establish a broadcast brand identity:

✔ Establish a broadcast ad style, such as ads consisting of a dialogue between two people, ads that feature testimonials, ads with the same voice or actor, and ads that convey a consistent mood and message.

✔ Use music, sound effects, and visual techniques to help people recognize and identify your brand by the its look or sound alone. (The Progressive television ads and Oreo social-media ads are good examples.)

✔ Seriously consider hiring professional broadcast resources for everything from ad concept development to studio production to talent.

See Chapter 11 for advice on shooting, editing, and uploading video and microvideo pieces to your YouTube channel for sharing on social-media pages.

Especially if you're producing video for an ad that will run alongside the ads of major brand advertisers, hire professionals to create an ad that will make you look like able competition; a do-it-yourself ad may well flag your brand — in seconds — as an also-ran. Turn to the upcoming section, "Where to turn for creative help" for information on hiring professionals.

Digital ads

You don't need a book to tell you that people love to hate ads — especially ads that interrupt them with loud-volume, fast-talking messages that have nothing to do with them or their interests. On the flip side, people also love to watch, read, and talk about ads, evidenced by viewership of World Cup, Super Bowl, and award-ceremony ads and viral sharing of ads on social media.

The difference between an annoying and an astonishingly effective ad hinges on whether or not it reaches and wins interest from the person viewing it. And no medium does customer targeting better than digital ads, which is why advertising investments keep shifting toward the online channel. Online ads are among the least expensive to run and among the easiest to target and monitor for return-on-investment, because they generate measurable clicks through to your website. Here's a look at the digital-advertising menu:

- **Banner ads** run across the top of third-party sites. They almost disappeared due to customer resistance but made a comeback thanks to inclusion in the Google AdSense program. They rely on a creative concept that prompts consumer to click the ad, at which time the advertiser gets charged and the website owner gets paid.

- **Pop-up and pop-under ads** sit over or hide under third-party websites. They vie with robo-call telemarketing for the most-annoying forms of advertising. Pop-up blocking software is in wide use and Google, for one, doesn't allow pop-ups on its sites.

- **Pay-per-click (PPC) ads** are small ads in the margin of search engine or social-media pages. The advertiser pays only when someone clicks the ad to reach the advertiser's site.

- **Search ads** are all-word ads that display on the screens of search-engine results because they focus on the same keywords as those in the search. Google AdWords and Microsoft adCenter (representing Bing and Yahoo!) are the leading search ad programs. Like pay-per-click ads, the advertiser pays each time someone clicks on the URL presented in the ad.

  A companion program to Google AdWords is the AdSense advertising program, which allows high-traffic information sites to earn revenue by displaying AdWords ads on their web pages.

✔ **Social-media PPC ads** work a lot like search ads, except they target people rather than keyword topics. Almost every social-media network has a way to let you place ads. Visit the network's help center or enter the name of the network you're interested in, along with the word "advertising," in a search engine to find the latest advice to follow. Success in social-media ads follows the same rules as success in any other effective ad:

- **Target your audience.** If you're selling high school graduation photo packages, target high school graduates or their parents.

- **Match content to the format of the social network you're using.** The word for this match is *native* advertising, because it's advertising that looks like it's part of its media environment.

- **Grab attention with interesting, informative, humorous, or entertaining information.**

- **Advance your brand message.**

- **Make people want to know more.**

- **Give people a reason to take action, including clicking and sharing.**

✔ **Social-media posts** display in your followers' feeds — if algorithmic forces are with you. Promoted content — called *paid reach* — gets seen by a wider audience than regular posts — called *organic page reach* — because it doesn't get weeded out by Facebook's sorting algorithms or buried in the deluge of Twitter or other social-network posts.

Direct mail

Direct mailers carry brand and promotional messages straight to the in-boxes or mail boxes of those in your target audience rather than reaching them through paid ads.

✔ **Direct surface mail** is often considered junk mail. That's the downside. The upside is that, unlike direct email, surface mail can be sent to anyone you want. Typical response rates are 3 to 4 percent if you're mailing to your own list of customers and prospects and lower if you're using a rented list.

✔ **Direct email** is often blocked as spam, gets delivered to crowded inboxes, and can be sent only to people who have opted in or had previous contact with your business, yet it's still among the most effective ways to develop business. Build your mail list by committing to an opt-in policy, never publish your mail list addresses, protect your customers by hiding their addresses on mass mailings, and keep your mailings useful to recipients. Above all, keep your mailers out of the dreaded spam category — both for legal reasons and to protect your brand reputation, by going to the CAN-SPAM Act website (`www.fcc.gov/guides/spam-unwanted-text-messages-and-email`) and following the guidelines to a tee.

Both forms of direct mail rely on the same necessary ingredients: A targeted list that reaches genuine prospects interested in your product, service or message; a compelling offer that's capable of triggering action; a free response mechanism; and an attention-getting presentation.

Both also require prompt follow up. Immediately capture every response in your customer database and quickly respond by thanking the person, fulfilling your offer, introducing your brand, and prompting the next step in the purchase or customer-relationship process.

Where to turn for creative help

When you're creating a long-lasting marketing piece or launching a major campaign on which you're pinning high expectations, think seriously about hiring pros to help you do the job right. Consider the following resources:

- **Free or almost-free resources:** Media outlets and marketing suppliers such as printers, sign makers, and publishers often offer free or close-to-free design tools. If you're updating existing materials, free is a great price. But beware: If you want a unique, creative concept or ad look, turn to professionals who can devote the time and talent necessary to do the job, at a price.

- **Crowd-sourced solutions:** Sites such as 99designs.com and www.CrowdSpring.com have enlisted tens of thousands of designers to provide rapid response to client requests that are treated like design contests. Designs address the needs outlined in a creative brief you'll be required to complete, and they usually cost less than traditionally purchased creative services. But be careful: Realize that designers participating in a contest don't commit the time or participate in the collaborative discussions you can expect from a typical client-professional relationship. Also, be aware that you can't use the designs you receive until agreeing to and signing the site's terms of service.

- **Marketing professionals:** Consider using freelance professionals, design or production studios, full-scale agencies, and brand consultants. When working with marketing professionals, be sure to do the following:

    - **Match services to your needs.** If you're seeking one-time assistance, a freelancer may work fine. If you want to acquire a long-term creative-development or branding partner, an ongoing relationship is a better choice.

    - **Set your priorities.** If you're seeking cutting-edge creative ideas, find an agency that reels in creative awards. If your emphasis is online marketing, head toward a group with proven experience in the digital communications arena. If you want help from someone with deep knowledge of your industry or market sector, or someone with government, business, or even social or client connections, state that priority before you start interviewing potential resources.

- **Define and be ready to share the budget you plan to commit.** If your budget doesn't fit with the professional's client profile, better to know sooner than later.

When you identify professionals whose expertise match your needs, make your decision by following these steps:

1. **Decide how many professionals you want to interview.**

   If your project is simple or your budget is low, talk to one top-choice supplier and save yourself and other professionals the drill of a competition that will eat up the time and money on all sides.

2. **If you interview multiple professionals, follow this process so that you compare apples to apples:**

   1. Share your needs, priorities, budget, and timeline with each firm's CEO, and determine the firm's interest and whether its capabilities fit well with your needs.

   2. Review each firm's presentation and then make your selection.

   3. Get a professional services agreement in writing

Turning Packaging into a Powerful Brand Touchpoint

Packages are the physical interface between your brand and your branded product. They're the point of contact at the moment your customer is shifting from the mindset of a shopper to that of an owner of your brand offering. They need to affirm positive beliefs about your brand, reflect the price and value of your offering, dominate in retail settings, and, as if that's not enough, they also have to be efficient and affordable to manufacture. Product packages are a combination of form and function.

- ✔ **Form:** The *form* of your package involves design, shape, and a look that captures consumer attention and conveys and reinforces your brand image and promise.

- ✔ **Function:** The *function* of your package involves usability. In addition to looking good on a shelf, your packaging has to work. It has to be easy to pick up, read, study, carry away, use, and, hopefully, recycle.

Even if you don't have a consumer product, you still package your offering, perhaps in a shopping bag, a folder or envelope containing a cost estimate or proposal, or a take-home bag for diners to carry home leftovers.

Regardless of the form your packaging takes, make sure that it accurately reflects the promise of your brand and that it makes an appropriately strong and consistent impression for your business. Chapter 17 includes information on redesigning packaging as part of revitalizing a brand.

Matching Promotions to Your Brand Image

Promotions are time-sensitive, attention-generating events that aim to alter customer perception or behavior. Most involve price incentives, trial offers, coupons, rebates, or event invitations.

Buying brand awareness with daily deals

Coupons were a dying breed until Groupon and other sites turned discount redemptions into a social craze. You know how they work: An advertiser offers a deep-discount deal that's good only if a minimum number of people buy, inspiring people who are interested to pass the word along to friends, creating viral sharing of the message and viral introduction of brands. If you decide to achieve brand awareness through daily deals, here's what to keep in mind:

✔ **Don't expect to make money:** When you're offering two-for-one or half-price deals, as group-buying coupons usually involve, you're not going see a profit margin, especially not after the coupon site takes 40 to 60 percent as its fee. What you'll earn is brand exposure, which is great if (and only if) you can turn the exposure to bargain seekers into a message that's in alignment with the brand image you want to achieve.

✔ **Be ready to manage the volume:** When they work, daily deal sites can overwhelm restaurants or service establishments. Be careful to offer date- or time-specific deals that drive traffic when you know you can manage it best.

✔ **Design a deal that fits customer interests *and* your business model.** A wine shop that introduced itself through Groupon offered wine flights, a customer favorite that nearly always leads to the profitable purchase of bottles of wine. Later, the owners further refined their deal offering discounted wine classes that developed awareness and loyalty from new customers during slow-period evenings.

Remember: While successful coupons can help you develop brand awareness and draw people to your business only a great product and positive brand experience will bring them back.

As you introduce and strengthen your brand, be sure that any promotion you stage matches your brand character and promise. For example, if yours is the most exclusive brand in your category, a price promotion is probably out of character, whereas an event featuring celebrities or authorities in your field is more compatible with your image.

Also, take care to protect your brand image when entering cross-promotions that tie your brand to another brand. Chapter 16 includes a section on how to cross-promote without diluting the value of your own brand. The sidebar "Buying brand awareness with daily deals" offers tips for staging price promotions using group buying coupons.

Using Public Relations to Build Your Brand

Public relations (PR) is a term that's often misused. Public relations isn't a fancy name for publicity, although publicity is the element of public relations that most brands work the hardest to achieve. For that matter, even the term *publicity* comes with a set of misconceptions, including the idea that publicity is a free substitute for advertising or a way to fix a brand image through — to use the term you've no doubt heard — *spin*.

To set the record straight, public relations involves activities that develop a favorable image among all the audiences that contribute to a brand's success.

Most brands ride into public view on the magic carpet of a public relations program, mainly for the following reasons:

- ✔ Most brands are launched by entrepreneurs and small businesses with niche markets easily reached by presentations, events, and publicity.

- ✔ New brands benefit from the awareness and credibility they gain through public relations and publicity efforts, which also usually cost less to implement than advertising programs.

- ✔ Brand owners know that publicity needs to precede advertising, because after a brand is announced through advertising, it falls out of the breaking news category and enters the realm of promotional marketing.

As you launch or reintroduce your brand, the following information can help you assemble your public-relations game plan.

Covering all the public-relations bases

The *public* in public relations is divided into the following interest or stakeholder groups.

Employees or members

Employees and members (in the case of cooperatives or associations) comprise the audience your brand launch targets first. Through what's called *internal relations,* it's important to communicate with this group before all others so they know and are trained to represent your brand message and promise before your take your brand message to your broader audience.

Refer to Chapter 9 for help preparing for your internal launch. Then turn to Chapter 13 as you use internal relations on an ongoing basis to turn your employees into a team of champions for your brand.

Community

You'll want to create visibility and understanding for your brand in your home community if your market is local or if you want to establish your business and brand as forces in your own backyard. To gain community awareness, follow these steps:

1. **Introduce your brand through regional news stories.** Target and provide news stories to local media outlets.

2. **Introduce your brand to regional leaders and customers.** Host brand-launch events or perhaps time your brand launch to coincide with a regional economic development or business fair that brings regional leaders, customers, and media representatives together.

3. **Get and stay involved in community programs.** Use your brand launch as the beginning of an ongoing effort to establish and keep your name, message, and brand promise in the minds of community residents and leaders by joining groups, participating in charitable efforts, and contributing time, products, services, or funds to support projects that benefit your home market region.

Your brand launch or relaunch provides an ideal opportunity to introduce — or reintroduce in the case of brand revitalization or rebranding — your brand in your community.

Industry associates

If your brand serves a *vertical market* — a market with specialized interest in a particular industry or area — industry relations deliver the following benefits:

- ✔ You stay at the forefront of industry advances.

- ✔ You acquire industry information to share with local and business media and with customers and other leaders, resulting in a reputation for thought leadership and valuable brand exposure.

To achieve industry awareness, consider timing your brand launch to coincide with a major industry conference or trade show to gain awareness among customers, suppliers, industry leaders, and representatives of industry-specific media outlets all in one fell swoop.

Also, join industry associations, participate in industry events, and cultivate industry-specific media relations and resulting publicity using the tips throughout "Leveraging media relations and publicity" later in this chapter.

Government representatives

If your business is regulated or depends on relationships with elected officials, move government relations high on your public-relations objectives and treat your brand launch as a good opportunity to make important introductions. Provide information to government leaders, invite officials to brand launch events, and stay in contact by sending copies of news releases, reprints of favorable news features or articles, annual reports, or other indicators of success.

Media

Media relations are the pathway to publicity, and generating publicity is a priority for nearly all brands for these reasons:

- ✔ Publicity is a cost-effective way to gain media exposure. Sure, it costs money to write and distribute news releases and to cultivate media relationships. But unlike advertising, publicity isn't purchased.

- ✔ Publicity contributes to brand credibility for the simple reason that people find editorial content more convincing and believable than similar information delivered through paid ads.

- ✔ You can reproduce and repurpose news articles or segments to post on your website, include in social-media content, feature in direct mailings, highlight in presentations, and add to your online media center.

Successful media relations rely on established editorial relationships, distribution of newsworthy releases and story ideas, and ongoing availability as a reliable and trustworthy news resource. The upcoming sections give you advice to follow for meeting these requirements.

Leveraging media relations and publicity

As you work on your brand launch, you welcome all good publicity, but you benefit most from publicity that carries your story to your highest-priority audiences, which are the audiences whose positive opinions are most likely to contribute to your success. The following sections help you direct your publicity in the right way to the right channels.

Matching publicity efforts to your branding objectives

To set your publicity generation efforts off in the right direction, define who you most want to reach via publicity, the story you want to convey, and the type of media that's most likely to carry your news to your target audiences.

In brand launch after brand launch, we've learned this lesson: Unless your brand already enjoys a sky-high level of public awareness and interest, audiences don't care that you have a new or revitalized brand identity. What they care about is how your brand announcement affects them and their lives.

Make your brand announcement newsworthy by creating a launch story of genuine news value. The opposite of newsworthy information is information that belongs in sales pitches. The minute your "news" becomes promotional, it's labeled as hype and trashed accordingly.

In planning your publicity approach, ask yourself, "How is our brand announcement important to the audience of the media outlet where we want a story to post, run, or air?" When you have clear answers, prepare to generate publicity by following these steps:

1. **Target the audiences you want to reach and the nature of the story you want to convey about your brand launch.** You may want to get your story to the financial world, to those in your industry, to your local community, or specifically to those who are or are likely to become customers of your business.

2. **Target media outlets by researching and selecting media outlets that reach the audiences you're trying to reach.** If your objective is to reach customers but you're not completely certain about your customer profile, flip to Chapter 5 and complete the Customer Profile Worksheet.

3. **Prepare and distribute your news, either through personal calls or with news releases to editorial contacts.**

Refer to Table 12-2 as you create your publicity game plan.

Table 12-2	Planning Publicity Objectives and Approaches	
Publicity Objective	**Media Channel**	**Nature of Story**
Heighten awareness among business leaders and the financial industry.	Business and financial publications, business sections of daily newspapers, business segments of broadcast outlets, business websites	Announcement of a new brand, business, product, or strategic direction, including forecasts for market opportunity, new jobs, and business growth
Heighten awareness in local or regional market areas.	Local and regional news outlets, newspapers, radio and TV stations, alternative press, and websites distributing local/regional information	Announcement of a new brand, business, products, services, or opportunities of interest to local/regional residents
Heighten awareness in the national/global market.	Network radio and television channels, national and major metro newspapers, news wire services, consumer and lifestyle magazines, major websites and news portals, social-media networks	Announcement of a new brand, product, service, new business direction, or other news of high impact and interest to national and international consumers and investors
Heighten awareness within your industry or trade group.	Trade, technical, and professional publications and websites	Announcement of a new brand, product, service, production process, distribution method, or marketing campaign of interest to industry leaders, suppliers, wholesalers, and retailers

Targeting media outlets

Your *media list* is the list of outlets that you want to cultivate for editorial relationships. The media list for your brand-launch publicity program may include only the few news outlets in your hometown or it may be long enough to list all the publications, broadcast outlets, wire services, and websites that reach your market locally, regionally, nationally, and globally.

Long or short, limit your list to media outlets that reach your target audience with news of the nature you're working to spread. Put media outlets on your list only if they match your needs on the following fronts:

- They serve audiences in the geographic market areas you aim to reach.

- Their audiences are comprised of people with the lifestyle interests and demographics — age, gender, education level, income level, and so on — of those you're trying to reach.

- ✔ Their editorial focus aligns with the nature of your story.
- ✔ Their audiences are likely to be interested in your news.

Rank relevant media outlets so that your top priorities are listed first. Although all media outlets on your target media list are valuable and important to your publicity program, your high-priority editorial contacts are the ones to whom you'll give special attention. They're the ones most apt to deliver coverage that goes straight to your most important audiences. Find out everything you can about these outlets so you can match your stories and pitches accordingly.

Want to know the quickest route to a news editor's trash bin? Lack relevance. Send a community news outlet a story with no local news slant. Send a national outlet a story that lacks broad-reaching impact. Or send a special-interest media outlet news of no significance to the audience it serves. Save your news from rejection by researching news outlets to be sure they match up with the nature of your news and then crafting your news to match up with the needs of the writers, editors, and audiences you're seeking to influence.

As you develop your media list, turn to the Bacon's Media Directories and the Standard Rate and Data Service (SRDS) Media Source books, both available by subscription online and in the reference section of major libraries.

Pitching your story

Instead of just sending a news release and crossing your fingers, lay some groundwork to establish a relationship and help your story's chances of being picked up.

First, conduct advance research. Read the publication, watch or listen to the station, subscribe, follow, and participate on the blog. Get familiar with the nature and tone of the stories covered by the outlet you're targeting, then go to the media website to learn story angle and submission guidelines, required lead times, and contact information for the editor, writer, blogger, or reporter you should contact for stories like the one you're aiming to place.

Then contact high-priority contacts and pitch your story. Your goal is to provide a heads-up about your news and to persuade each contact to cover the story. When pitching stories, keep these points in mind:

- ✔ **Be timely and newsworthy.** Tell your contact how the story you're proposing will interest their audiences, fit well within their editorial format, and match the current interests of their audience members.

- ✔ **Be concise.** Your contacts are on tight deadlines, so be ready to pitch your story and its significance quickly and completely.

- ✔ **Be professional.** Don't hem and haw, stumble to find words, or sound uncertain about the story you're proposing.

⮌ **Find out how to follow up.** Obtain information about how to deliver your news — in person or by mail, fax, or email — in what format and by what deadline.

After introducing your proposed story and summarizing what makes it newsworthy, be ready to describe how you can assist in story development by providing a news release, a guest editorial or blog post, audio or video files, artwork or photos, and background information on your company, market trends, research findings, or other useful information. Confirm specifications and deadlines for submitting material, and send a follow-up note confirming your understanding.

Preparing and distributing news releases

News releases are the standard currency in the publicity realm. Whether you're delivering news in person, at a news event, or by hand, mail, or email, the minimum standard is to pass along a news release that summarizes your story and offers to provide more information on request.

In the past, nearly all news releases were printed on paper and delivered by hand, mail, or fax to editorial contacts. Today, most news releases are created electronically and delivered via email with hard-copy versions available for subsequent handout and follow-up. Additionally, a growing number of companies now package news into audio or video form for ready-to-go transmission to broadcast audiences.

⮌ **Hard-copy news releases** generally fit on no more than two double-spaced pages that provide the following information, in the following order:

1. **Contact information:** Along the top of the page, type, "For more information:" followed by the name, telephone number, and email address of the person who can provide additional facts.

2. **Release date:** Most releases announce that the news is "For Immediate Release." If it's absolutely necessary to hold the news until a certain time, announce what's called an *embargo;* for instance, "Embargo until 12:01 a.m., January 15, 2015." If you embargo your news, be sure that to make the reason clear in the news release (for instance, "On January 15, Global Enterprises announced its merger with Worldwide Business . . ."). Alert editorial contacts in advance to the time sensitivities, and see that your own organization keeps a lid on the news until the date that you authorize the media to announce it.

3. **A headline:** On no more than two lines, summarize the topic of the news release in a statement that uses active voice as opposed to passive voice. For example, use "New ABC Brand Identity Appeals to Expanded Global Marketplace" instead of "New Logo Unveiled."

4. **Dateline:** The body of the release begins with the name of the city and the abbreviation of the state from which the news originates, followed by the date (for example, "CHICAGO, IL, January 15, 2015").

5. **The news:** Present your news in an inverted pyramid style that tells who, what, where, when, why, and how. Keep the most important news high in the release so it remains intact if an editor cuts the release from the bottom up.

6. **Quotes:** Include brief quotes from executives, industry leaders, or other authorities, along with complete attribution.

7. **Boilerplate closing:** End your release with a one-paragraph summary of your company's mission and background, including facts about the size and purpose of your company and your brand promise.

8. **Accompanying photos and artwork:** Provide only high-quality and professionally produced graphics that meet the specifications of the media outlet, each with a caption titling the image and a cutline providing details.

Deliver hard-copy news releases by mail, fax, or in person, directly or through a public relations firm.

✔ **Email news releases** convert hard-copy news releases for digital delivery. First, confirm that your editorial contact will accept your release and confirm whether to send it within an email message or as an attachment. Most news outlets won't open unsolicited attachments, so definitely check first. When converting releases for transmission as email messages, follow this format:

1. **Email subject line:** Enter a benefit-oriented headline in 50 or fewer characters, using upper- and lowercase.

2. **Message:** In the message portion of your e-mail, begin with a customized introduction to the content that follows, for example, *News Release for [name of media contact] at [name of media outlet].* Then paste in a single-spaced version of your hard-copy news release (with double spacing between paragraphs). Provide hyperlinks that lead to supporting information or product landing pages on your website, if that information will be helpful. End with how to obtain additional information (for example, "To schedule interviews . . ." or, "To obtain photos and artwork . . ."), the contact person's name, phone number and email address, and your company web address.

Prepare your message in plain text rather than HTML or other markup language, because they reduce readability. For simultaneous broad distribution of your electronic release, use a news distribution service such as PR Newswire (www.prnewswire.com),

Business Wire (www.businesswire.com), or other distribution services listed at www.ereleases.com, www.prweb.com, and www.internetnewsbureau.com.

3. **Accompanying photos or artwork:** Always inquire with your editorial source before submitting artwork, video, or photos, both to confirm submission specifications and because few media contacts will open unsolicited attachments.

✔ **Audio, video, and multimedia news releases** present prepackaged news stories to broadcast outlets.

- *Video new releases* (VNR) either package news in the same style as that used in television news reporting or provide video footage for use by broadcast outlets when producing news segments.

- *Audio news releases* (ANR) usually take the form of 60-second news stories tailored for use by radio stations and networks.

- *Webcasts* allow marketers to present portions of offline events — such as major presentations or announcements — to online audiences.

Audio and video releases require a high level of production capability. Contact advertising agencies and broadcast professionals for assistance, and visit www.prnewswire.com for information.

Building an online pressroom or media center

Journalists and others seeking brand information increasingly turn to your website to find company contacts, facts, information, and downloadable images. Before launching or relaunching your brand, consider adding a media center to your website. Here's what to include:

✔ Your brand story and business facts, including company history, product information, and descriptions of the markets you serve.

✔ Head shots and 100-word, 50-word, and 20-word bios of owners and key executives.

✔ Downloadable high-quality photos and graphics, including high-resolution versions of your logo in several sizes and prototypes that show applications of your new brand identity.

✔ Samples or links to recent media coverage.

✔ Links to your social-media pages and other useful sites.

✔ Background information, such as annual reports, research reports, transcripts of speeches or presentations, and other information that presents your position or philosophy on topics important to those in your target audience.

✔ An invitation welcoming requests for guest posts and original articles.

✔ An invitation for media interview requests.

✔ A calendar of scheduled events worthy of media coverage.

✔ Contact information, including names, phone numbers, and email addresses of those who can be reached for additional information.

Staging news conferences

News conferences are more popular among companies and people seeking publicity than they are among those covering, writing, and producing news. Many journalists shun ribbon cuttings, groundbreakings, and announcements that can just as easily be explained in a news release or phone conversation.

Stage a news conference only in the following situations:

✔ Your launch includes important news that should be announced simultaneously to all media outlets.

✔ You're presenting an important speaker or celebrity.

✔ Your launch includes displays and presentations that require personal attendance.

If you decide to schedule a news conference, hold it at a time and place convenient to most journalists, start it on time, hold speakers to short time slots, minimize speeches in favor of demonstrations, and have hard-copy news releases ready for attendees (and ready to be delivered to media outlets not in attendance).

There's no such thing as bad publicity, right? Wrong!

Sorry, but sometimes publicity gives a brand a black eye. Bad publicity can be the result of bad luck, bad timing, a bad product or service, or a bad mistake made in the process of a media interview, customer encounter, or marketplace mishap.

Chapter 18 tackles the topic of what to do if you run into trouble, but to stay out of trouble in the first place, follow these tips:

✔ **Before meeting with media, be clear about your brand promise and brand character, and stay true to your brand at all times.** Even if you're asked to comment on something that has nothing to do with your brand message (recent news or politics, for example), when people read or hear your news, your response contributes to the way they experience your brand. If the voice, message, or character you convey is inconsistent with what people expect from your brand, then the resulting publicity can be harmful to your company and brand.

✔ **Watch your words.** Don't get flip, don't go off-message, and don't disparage others. If you attack someone else, the least that can happen is that you erode your brand image. The most that can happen is that you face a libel suit if an untrue statement ends up in print or a slander suit if an untrue statement ends up on air.

Part IV
Caring for Your Brand

A Brand's Life Cycle

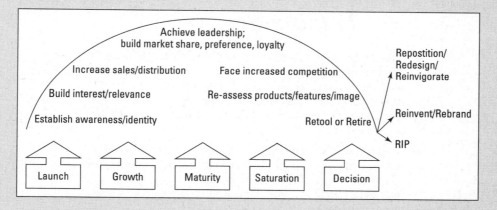

Achieve leadership;
build market share, preference, loyalty

Increase sales/distribution

Face increased competition

Build interest/relevance

Re-assess products/features/image

Establish awareness/identity

Retool or Retire

Repostition/
Redesign/
Reinvigorate

Reinvent/Rebrand

RIP

Launch | Growth | Maturity | Saturation | Decision

To find out how to go the extra mile with your brand experience and service, head to
www.dummies.com/extras/branding.

In this part . . .

✔ Kick the brand-management process into high gear by creating a brand experience that results in devoted, passionate customers and ever-increasing brand value. Follow steps, tips, and advice to develop brand champions, brand trust, and consistent brand encounters that consistently deliver on your brand promise at every point of contact.

✔ Cultivate an avid brand following by developing and nurturing lasting customer relationships that lead to brand loyalty, marketplace passion, and the kind of customer-to-customer sharing that gives your brand viral buzz and a free ride into consumer minds and hearts.

✔ Assess your brand equity and develop its value by following advice for smart brand innovations, well-chosen co-branding partnerships, and careful brand extensions.

✔ Keep your brand hale and hearty by conducting a brand-health review to spot brand aging signs and warning signals. Use diagnostic steps and tools to decide whether your brand repair requires a minor update, a broad-scale revitalization, or an out-and-out rebranding program — and how to implement a change that protects valuable brand assets while achieving new brand goals.

Chapter 13

Perfecting Your Brand Experience

. . . .

In This Chapter

▶ Generating organization-wide brand buy-in

▶ Creating brand champions

▶ Developing and delivering a great brand experience

. . . .

*P*eople power brands.

Brands are made or broken by human encounters that either advance or erode brand promises. The difference between well-launched brands that fizzle and well-managed brands that soar to great value lies in the customer's brand experience, which is the result of everyday contact with your name, your product, your organization, and, most of all, your people.

A great brand name, logo, promise, and communication program are essential ingredients for brand success, but to hit a branding home run you need a committed team of brand champions who embody your brand and who consistently deliver a brand experience worthy of customer praise and loyalty.

The brand experience runs from a person's very first encounter with your brand through the pre-purchase experience, the purchase process, and post-purchase, when brand contacts take the form of product usage, customer service, repeat purchases, and ongoing encounters with your brand. As you develop your brand experience, this chapter outlines the game plan to follow.

Making an Organization-Wide Commitment to Your Brand

Great brands need great leaders. Leading a great brand takes courage and decisiveness. It requires commitment to the brand promise, discipline to build an organization around fulfillment of the promise, and perseverance to keep the promise through all customer contacts and market conditions.

The person whose name sits at the very top of your organizational chart needs to be your brand's evangelist-in-chief.

✔ **If that person is you,** be prepared to serve as your brand's primary champion, your organization's brand coach, the mirror of your brand's promise, and the driving force behind the quality of your customer's brand experience.

✔ **If that person is your boss,** gain top-tier involvement before taking another step in the branding process. Without buy-in from the person on the highest rung of the management ladder, your brand will never reach its potential.

Great brands reflect values and commitments that reach from the most visible leader all the way to the core of an organization. They're embodied by brand representatives and by enthusiastic customers who don't just buy the brand. They own the brand.

Writing your branding playbook

To make branding an organization-wide commitment, take three steps:

1. **Clearly communicate your organization's mission and vision.**

   Your mission defines what you intend to do and the approach you'll follow to achieve your aspirations. Your vision defines why your company does what it does and the ultimate good you aim to achieve through your success. Together your mission and vision orient all who work with your organization to the ultimate aim you're working toward and the route you'll take to get there. For help putting your statements into words, see Chapter 6.

2. **Build organization-wide understanding for your brand statement.**

   Your brand statement encapsulates what you do, those you serve, how you differ from similar solutions, and the promise you make to all who deal with your organization.

3. **Make your brand promise an organization-wide commitment.**

   Your brand promise is the statement upon which you stake your reputation. It's the essence of your brand and the quality you assure to all who come into contact with your organization. Be sure that your entire team knows the promise they're helping to keep.

True brand culture stems from the beliefs, personalities, and values of those leading the brand. It's so authentic and heartfelt that it's caught, not taught, throughout the organization.

You can't impose your brand mission or promise onto employees. We've heard about companies that assemble their staffs to recite the mission statement each morning (or worse, to sing it in staff meetings — believe it or not, we've seen this firsthand, much to the embarrassment of the assembled employees). The only way to gain company-wide buy-in is to start with buy-in at the top and to spread it with such enthusiasm that a strong sense of culture naturally follows.

To test how well your promise is known, embraced, and implemented in your organization, answer the questions posed in Figure 13-1.

Putting Your Brand Promise to the Test

How do you define your brand promise?

State how your offering stands apart from all others in terms of features but more important in terms of consumer benefits. (See Chapter 6 for steps to follow.)

How do those in your organization define your brand promise?

Benchmark current awareness of your brand promise by asking individuals at different levels of your organization — from top management to service front lines – to describe how your organization differs from competitors and the unique promise that consumers can count on only from your organization.

How do you communicate your brand promise within your organization?

Is your brand promise the basis of your company name or slogan? Is your brand promise explained during employee training sessions? Is your brand promise – and its delivery – discussed during management planning sessions? Do you have programs that recognize and reward employees for actions that exemplify your brand promise?

How have you coordinated the delivery of your brand promise?

Have you studied how well your promise is conveyed and kept at each customer encounter point, whether through advertising, online, upon first call or visit, during the purchase transaction, at the point of billing, during delivery and after-purchase transactions, at the point of customer service or concerns, during post-purchase follow-up, through customer loyalty programs, and at all other points where the customer has an experience with your brand?

How well do your customers know your promise?

To really test whether your promise is clear, compelling, and well delivered, ask customers how they find your organization different from all competing entities. Ask how they would describe the promise they count on your business to keep. Ask what one attribute they most rely on from you; what one thing they would miss the most if your organization disappeared tomorrow. (Chapter 4 offers advice for conducting research.)

Figure 13-1: Test your organization's commitment to your brand promise by using questions like these.

Becoming your brand's MVP

"Walk the talk" may sound like an overused phrase, but it's a tenet that could be far better employed in today's business world.

How many times have you entered a business that promises friendly service only to stand around waiting for someone to look up and recognize your existence? How many times have you been assured by a company's communications that "to us, you're a name, not a number" only to place a phone call that burns ten minutes in an automated menu maze that repeatedly requests your account number, interspersed by blasé background music and an occasional prerecorded voice reminding you that your call is important?

Following are some suggestions for developing organization-wide passion for and commitment to your brand promise:

- ✔ **Keep the same promise that you make to your customers with your employees.** If you promise customers friendly service, promise your employees a friendly employment setting. If you promise the highest-quality offering, promise your employees the highest-quality work environment. If you promise a super-creative product, promise employees super-creative work surroundings. Let employees and customers experience the same brand promise.

- ✔ **Make your work environment a mirror image of your brand experience.** If you promise that customers are served by your full business team, break down the barriers of cubicles and closed doors to create an atmosphere of teamwork. If you promise the most creative solutions, foster a creative work environment (no uniforms, please!). We heard of an ad agency that took its creativity promise so far as to say they wouldn't hold company gatherings at an establishment that served sugar in cubes — a sign of regulated servings and traditional delivery that ran counter to the agency's culture and promise.

- ✔ **Be sure your brand promise starts at the top and runs through to the core of your organization.** Make an organization-wide commitment to your brand promise, and then make every business decision with the promise in mind, including decisions about how you'll create a work environment, employee training, and employee rewards that help you walk the talk of your brand promise within your organization.

Suiting Up a Team of Brand Champions

If you're launching a new brand, before your brand makes its public debut, prepare all players for their roles. Follow the step-by-step advice in Chapter 9, which covers the topic of training and inspiring your staff.

If you're managing an existing brand, your training needs are twofold: To recruit and train new employees into the brand culture and to enhance and reward commitment to the brand among existing employees.

What everyone in your organization needs to know about your brand

When training employees to be brand champions, make sure they understand the market position, promise, and character of the brand they represent.

- **Presenting your brand's market position:** Put your brand on a map using a device such as the positioning matrix (shown in Chapter 5) to illustrate and gain understanding for the unique place your brand holds in its market.

- **Promoting your brand promise:** Describe how your organization delivers on its promise at every point of the customer's brand experience. Cite examples for how the promise is upheld upon arrival by phone, in person, or online; in correspondence and email; in marketing materials; at the point of customer purchase, billing, or service; and even when handling concerns and complaints. Turn to Chapter 6 as you define your brand attributes and write your business promise.

- **Conveying your brand character:** Your *brand character* is the personality of your brand that's reflected through the look and voice of your brand expressions.

Especially if people have face-to-face contact with your brand, the people you employ are the most important representatives of your brand character. If you convey one brand character in marketing communications and then deliver service through a staff member who reflects a completely different character, you're in line for a credibility train wreck. The following are ways to train your staff members to represent your brand character:

- During orientation, explain your brand character as a look and voice — a personality — that's based on your organization's values, vision, and brand promise.

- Explain that every employee represents the brand character. Describe your brand character in a statement such as, "Our brand character is [*a description using words that you'd use to describe the personality of your brand if it were a person or a car; for instance, sophisticated, fashionable, revolutionary, innovative, professional, elegant, or refined*]. We reflect our character through brand expressions that are [*a description of the mood, voice, and tone that your marketing will project; for example, chic and stylish, cutting-edge creative, calm and subdued, high-quality and professional*]."

- Define how your organization manages its brand character through company dress, customer contact, office décor, correspondence, background music, aroma, color, and any other way that the personality of your organization is expressed. Create policies where appropriate, but focus on creating a brand promise and culture that runs so deeply that employees naturally adopt it as their own.

For an example of pervasive brand character, walk through the lobby of a W Hotel. The brand describes itself as "W . . . for warm, wonderful, witty, wired, welcome." More than words, though, the brand expresses its identity at every presentation point, especially through employees — called *talent* — who, within weeks of joining the hotel team, seem to transform their looks to represent W's "young, hip" culture.

Gaining team buy-in

To win staff understanding and enthusiasm for your brand, treat brand training as a function worthy of time and effort by doing the following:

- ✔ **Stage a formal brand training session that presents the following:**

  - A snapshot history of your organization

  - A description of your market and how you provide the best solution to the customer's wants or needs

  - Your brand definition

  - Your brand's unique position in your competitive arena

  - Your brand's distinguishing attributes and how they translate into meaningful customer benefits

  - Your brand's character and how it's reflected through employees and at each customer contact point

  - How your brand is key to your business success

- ✔ **Immerse staff members in your brand culture.** Arrange for new employees to experience your brand as a customer does, beginning with a review of marketing materials and moving through contact with all departments. Help each employee see how various employees uphold the brand promise and exceed customer expectations.

- ✔ **Arrange opportunities for employees to watch others make brand presentations.** Let them see how the brand is described and translated into customer benefits.

- ✔ **Make brand training an ongoing effort.** Periodically ask employees questions such as

- Which brand attributes do you think customers most appreciate?

- From your encounters with customers or from your vantage point within our organization, do you think our customers understand our brand's distinctions and how we differ from competitors?

- If you were one of our primary competitors, how might you describe the greatest weakness of our brand?

- What one customer contact point seems to you to be least effective at conveying our brand promise?

- If you could wave a magic wand and fix one thing that causes customer frustration or erodes brand confidence, what would it be?

✔ **Give employees authority to go the extra mile to keep brand promises, and reward them for their innovation and responsiveness.** Nordstrom is a shining example of an empowered team of confident brand champions who are encouraged to use their own good instincts to offer customized solutions, to right wrongs when they see them, and to go overboard to deliver a great customer experience. The result? Passionate customers who spread the good word with far greater impact than any company-generated communication could achieve.

✔ **Regularly ask yourself and your staff: What kinds of stories are customers telling about our service?**

If you're not totally proud of what you believe is being said about you, spend extra time with the upcoming section on developing an outstanding customer experience.

Building Brand Trust at the Point of Sale

The best brand owners make sure that salespeople are steeped in brand culture and armed with tools and scripts that help them share and inspire belief in the brand promise.

For example, Victoria's Secret sells underwear, but salespeople know that what people are really buying is the idea of sexy romance. Harley Davidson sells motorcycles, but people are really buying association with an independent and rebellious spirit.

Even more than your product, it's your brand promise that inspires your customer's purchase decision. So arm your sales team with scripts for sharing your story, brand testimonials and endorsements, techniques for overcoming objections, and approaches for negotiating terms and closing sales without ever varying from the brand message and promise.

Developing and sharing brand testimonials, endorsements, and reviews

At the moment of purchase decision, customers need a final hit of inspiration and reassurance that the brand's offering will deliver as promised. This is true when customers are purchasing in-person and even more essential when they're purchasing from websites or mobile apps that guide their choices.

To underscore that a branded product is as good as it's touted to be, amass positive reviews, testimonials, and endorsements.

Personal testimonials

When obtaining and presenting customer testimonials, follow these tips:

- Wait until purchase transactions are completed before asking a satisfied buyer if he or she would say a few words on behalf of your brand.

- Encourage frank comments. Even if the words aren't suitable for a testimonial, they'll be valuable as you refine your offering and brand experience.

- Whether customers speak or write their comments, ask them to focus on the aspect of their experience that they found most compelling. Whether they cite service, product selection, convenience, guarantee, or after-sale assistance, specific praise makes the comments more believable.

- Ask customers to describe details about their experiences. Consider the difference in impact between, "I'm impressed by your willingness to go the extra mile" and "We were leaving town and needed to pick up our new widget late on a Thursday evening. We still can't believe that you worked long past closing hours and then made our pick-up unnecessary by delivering the widget to our doorstep. Thanks!"

- Obtain written permission to use the testimonial. Then identify the praise with at least the customer's first name, hometown, title, and business affiliation if possible and appropriate.

When dealing with customer testimonials, avoid these mistakes:

- Never offer cash, product, or favors in return for customer testimonials.

- Don't invent testimonials. They're likely to sound phony (which they are), and the practice is unethical and sometimes illegal.

- Don't prompt customers. Let them speak freely. You want to collect genuine opinions about how they view the attributes and benefits of your offering and the experience of dealing with your organization.

Celebrity endorsements

Celebrity endorsements link star-powered statements of support (increasingly in the form of social-media mentions) with brands that somehow match up with the celebrity's personality and reputation — for a price. Usually celebrity endorsements are purchased with cash, product, or stock options.

Consider these points when using celebrities in your brand-building program:

- The most credible endorsements convince people that a respected personality uses and benefits from your offering.

- The best celebrity representatives align perfectly with your brand image and actually use and support your offerings. Aim for a relationship that goes beyond endorsement and involves product usage and affinity.

- Celebrity endorsements are worthy of legal contracts that define the relationship, the compensation, and what happens should the celebrity's integrity be damaged by scandal. Don't proceed on a handshake.

Expert endorsements

When experts test, evaluate, and offer positive opinions on products, the endorsements are valuable in developing consumer confidence as long as you follow a few precautions:

- The expert must have clear and well-recognized qualifications.

- The expert must conduct a product test that conforms to testing standards in your industry. If the test proves that your offering is superior to a competitor's offering, keep records that support the claim.

- The expert must have no relationship with your business, or if a relationship exists, you must describe the relationship in all materials that reference the test.

Organization endorsements

An organization endorsement is a seal of approval from a reputable organization. The Good Housekeeping Seal is a well-known example.

Feature endorsements *only* from actual, independent organizations that have credibility with your target audience, never from organizations created solely for use in your marketing program. Always check with the organization about how you may use the endorsement and what restrictions apply.

Customer reviews

Customers post reviews for all kinds of products and services at review sites like Yelp, TripAdvisor, CitySearch, and other networks. At many sites, the difference between a four-star or four-and-a-half-star rating can cause dramatic swings in customer decisions.

Nearly every business benefits from positive reviews and is susceptible to damage from bad reviews. Don't leave it to chance. Claim presence for your business on the review sites prospective customers are likely to check out. Encourage customers to post good words. And keep your cool but double your efforts when an occasional bad review shows up. See Chapter 11 for steps to follow and mistakes to avoid.

Spreading the good word

Gain mileage out of good words by presenting them in the following ways:

- ✔ **Provide testimonials and endorsements in sales presentations.** Share praise from past customers as well as details on expert test results.

- ✔ **Include accolades in sales letters and literature.** Intersperse testimonials and endorsements with sales points rather than isolate testimonials to a single page.

- ✔ **Feature testimonials on your website and social-media pages.** On your website, create a page of testimonials and endorsements, but also incorporate them throughout your site. On social media, share phrases from positive comments, with thanks, as posts or status updates.

Intercepting and overcoming objections

It sounds counterintuitive, but objections can open the door to brand-building opportunities. When customers share concerns or objections with your company's representatives, at the very least they're involved in the sales conversation and, at the most, they're providing input that allows your company to clarify misunderstandings and overcome buying obstacles.

Most objections stem from one of three areas of concern.

- ✔ **Lack of trust in your brand:** Here's where testimonials and endorsements can come to the rescue.

- ✔ **Preference for a competing brand:** Be ready with a recap of the benefits and value your brand delivers in order to present a positive comparison without taking any digs at competitors.

- ✔ **Concern over your offer:** Probe the concern and avoid jumping to the conclusion that price is the issue. Often concerns have as much to do with questions about ease of use, appropriateness of the offering, perceived risk in dealing with a new product or brand, or even lack of authority to make the purchase.

  - • **Price concerns:** Demonstrate worth, present product value, show cost/value ratios, and show cost- or time-saving potential. Also provide purchase options — from trial offers to bulk discounts to special terms or installment plans — to address price barriers.

- **Time concerns:** Demonstrate ease of use, installation, product adoption, training, or other time concerns.

- **Risk concerns:** Demonstrate ease of use and make trial offers, no-risk guarantees, or service assurances to minimize perceived risk. Also, present testimonials, endorsements, and case studies that replace risk concerns with product assurances.

In addition to dealing positively with concerns, log concerns so when it's time to revitalize your brand, you know the kinds of issues to address.

Delivering a Brand-Building Experience

Be the brand isn't just talk; it's the key to branding success. Brand strategy doesn't move markets, but brand experience does. To build the brand you want, create an experience that reaffirms your promise during every encounter with your brand.

Testing your brand experience

The first step in managing your brand experience is to experience your brand firsthand. How? Follow these suggestions:

- **Arrive like customers arrive.** Forget your insider shortcuts. Imagine you're a first timer trying to reach your front door or website; see if your business is findable and accessible and what first impression it makes.

- **Shop like they shop.** Go through the buying experience exactly as a customer would. Ask to see samples, request cost estimates, and compare options both within your company and with competitors. Then go through the trial, customization, and purchase-decision process.

- **Pause where they pause.** Notice where and how long you wait during the purchase process. How long does it take to receive a greeting? Is the greeting appropriate? What do you do while you wait? Are you comfortable? Do you receive positive brand messages and an experience that fits your brand image and promise?

- **Use your product just as customers use it.** If they sign an estimate or a contract, notice how the information is presented, whether it's perfectly clear or whether questions come to mind. If they have to unpackage or assemble your product, follow the instructions to see if they make sense. Dial your help line to check out your support functions. Then put the product to use to assess the user experience.

Use your findings and do the following to smooth the customer experience:

- ✔ **Create a map of how customers arrive at, buy from, and follow up with your business.** This information helps as you conduct your more formal brand experience audit (see the next section).

- ✔ **Recognize and make plans to eliminate customer barriers,** whether they're physical (lack of parking), emotional (undue waits), or product-oriented (packaging is hard to open; instructions are confusing).

- ✔ **Note and make plans to address opportunities for service or product enhancements.** For example, if you find that customers are consistently tailoring your product to suit their particular needs, include customization as a free or low-cost option.

Auditing your brand experience

Brand experiences are the result of brand encounters, and brand encounters are affected by

- ✔ How easy it is to find and reach you in person, by phone, or online

- ✔ Your business location and appearance, including signage, displays, staff, waiting areas, and even the look of other customers

- ✔ The caliber and cleanliness of your business vehicles

- ✔ The quality of your advertising and other communications

- ✔ The nature of your publicity

- ✔ The look and speed of your website

- ✔ The speed of service, including the length of time phone calls are left on hold, how long messages go unanswered, and how long people wait in line or for product delivery

- ✔ The friendliness and experience of customer-service staff

- ✔ The flexibility of your policies

This list barely scratches the surface of the ways that people form impressions about your brand, but you get the idea. With so many encounter points, it's no wonder that brands have trouble maintaining a consistent image. With each lapse, though, no matter how minor, consumers lose confidence in the brand's ability to keep its promise and to maintain its distinction.

To develop the quality of your brand experience, take these steps:

1. **Determine every brand impression point that prospects and customers encounter when dealing with your business, from the prepurchase stage through the purchase experience and post-purchase contact. (The form in Figure 13-2 helps with this step.)**

2. **Create an experience that conveys your brand promise without fail or hesitation through encounters that consistently advance your brand message, voice, look, and character.**

3. **Audit your brand experience on a regular basis to insure against reputation-eroding communication or service lapses.**

4. **Take action immediately if you discover impression points that compromise the consistency and value of your brand.**

Pre-purchase impressions

Pre-purchase impressions take the form of web searches, website visits, social-media posts and interactions, advertising, direct mail, displays, publicity, presentations, reviews, word-of-mouth comments, and more. Some you control; others are outside of your control. All contribute to awareness of your brand and its distinctions, market perceptions, and relevance to customer wants and needs.

Pre-purchase communications reach prospective, new, or lapsed customers with messages that, if all goes well, prompt inquiries, product sampling or trial, and, ultimately, purchases.

Purchase experience impressions

During the purchase process, people form impressions based on the location of your business, the design of your physical or online setting, the style and attitude of your employees (and even that of other customers), the design of your packaging, the nature of your pricing, your service style and systems, and the way they're treated by sales and service staff.

This is the point when you want to reinforce your brand promise. You also want to heighten consumer confidence, overcome doubts, underscore brand distinctions and competitive advantages, build trust, and convey your product value and positive price-value relationship.

Post-purchase impressions

The best post-purchase impression comes from delivery of a branded product that matches or exceeds the customer's quality and performance expectations.

The post-purchase experience also includes follow-up service, customer communications and engagement, loyalty programs, and customer events.

At each post-purchase encounter point, be sure the experience deepens your brand promise while also demonstrating appreciation, exceeding customer expectations, addressing customer needs, and encouraging involvement and brand ownership. How you handle compliments and concerns and how you encourage customer involvement to tailor the brand experience to their unique wants and needs tips the balance between satisfied customers and raving fans. (See Chapter 14 for information on this point.)

Making use of your findings

As you conduct your brand experience audit, use the worksheet in Figure 13-2 as a guide and follow these steps:

1. **Identify all brand impression points.**

2. **Evaluate the strength of each impression point based on how well your organization currently performs and whether your performance has improved or slipped in the recent past.**

3. **Identify gaps between your brand promise and brand experience.**

4. **Prioritize which gaps need immediate attention based on the seriousness of the experience lapse and the prominence of the impression point.**

5. **Set improvement objectives, monitor progress, and reward your staff for performance advances.**

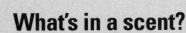

What's in a scent?

Want an example of a strong brand experience? Think of Cinnabon. Within a football field's distance of the shopping mall food court, you know whether or not it has a Cinnabon. The brand has perfected what's called an *olfactory signature* — a *scent* — that announces its presence and lures customers into what has become a highly predictable brand experience.

Brands are comprised of memories, and smell is the sense that most effectively triggers memory. Cinnabon manages its brand around its scent so carefully that it sites its stores far from outlets that may compromise its aroma.

More and more brands are getting into the scent-as-brand-experience arena. Hotels perfume their lobbies with stress-reducing brand aromas or waft smells from the espresso bar toward waiting areas — establishing a brand scent while also generating coffee bar revenues.

So how does your brand smell? Even if you don't have or need a brand scent, a pleasant smell makes a positive, lasting customer impression.

BRAND EXPERIENCE AUDIT **Impression Point**	Rate quality of brand experience at this impression point (1=low, 5=high)			✔ For priority attention
	Brand Look/Tone	Brand Promise	Brand Character	
Pre-Purchase				
Web search results and presence	1 2 3 4 5	1 2 3 4 5	1 2 3 4 5	☐
Newspaper ads	1 2 3 4 5	1 2 3 4 5	1 2 3 4 5	☐
Magazine ads	1 2 3 4 5	1 2 3 4 5	1 2 3 4 5	☐
Broadcast ads	1 2 3 4 5	1 2 3 4 5	1 2 3 4 5	☐
Posted video, audio, webcasts	1 2 3 4 5	1 2 3 4 5	1 2 3 4 5	☐
Directory ads	1 2 3 4 5	1 2 3 4 5	1 2 3 4 5	☐
Direct mailers and newsletters	1 2 3 4 5	1 2 3 4 5	1 2 3 4 5	☐
Transit and outdoor ads	1 2 3 4 5	1 2 3 4 5	1 2 3 4 5	☐
Business signage	1 2 3 4 5	1 2 3 4 5	1 2 3 4 5	☐
Vehicle signage	1 2 3 4 5	1 2 3 4 5	1 2 3 4 5	☐
Product samples	1 2 3 4 5	1 2 3 4 5	1 2 3 4 5	☐
Marketing literature	1 2 3 4 5	1 2 3 4 5	1 2 3 4 5	☐
Tradeshow/expo displays	1 2 3 4 5	1 2 3 4 5	1 2 3 4 5	☐
Presentation materials	1 2 3 4 5	1 2 3 4 5	1 2 3 4 5	☐
Reviews and ratings	1 2 3 4 5	1 2 3 4 5	1 2 3 4 5	☐
Word-of-mouth comments	1 2 3 4 5	1 2 3 4 5	1 2 3 4 5	☐
Purchase Experience				
Building and entry signage	1 2 3 4 5	1 2 3 4 5	1 2 3 4 5	☐
Website navigation, usability, and purchase security	1 2 3 4 5	1 2 3 4 5	1 2 3 4 5	☐
Business environment	1 2 3 4 5	1 2 3 4 5	1 2 3 4 5	☐
Product presentation online and in catalogs, literature, point-of-purchase displays	1 2 3 4 5	1 2 3 4 5	1 2 3 4 5	☐
Staff interaction from reception through purchase transaction	1 2 3 4 5	1 2 3 4 5	1 2 3 4 5	☐
Waiting areas	1 2 3 4 5	1 2 3 4 5	1 2 3 4 5	☐
Product packaging	1 2 3 4 5	1 2 3 4 5	1 2 3 4 5	☐
Product customization	1 2 3 4 5	1 2 3 4 5	1 2 3 4 5	☐
Price presentation	1 2 3 4 5	1 2 3 4 5	1 2 3 4 5	☐
Checkout and billing processes	1 2 3 4 5	1 2 3 4 5	1 2 3 4 5	☐
Samples and trial offers	1 2 3 4 5	1 2 3 4 5	1 2 3 4 5	☐

Figure 13-2a: Regularly monitor and improve your brand experience impression points.

BRAND EXPERIENCE AUDIT	Rate quality of brand experience at this impression point (1=low, 5=high)			✔ For priority attention
Impression Point	Brand Look/Tone	Brand Promise	Brand Character	
Post Purchase				
Product quality and usage	1 2 3 4 5	1 2 3 4 5	1 2 3 4 5	☐
Use and warranty information	1 2 3 4 5	1 2 3 4 5	1 2 3 4 5	☐
Invoices and statements	1 2 3 4 5	1 2 3 4 5	1 2 3 4 5	☐
Post-purchase service/policies	1 2 3 4 5	1 2 3 4 5	1 2 3 4 5	☐
Customer surveys	1 2 3 4 5	1 2 3 4 5	1 2 3 4 5	☐
Customer communications	1 2 3 4 5	1 2 3 4 5	1 2 3 4 5	☐
Loyalty programs	1 2 3 4 5	1 2 3 4 5	1 2 3 4 5	☐
Events and promotions	1 2 3 4 5	1 2 3 4 5	1 2 3 4 5	☐
General				
Web presence	1 2 3 4 5	1 2 3 4 5	1 2 3 4 5	☐
Social-media presence	1 2 3 4 5	1 2 3 4 5	1 2 3 4 5	☐
Correspondence (mail/email)	1 2 3 4 5	1 2 3 4 5	1 2 3 4 5	☐
Publicity	1 2 3 4 5	1 2 3 4 5	1 2 3 4 5	☐
Quality of brand identity and logo applications	1 2 3 4 5	1 2 3 4 5	1 2 3 4 5	☐
Clientele (how well customers reflect brand image)	1 2 3 4 5	1 2 3 4 5	1 2 3 4 5	☐

Figure 13-2b:
continued

© Barbara Findlay Schenck

Chapter 14

Winning Brand Loyalty

In This Chapter

▶ Reaching beyond expectations to create brand loyalists

▶ Igniting customer passion for your brand

▶ Generating buzz and viral marketing for your brand

Creating a brand name, a brand identity, and a brand promise are the beginning steps in the branding process. They're like the ante you pay to play in the high-stakes branding arena. They're the down payment required to rise above the noisy floor of me-too offerings and to win a chance at a preferred place in customers' hearts and minds, where great brands live and thrive.

But you can't just register a terrific brand name, design an award-winning logo, craft a great brand promise, and then sit back and wait for the magic to happen. Sorry, but even the greatest brand framework, of and by itself, isn't enough to build a great brand success story. Even high market awareness and strong sales aren't enough.

The highest level of brand success requires one more essential ingredient: loyal customers with brand passion so powerful that their association with the brand becomes a reflection of how they see themselves — or how they wish to be seen by others. This loyal connection, called *brand association,* is the pinnacle of branding success and the focus of this chapter.

Developing Loyalty through Customer Relationships

Great brands generate sky-high customer enthusiasm that results in nothing short of brand passion.

For good examples of the power of customer enthusiasm, consider the brands whose logos you see displayed on car windshields or whose labels are worn on the outside of clothes as badges of association and pride of ownership. They're the brands that win allegiance and reap the incalculable value of customer affection, word-of-mouth, online sharing, and loyalty.

Passionate employees and passionate customers (in that order) power great brands. You can't put the cart before the horse. You can't create passionate customers without first creating passionate employees and the kind of brand experience they're proud to deliver. For help turning your employees into a team of brand champions, flip back to Chapter 13.

When your organization's ready to deliver awe-inspiring service that fulfills your brand promise at every customer encounter point, you're on your way to developing not just customers but customer relationships and brand passion.

Why customer relationships matter

It costs a lot to attract a first-time customer. If that person buys once and heads out the door never to be seen again, the one-time purchase represents the only revenue you'll realize from your customer-attraction investment.

On the other hand, if the customer buys again and again, your marketing investment gets amortized and the profitability you enjoy from your initial investment grows higher and higher. Researchers have even quantified the value you reap, finding that by winning repeat business from just 5 percent more customers, a business can improve profitability by 75 to 100 percent.

Unquestionably, profitability is a major reason that customer relationships matter. Additionally, customers who develop a relationship with your business contribute so much more:

- Loyal customers account for higher purchase volume and lower costs than other customers because they're easier to reach and require lower sales and service assistance.

- Loyal customers involve fewer problems because you know their credit status, purchase preferences, and buying patterns.

- Loyal customers are a good source of positive reviews, favorable word-of-mouth, and qualified referrals. They're most apt to spread their brand affection to others.

✔ Loyal customers help develop loyal staff — and loyal staff help develop loyal customers — because lasting, positive relationships enhance your brand and your business environment for employees and customers alike.

✔ Loyal customers who are treated well and who receive consistently good brand experiences are most apt to make repeat purchases, even when promotions and discounts aren't involved. What's more, loyal customers who are treated like insiders and who gain a feeling of brand ownership turn into *passionate customers*.

✔ Passionate customers who are treated well and who receive consistently good brand experiences become *brand ambassadors*.

✔ Brand ambassadors spread good words on the brand's behalf, increasing marketplace awareness, positive perceptions, and brand value. Even more valuable, they become so engaged and so associated with the brand and what it stands for that it becomes an expression of how they see themselves.

A *BusinessWeek*/Interbrand report concluded that "a sense of ownership in near-fanatical customers" was a key contributor to the success of the most valuable global brands. See the sidebar "Sharing ownership of your brand with your most loyal customers" for a description of the invaluable associations between brands and those who love them most.

Sharing ownership of your brand with your most loyal customers

Why do people affix an Apple logo on their cars? Why do they pay premium prices for Ray-Ban sunglasses? Why in the world do they applaud, scream, and paint their faces the colors of a local sports team when they don't personally know a soul in the organization?

They do it, instinctively and without even thinking deeply about it, to telegraph the association they have with the image of the brand. They do it to align themselves with what they believe about the brand. They do it to borrow from the brand's identity and meaning as they define who they are and what they stand for, both to themselves and to others. That may seem a bit philosophical to some — even silly to others — but it explains why brands with resonant, powerful, meaningful brand stories and images generate almost crazy levels of brand association, followed by strong brand loyalty and resulting brand value that few brands attain and all should aspire to achieve.

Sparking customer relationships

The first step in developing brand allegiance is sparking a customer relationship. Most customers fit into one of two categories:

- ✔ **Transaction customers help build your bottom line.** They approach your business seeking a good deal, and their expectations usually are based on price coupled with outstanding features or convenience. Transaction customers' primary interest is in the deal rather than the relationship. Although they may be happy enough with your business to pass along positive word-of-mouth comments and even to make repeat purchases, in most cases they'll leave you in a heartbeat if a deeper discount or better-sounding deal comes along.

  Most transaction customers remain in that category. But sometimes, if you ignite their interest, enthusiasm, and trust, they surprise you (and themselves) by becoming entranced by your brand experience and moving into the *relationship customer* category. The moral of the story: Never assume a price-shopper is there only for the deal. Deliver your brand story and experience, and you may convert the one-time interaction into a valuable lasting relationship.

- ✔ **Relationship customers help build your brand.** They value loyalty, commitment, and trust even more than they value good deals. They prefer to do business with those whose reputations they know and trust and whose promises they believe in.

  When relationship customers choose a brand, they're inclined to stick with it *if* — and this is a big *if* and the whole point of this chapter — you give them the kind of brand experience that turns them into spread-the-word ambassadors for your brand.

All customers are important because all customers represent revenue and the potential for good or bad word-of-mouth. But relationship customers deliver a more powerful benefit. Through their commitment to your brand, loyal, long-term customers become brand ambassadors and even brand zealots who create awareness and develop positive perceptions for your brand in the minds of others, which is where brands live and thrive.

Igniting Customer Passion

Customers don't fall in love with a brand overnight. They need a little wooing. In the matchmaking process, your brand needs to help customers through these stages:

- ✔ **Meeting a brand that interests them:** They need to hear a name, see a logo, and encounter a brand message that somehow makes them think, "Hey, this could be for *me.*"

✔ **Being presented with a brand promise that compels them to get further involved:** Your brand promise is the pledge upon which you stake your brand reputation. It's the essence of your brand. It's the reason people choose you, your business, or your offerings over all others and, when it's consistently upheld, it's the reason they fall in love and stay faithful to your brand — forever after. Chapter 6 helps you develop a promise that follows this template:

> [*Name of your business, product, or service*] is the [*your distinction and the generic term for your type of offering*] to provide [*your unique features or benefits*] to [*your customer profile*] who choose our offering in order to feel [*your customers' emotional outcome*].

✔ **Having a brand experience that heightens their interest while confirming their initially formed positive impressions:** The brand experience (the sole focus of Chapter 13) is where trust happens — or doesn't. *Trust* is one of the most-frequently used words in this book for the simple, never-contested fact that brands are built on trust. They're built by making, keeping, and continuously living up to the promise customers believe about who you are, what you stand for, and what unique and meaningful benefits you deliver — without fail.

✔ **Being overwhelmed by the pride they feel in simply saying that the brand is "theirs."** To adopt and stay loyal to a brand, customers need to believe that everything about the brand is so right and that everything about the brand's products, service, promise, people, and clientele is so consistently ideal that the brand association is somehow capable of enriching their lives on a personal level.

Nurturing Brand Loyalists

Online or in-person, customers really don't ask for that much. Here's what they want:

✔ They want to be served quickly, whether on the phone, at a physical location, or online.

✔ They want their requests or problems addressed efficiently and effectively.

✔ They want to deal with experienced, friendly people who they feel relate to and understand their needs.

✔ They want clear communication from knowledgeable people.

✔ They want solutions that make them feel heard, understood, important, and valued.

Here's what they don't want: They don't want to wait. In person, they consider two-minute waits total service failures, and online they're gone in a matter of seconds if a website doesn't load and hook their interest at lightning-speed. (Turn to Chapter 10 for website-building advice.)

Meet these pretty basic standards, and chances are good that you'll win business. If you want to develop valuable, profitable, brand-building loyalty, though, you need to go farther. You need to deepen and reward customer relationships through ongoing interaction, engagement, recognition, and loyalty incentives that glue them to your brand because they're stuck on the way it continuously exceeds their already high expectations.

Increasing accessibility and interaction

Customers grow and stay loyal to brands that reach out to them with valuable, interesting, entertaining, rewarding messages that invite and foster two-way communication and ongoing relationships. Social media — the focus of Chapter 11 — makes this now-requisite interaction possible, affordable, and scalable to an ever-growing clientele. Here's why:

- ✔ **Social media is the great marketing equalizer.** It gives the smallest brand the same free or nearly free communication opportunity as the biggest brand. But it also offers a huge equalizing benefit to big brands, because it allows them to establish the kind of ongoing conversational customer rapport that previously happened only over-the-counter or at the cash register of small, friendly, locally owned businesses.

- ✔ **Social media is the great brand truth-teller.** It presents brands as most people see them. Activated by social media, customers become brand mouthpieces, spreading praise or pans and affecting brand perceptions for better or worse. In today's customer-empowered marketplace, satisfaction and loyalty levels hinge on brand awareness of and responsiveness to their wants, needs, comments, concerns, and especially complaints.

The only way to successfully develop brand loyalty via social media is to begin with a true interest in developing customer relationships, to make your brand accessible for two-way communication with customers, and then to communicate directly with messages that are relevant, useful, interactive, and most of all authentic. For help, scan this list of tips:

- ✔ **Establish a social media voice people like and want to hang out with.** Present brand posts by individuals, or at least present them in a voice that sounds like it comes from a person — not a faceless corporation — that people find authentic and likable.

- ✔ **Listen more than you talk.** This guideline applies to all communication channels but gets ignored most frequently where it matters most: on social media networks.

- ✔ **Be conversational.** Instead of spewing sales messages through posts, robo-direct mails or other means that border on spam, share meaningful, useful, relevant messages that ask questions, invite input, prompt sharing, or, at the very least, strike the recipient as truly interesting.

✔ **Give credit.** Quote other sources or people, share content posted by others, pass along good ideas you've heard from others, and always give credit and thanks for the content you curate and pass along.

✔ **Watch comments more closely than metrics.** Put differently, value interaction more highly than engagement. The number of followers, shares, leads generated or other quantifiable statistics are important, but a conversation with a customer, sparked by a comment and kindled by a response, is where loyalty catches fire.

For a case study demonstrating the success of developing customer loyalty, see the sidebar "How SOL REPUBLIC enlists and rewards loyal SOLdiers of Sound."

Generating buzz that spreads virally

We're not talking about stinging insects or infectious diseases here. Instead, viral buzz comes from developing passionate customers through messages that make noise, get people talking, magnetize interest, and spread on their own because of the nature of their content.

In the first edition of *Branding For Dummies,* we called *buzz marketing* high-powered word-of-mouth that aims to get people to tell other people who then tell other people about your brand and its products and service, spreading the message like a virus that transmits on its own far and wide. Digital communications have skyrocketed viral marketing up the list of branding priorities because brand-builders want the high levels of awareness, interest, and passion it generates so effectively. But with the enthusiasm comes confusion about the terms involved. These definitions help:

✔ **Word-of-mouth** is age-old. It's the result of one person telling another person an opinion or a recap of an experience about your brand, business, or product. In person, the word may get passed along dozens or hundreds of times. Online, it can reach thousands — at least. You can encourage customers to pass along good comments, but you're a passive player in the game and have to take whatever word-of-mouth you get.

✔ **Buzz marketing** involves planned efforts to place, post, or air communications aimed at generating high levels of interest, conversation, and excitement. When someone sees an ad, video, post, or other brand communication and feels compelled to talk about it or spread the word, that's buzz marketing in action.

✔ **Viral marketing** takes buzz marketing a step further. Viral marketing turns customers into your brand-marketing channel. It involves attention-seizing, brand-enhancing messages that break rules, make waves, and so highly engage customers that they follow your call to action and use easy-to-use sharing prompts that drive social-media exposure, more views, more sharing, and, best, more sales.

Takeaways from best-of-viral case studies

Creating a video or post a graphic that goes viral and gets shared and viewed millions of times is one thing. It's another, far preferable, thing to reach those in your target audience with a communication capable of getting them to not only enjoy or benefit from your message but also to take the action the piece intends to prompt *and* transmit it to others.

When aiming to generate customer-to-customer viral marketing for your brand, keep these proven tips in mind:

✔ **Be cool and ride a trend.** Strike a chord by tying your message into conversations that are trending on social media or strongly on the radar screens of customers. Blendtec's "Will It Blend?" videos garnered 15 million YouTube views in part by blending an iPad in a video that tied into the fascination with destruction and the popularity of the then-new tablet device.

✔ **Be provocative.** As the saying goes, give 'em something to talk about. In your communication, do or say something unexpected, stunning, or, as the maker of the virally developed MillionDollarHomePage.com put it, announce "something crazy enough to work." An example: The bacon coffin, by the makers of Baconnaise and Bacon Salt, was announced on April Fool's Day (talk about tapping into social interest) and was so amusing to those who "love bacon to death" that the news clip announcing its availability took on a life of its own.

✔ **Give something away.** Or if you don't give it away, include an offer that's such a good deal it's too good to overlook. Hotmail is an example of a virally transmitted free deal. It broke rules by offering the first free email service. What's more, every free message sent included the invitation, "Get your private, free email at `http://www.hotmail.com`," ensuring that early adopters virally spread the word.

✔ **Prompt interaction.** Invite input, responses to poll questions, photos of fans wearing logo apparel, suggestions for next-generation offerings, participation in contests — always posting responses to showcase customer passion and inspire viral sharing of the brand message.

✔ **Make sharing super simple.** Comments, contests, and click-to-share invitations drive media exposure. Offers that gain value through sharing (Groupon deals are a good example) help early adopters bring their friends into your customer circle. Always the goal is the same: Make sharing effortless, or at least as easy as a single click.

REAL WORLD

Gamifying brand spirit

In 2004, when the Mozilla Foundation introduced the open-source web browser Firefox, it launched a user-organized viral campaign titled *Spread Firefox* that did exactly as its name implied. Within days of the browser launch, Firefox was generating a million downloads a day. Tens of thousands of brand fans signed up to serve as marketing volunteers on a quest to get websites to display Firefox promotional buttons and banners and to spread the Firefox word through blogs, chat rooms, mainstream media, and even a full-page ad in *The New York Times,* paid for with donated dollars.

As the brand evolved, Firefox created a brand-fan leaderboard that affiliates could climb based on clicks generated, winning Firefox gear along the way in a gamified rewards program that as of mid-2014 involved nearly 70,000 affiliates posting brand banners in more than 30 languages. To get an idea for how the Firefox viral marketing campaign is presented and used, visit www.spreadfirefox.com.

Loyalty program do's and don'ts

Loyalty programs reward repeat purchasers with discounts, rewards, or added value offers.

Chances are good you're a member of an airline frequent flyer rewards program and that you carry at least one loyalty reward card for a local business in your billfold. Most loyalty programs take one of these forms:

- ✔ **Buy-ahead discounts** that a customer pays for upfront, receiving an immediate bonus at the time of purchase and the promise of ongoing discounts thereafter. The business benefits from upfront revenue and by locking in customer commitment, but because a purchase is involved the customer tends to view the program more as a financial benefit than a customer reward that fosters brand love and loyalty.

- ✔ **Purchase-level gifts, rebates, or discounts** reward customers with when they pass spending levels. The business benefits from increased purchases, but because the programs usually come with fine print about what kinds of purchases apply and over what time period, the programs lack the kind of simplicity that generates widespread appeal. They also attract attention from those who are most cost- and deal-sensitive unless the rewards are carefully crafted to appeal to the most loyal, passionate brand fans.

✔ **Upgrades and special treatments** are the loyalty-development sweet spot. Surprise rewards that seem individualized and spontaneous deepen brand passion like no other form of loyalty program. When you occasionally say, essentially, "this one's on us," or "this is just to say thanks," about the only caution to consider is that customers will anticipate and expect acknowledgement again in the future. But if that happens, 1) they're returning to your business, which is the point of a loyalty program, and 2) you get the chance to dream up an even more inspired demonstration of appreciation to win an even higher degree of enthusiasm for your brand.

Be sure any loyalty program you host gives customers valued rewards that show your appreciation and exceed their expectations. Avoid any program that resembles a purchase-inspiring promotion with strings attached ($10 off your next purchase of any regularly priced product of $25 or more through the end of the month) or that looks more like a benefit to your business than a gift to your customer.

How SOL REPUBLIC enlists and rewards loyal SOLdiers of Sound

Brands that win fan loyalty start with fan loyalty in mind. The global consumer electronics company SOL REPUBLIC (solrepublic.com) is a good example.

The brand name — SOL stands for Soundtrack of Life — deserves a shoutout in the naming chapter of this book, and its brand promise provides a real-world template that any brand would be smart to follow: celebrating the people who make music, love music, and are devoted to music. The company declares its commitment to creating a community where music fans, athletes, and all dreamers are welcome to put a voice to their ideas, share their sound, and be heard.

The brand launched not with a website but with a Facebook page that aimed to generate viral sharing among what it called SOLdiers of Sound. It worked. By mid-2014 the brand had 30,000 Twitter followers, 30,000 YouTube subscribers, 45,000 Instagram followers, and a half million Facebook fans, a contingent that now has its own active online community.

To generate similar engagement, SOL REPUBLIC's Director of Social, Nora Walker, shares this advice:

✔ **Be authentic:** "We stay true to who we are. We're a brand created by and for music lovers with on-ear and over-ear products for everyone, all completely customizable (our Remix offering), at very affordable price points, and virtually indestructible so they're made to last." *Takeaway:* Know and convey your brand, your brand position, your brand voice and language, and your brand promise.

- **Reach the right people with relevant content:** "As Facebook became more pay-to-play, we shifted to using targeted promoted posts rather than fan-acquisition ads. We're a music-lifestyle brand and find promoted posts the best way to reach a relevant audience, target against our competitive set, raise awareness, and drive the greatest purchase intent amongst fans and non-fans alike. Our approach on Twitter, which is still refining its product suite, is to get relevant content in front of consumers based on real-time signals of context — whether they're talking about broken headphones, searching for competitors, commenting on artists we work with, or watching broadcasts for which we have a relevant product. We're always testing and measuring new approaches, creative, and copy for impact." *Takeaway:* Target your audience and message, engage with prospects, test effectiveness, adapt, stay authentic, repeat.

- **Measure success:** "As a newer brand in the audio technology and music lifestyle space, we're still working to establish who we are as a brand and what sets us apart from our competitors in a rapidly growing marketplace. It's nice to have a million-plus Facebook fans, but for us the priority is to use our media dollars to reach the largest, most relevant audience for our brand and to drive engagement with the best content we can put forward. Awareness is a huge objective in our social program. We measure success primarily by exposure to and engagement with our content and recruitment into our SOLdiers of Sound community. Each month, we're able to reach millions of people on Facebook through this approach." *Takeaway:* It's not about how many people you reach. It's about how effectively you're reaching your target audience with meaningful content that engages their interest and draws them into your community where they make your brand their brand.

- **Control your brand's digital presence:** "The SOLdiers of Sound community is key to our brand strategy because it's an owned environment that we can adapt and where we can retain our most loyal and passionate brand audience. While social platforms evolve and change, our community lives primarily at SOLdierofsound.com." *Takeaway:* Don't leave your most-valuable communications to chance. Leverage media channels to reach your target audience, but establish and retain loyal customer relationships in a community you know you can control and protect.

- **Reward loyalty:** "Our SOLdier community collects limited edition headbands they can use to remix our Tracks headphones — some of which we sell on our website, others that we give away exclusively via social media. We're always looking to offer SOLdier discounts and special offers which they can earn through a wide variety of challenges." *Takeaway:* Create fans, reward fans, and retain fans by keeping the fan experience fun, exciting, and valuable.

- **Share. Don't sell:** "We try to strike a balance between lifestyle content and product- or sales-driving efforts. When discussing product, we use a conversational, engaging tone, and creative approaches that portray our products in a lifestyle context that feels natural without screaming, *buy, buy, buy.* Of course there are times we aim to drive sales, but we make sure our creative is on-brand and our messaging is timely and relevant. *Takeaway:* Use social to be social. Use content to pull interest. Use relevant, timely offers to convert interest to followers and followers to brand loyalists.

Recipe for a cult brand

Cult brands happen when customers take brand passion to the nth degree. They happen when customers adopt the brand as *theirs* instead of yours. When you hear people say *my iPod, my Google news page, my IKEA,* or *my Netflix queue,* they've assumed ownership of the brand and its product or service.

For as long as brands have existed, there have been cult brands. But in the past, most cult brands were small, underdog, or offbeat brands that attracted I'd-rather-fight-than-switch customers who stood by their brands with pride even when hardly anyone else even knew the brand name.

Today, even the biggest brands inspire cult followings by using all or most of the following strategies:

- ✔ Start with a unique brand identity and promise that customers truly want to be part of. Then spotlight and stay true to your brand differences and distinctions.

- ✔ Offer products that customers not only *can* customize but that you prefer them to customize in order to adapt the products to their unique consumer preferences, no matter how far-out and unusual.

- ✔ Create a brand experience that's like no other and that never, ever, falls short of the customer's expectation.

- ✔ Emphasize viral marketing, buzz marketing, and good old-fashioned word of mouth over traditional advertising. (See the preceding section for more on viral and buzz marketing.)

- ✔ Create fans among your employees and customers, and support development of brand fan clubs, websites, forums, blogs, events, and any other channel that allows those who know and love your brand to share their opinions.

- ✔ Create or at least support the formation of a community of brand fans who personify your brand by displaying it on personalized items, talking about it, and sharing their enthusiasm with others.

Cult brand followers are passionate consumers. They're the kind of brand zealots Winston Churchill could have been talking about when he said, "A fanatic is one who can't change his mind and won't change the subject."

Keeping Your Best Customers

Even customers who trust and value their relationships with your brand will defect if their expectations aren't met. In fact, even those whose expectations *are* met will defect if they sense a *quality gap* (an experience that falls short of expectations) or if another brand wows them with an over-the-top brand experience that makes yours pale in comparison. That's why it's important to conduct a brand audit, following the steps and using the form in Chapter 13, on a regular basis to keep all customer impression points aligned and positive.

Protecting your customer base from defection takes work — and a strong brand. When customers believe in your brand promise, and when they consistently receive a clear brand message and a great brand experience, they're more likely to cut you some slack and remain true to your brand should one encounter fall short once in a rare blue moon.

To measure how well you're doing at delivering an exemplary brand experience, measure your customer satisfaction levels on a frequent basis. Figure 14-1 includes a chart to guide your assessment. Fill it out several times, once following your gut instinct, and again based on input you collect from those who work with customers and manage customer relation departments or functions. Periodically, you should also conduct customer satisfaction research, following the research advice in Chapter 4.

It's never crowded on the extra mile

You've seen the anonymous line that serves as this sidebar title in countless motivational messages, yet the extra mile remains wide open for those willing to double their service, triple their customer attention, quadruple their commitment to customized solutions, and build brand buzz and brand strength as a result.

To move into the elite group of brands that cruise to success by amazing customers with unfailing and exemplary experiences, follow these four steps:

- ✔ **Help employees to think like brand owners, doing whatever they feel is necessary to provide amazing customer experiences, to anticipate and preempt customer needs, to correct defects, and to create passionate customers — and brand enthusiasts — for life.** As an example, visit a page of the Ritz-Carlton website, at `http://corporate.ritzcarlton.com/`

`en/About/GoldStandards`, that shows how the hotel encompasses its values and philosophy through standards that serve as "the foundation of the Ritz-Carlton Hotel Company."

- ✔ **Empower employees to customize solutions and service innovations.** Give your staff parameters, including budget guidelines, to provide on-the-spot customer solutions without having to navigate frustrating management layers.

- ✔ **Recognize and reward outstanding service efforts.** Put a spotlight on team members who go out of their way to convey your brand promise, setting the bar higher for everyone.

- ✔ **Live your brand promise inside and outside your business.** Constantly find better ways to convey your brand message to employees, customers, and all in your community.

ASSESSING THE QUALITY OF YOUR CUSTOMER EXPERIENCE

1. *Assess current and past performance (1=low; 5=high).*
2. *Assess competitors' performance.*
Areas in which performance has slipped or competitors excel indicate potential expectation quality gaps.

Customer Experience Expectation	Your Performance		Competitors' Performance	
	Current	Previous	#1	#2
COMMUNICATION				
Clear/friendly/courteous/informed	1 2 3 4 5	1 2 3 4 5	1 2 3 4 5	1 2 3 4 5
Error-free	1 2 3 4 5	1 2 3 4 5	1 2 3 4 5	1 2 3 4 5
Prompt	1 2 3 4 5	1 2 3 4 5	1 2 3 4 5	1 2 3 4 5
Open to ideas/concerns/complaints	1 2 3 4 5	1 2 3 4 5	1 2 3 4 5	1 2 3 4 5
RESPONSIVENESS				
Customized solutions	1 2 3 4 5	1 2 3 4 5	1 2 3 4 5	1 2 3 4 5
Flexible, effective responses to requests	1 2 3 4 5	1 2 3 4 5	1 2 3 4 5	1 2 3 4 5
Prompt phone/mail/email follow-up	1 2 3 4 5	1 2 3 4 5	1 2 3 4 5	1 2 3 4 5
Prompt greeting by phone or in person	1 2 3 4 5	1 2 3 4 5	1 2 3 4 5	1 2 3 4 5
Lack of service/management barriers	1 2 3 4 5	1 2 3 4 5	1 2 3 4 5	1 2 3 4 5
COMPETENCE				
Relates to customer wants/needs	1 2 3 4 5	1 2 3 4 5	1 2 3 4 5	1 2 3 4 5
Experienced and informed staff	1 2 3 4 5	1 2 3 4 5	1 2 3 4 5	1 2 3 4 5
CONVENIENCE				
Easy phone/in-person/online access	1 2 3 4 5	1 2 3 4 5	1 2 3 4 5	1 2 3 4 5
Convenient location and parking	1 2 3 4 5	1 2 3 4 5	1 2 3 4 5	1 2 3 4 5
Convenient payment/delivery options	1 2 3 4 5	1 2 3 4 5	1 2 3 4 5	1 2 3 4 5
RELIABILITY				
Keeps/exceeds commitments	1 2 3 4 5	1 2 3 4 5	1 2 3 4 5	1 2 3 4 5
Delivers quality	1 2 3 4 5	1 2 3 4 5	1 2 3 4 5	1 2 3 4 5
Good reputation	1 2 3 4 5	1 2 3 4 5	1 2 3 4 5	1 2 3 4 5

Figure 14-1:
Analyzing the quality of your customer experience.

© Barbara Findlay Schenck

Chapter 15

Valuing and Leveraging Your Brand

*I*t seems almost too good to be true that a name, a promise, and a great reputation can be worth thousands, millions, or even billions of dollars, but it's a fact you can bank on when you build and manage a great brand.

Often, when companies are bought and sold, as much as half of the money that trades hands covers the purchase of the brand name and all it means in the marketplace. That means that roughly 50 cents out of every dollar exchanged in many business sales goes not for inventory, buildings, physical items, business contracts, accounts receivable, or other tangible assets but for the purchase of the brand — something no one can actually see or touch, which is why brand equity is called an *intangible asset*.

Brand equity is so important that, in the world's most successful businesses, the most valuable single intangible asset is the brand.

Great brands are great assets. This chapter helps you get your money's worth by defining what it takes to build the value of your brand, how to convert brand value to brand equity (and how to protect that equity), how to measure and enhance your brand's worth, and how to leverage the value of your brand through cautious and smart co-branding, brand extensions, and brand licensing opportunities.

The Brand Value–Brand Equity Connection

The value of a brand results from two elements:

- ✔ **How your brand is valued by consumers:** Your brand's value in consumer minds is the result of public perception formed by all the impressions your brand makes in its marketplace. If you're making impressions that are positive and consistent, your brand's value is likely to be positive and consistent, too. If impressions are erratic or even negative, brand value is likely to waver and sink.

- ✔ **How your brand is valued by investors or prospective brand buyers:** Your brand's value as an asset is called *brand equity*. Brand equity is determined by a complex process that assesses the monetary value of your brand based not only on current consumer perceptions but also on the ability of your brand to deliver economic advantages in the future.

Revving up the economic engine

From its invisible post deep in consumers' minds, brand value drives market activity. When your brand value is high, your brand enjoys a long lineup of economic advantages, including

- ✔ **Premium pricing:** When consumers in your target market hold your brand's attributes and promise in high esteem, they're willing to pay more for what they perceive is higher value and lower risk than they believe is represented by lesser-known or lesser-valued alternatives. As a result of high brand value, your brand enjoys the benefit of lower price sensitivity. What's more, customers purchase highly valued brands even when the price fluctuates, because their decision is based more on the perception of brand quality than on product price.

- ✔ **Lower cost of sales:** When people value a brand highly, their feeling of risk is reduced and their inclination to buy is increased because they believe in the brand's offerings and its well-accepted image. This leads to greater sales volume and greater likelihood of repeat purchases without the need for extensive and costly sales promotions, sales negotiations, and customer-retention efforts on your part. As a result, high brand value allows you to reduce initial sales-acquisition costs and, subsequently, to amortize a one-time sales expense across multiple purchases and a longtime client or customer relationship.

- ✔ **Lower cost of promotion:** Customers who value your brand highly become brand ambassadors. They enhance your brand's marketplace visibility by speaking well on your behalf, spreading positive word-of-mouth and online mentions, and recruiting others into your clientele at no additional promotional cost to your business.

✔ **Higher market share:** When customers stay loyal to your business — and recruit new customers to boot — you enjoy increased *market share,* which is the percentage of market activity captured by each competitor in a market arena. Dominant market share provides a two-pronged economic advantage: It reduces your brand's need for new business development expenses while boosting your brand's immunity from competitive attacks.

✔ **Lower employee turnover:** High brand value almost always exists in the minds of employees before it reaches the minds of consumers. (Chapter 13 is full of tips for instilling a sense of brand value and brand passion in your employee team.) When customers catch brand spirit from employees, they tend to pass their brand enthusiasm back to employees, making employees' jobs easier and far more enjoyable, thereby reducing employee turnover.

Gaining a competitive advantage

Strong brand value inoculates an organization against competitive threats it may otherwise face. It also provides a number of other competitive advantages, including:

✔ **Consumer recognition:** Brands with high brand value enjoy strong support and loyalty from customers. This loyalty results in long-term relationships that are resistant to overtures from competitors. It also results in higher sales volume, lower cost of sales, and greater return on investments in business development and customer retention.

✔ **Industry recognition:** Brands with high value enjoy stature in their industries or business arenas that results in advantageous leadership roles, trade media coverage, favorable relationships with suppliers, and preferential supplier terms.

✔ **Media recognition:** High brand value results in high levels of market awareness, including awareness among those who cover news stories. When seeking comments from industry leaders, news writers call on the names they know, catapulting high-value brands to even greater prominence.

✔ **Financial industry recognition:** The financial world monitors brand value as an indicator of the strength of an organization's management and corporate health. Analysts and investors see strong brands as reflections of strong businesses that they reward with higher levels of investment, lower cost of capital, and advantageous financial relationships.

To assess the current value of your brand, use the worksheet in Figure 15-1.

ASSESSING CONSUMER PERCEPTION OF BRAND VALUE: WORKSHEET

Circle responses and add up your score. Totals closest to 100 indicate high brand value.

Customers are willing to pay a premium to purchase your offering over a similar solution.	Rarely Frequently 1 2 3 4 5 6 7 8 9 10	
Customers typically return for additional purchases without promotional incentives.	Rarely Frequently 1 2 3 4 5 6 7 8 9 10	
Customers arrive at your point of purchase with confidence in your brand and consistently follow through with a product selection and purchase.	Rarely Frequently 1 2 3 4 5 6 7 8 9 10	
Your customers and business associates refer new customers to your business.	Rarely Frequently 1 2 3 4 5 6 7 8 9 10	
Customers change their minds and choose not to purchase upon close consideration at the point of sale.	Frequently Rarely 1 2 3 4 5 6 7 8 9 10	
Customers abandon your business for another in your market area, either due to discontentment or better deals.	Frequently Rarely 1 2 3 4 5 6 7 8 9 10	
Your sales have increased consistently over past years, with equally strong increases in profits.	Definitely Not Definitely 1 2 3 4 5 6 7 8 9 10	
Your brand is presented positively in industry reviews, business coverage, and other publicity.	Rarely Frequently 1 2 3 4 5 6 7 8 9 10	
When you raise prices, purchases by established customers decline.	Frequently Rarely 1 2 3 4 5 6 7 8 9 10	
Your highest-priced or highest-profit offerings are among your best selling items.	Definitely Not Definitely 1 2 3 4 5 6 7 8 9 10	

Figure 15-1:
Assess how consumers value your brand.

Estimating Your Brand's Equity

When a customer goes out of his way to buy a pair of sneakers bearing a certain logo, a cup of coffee from a certain outlet, jewelry in a certain pale blue box, a donut made while-you-watch at a certain bakery, or a reference book bound in a certain yellow-and-black cover, he does so because he believes the product he's buying offers a unique set of benefits. Those benefits translate into what consumers perceive as brand value.

When consumers go out of their way on a repeated basis, when they willingly pay a premium to obtain the set of benefits they attribute to a branded product, and when they encourage others to do the same, they deliver an economic advantage — brand equity — to the brand owner.

Brand equity measuring sticks

To measure brand equity, most brand evaluators assess a brand's ability to achieve premium pricing, lower costs, and business strength and growth.

Sales performance

As a starting point in evaluating the worth of your brand, assess whether your sales are going up and at what rate.

1. **Calculate the percentage of sales growth your brand has experienced for each of the past three years.**

   For example, if two years ago your sales totaled $3 million and last year they grew to $3.25 million, your business experienced one-year growth of 8.3 percent. (Sales were up $250,000, and $250,000 ÷ $3 million = 8.3 percent.)

2. **Calculate your average sales growth over the past three years by totaling the growth (or decline) of sales over each of the past three years and then dividing that number by three.**

   For example, if you experienced 5 percent sales growth three years ago, 5 percent sales growth two years ago, and 8 percent growth last year, your three-year average growth rate is 6 percent ([5 + 5 + 8] ÷ 3 = 6).

3. **Indicate if extraneous circumstances factored into the growth or decline of any of the past three years.**

   For example, if your business underwent a significant remodel that resulted in fewer customers and lower sales over a one-year period, note that factor and explain how the remodel contributed to brand worth even as it detracted from sales revenue.

4. Indicate if extraneous circumstances will affect the growth of sales over future years.

For example, if your business projects flat sales for the next few years as you complete development of a major new product, explain the development schedule and how the product launch will result in future sales and increased brand worth.

Unless you explain circumstances that affected your recent sales growth (or lack thereof), it's fair for brand evaluators to assume that your average sales growth over the past three years indicates the sales growth rate you'll achieve during the next few years.

Marketing strength

The size, growth rate, and composition of your market arena also affect your brand equity. Obviously, if the size of your market is decreasing, if consumer preferences are turning away from your brand attributes, or if new competitors are grabbing large slices of what used to be your share of market, the worth of your brand suffers. Measuring brand equity by marketing strength requires you to address the following questions:

✔ **Is your business arena one with growing or declining market interest?** For instance, the home sewing industry, the ski industry, and the tennis and golf industries are arenas that have seen consumer participation decline over recent years. In contrast, pet ownership, wine consumption, and healthcare usage are all up.

To assess trends in your industry, go to a major public library reference area and consult the *Lifestyle Market Analyst* from SRDS and Nielsen. The publication presents lifestyle and demographic information for residents of 210 major U.S. market areas. By obtaining your market area statistics for current and past years, you can determine whether the population of people who fit your customer profile is growing or declining.

✔ **Is consumer demand for your offering growing or declining?** Consult your own records first. Are your inquiries, your new customer accounts, and your customer purchase rates increasing or decreasing? Then obtain information from publications that serve your business arena. Are their subscription and circulation counts on the increase? Does your business association show increased or decreased activity in your business arena? Together, your findings can help you make a case regarding the strength of consumer demand for your brand's offerings.

✔ **Is your business arena getting more competitive, and is your brand faring better or worse in the competitive field?** List your top competitors for each of the past three years, along with how you ranked in terms of sales against each one. Note whether competitors have entered or left your market arena and whether competitors have gained or slipped in market share against your brand. The degree to which you're gaining business from competitors is a good indication of brand strength and worth.

Brand experience

Your *brand experience* is the means by which customers form impressions about your brand, and as such, it links directly to your brand's success. To assess your brand experience, use the worksheets that appear in Chapter 13. Also consider the following questions:

- Are your brand's distinguishing attributes clear and consistently conveyed?

- Are the benefits your brand promises ones of increasing value to consumers?

- Does your brand convey and keep its brand promise at every point of contact, whether with employees, prospects, customers, consumers, suppliers, investors, shareholders, or other stakeholders?

Brand value

To assess your brand value as a contributor to your brand equity, use the worksheet in Figure 15-1. If necessary, conduct research, following the guidelines in Chapter 5, to deepen your understanding of customer opinions and purchase tendencies. Use your findings to address the following questions. As you arrive at answers, realize that positive responses indicate that your brand value is strong, a mixed-bag set of responses indicates that your brand value is at risk, and a lineup of "no" answers indicates that your brand needs serious repair in order to restore its value.

- Is your customer base growing?

- Is your customer retention rate increasing? (Conversely, is your customer attrition rate — your *churn rate* — rising?)

- Is your brand awareness level increasing? When prospective customers are asked to name the top few brands that come to mind in your business arena, how many cite your name, and has that number grown or declined over recent years?

- Is your brand's mindshare increasing? When prospective customers are asked to name the *top* brand that comes to mind in your market arena, how many cite your name, and has that number grown or declined over recent years?

- Is your average sale price and profitability increasing?

  The degree to which consumers pay a premium for your offering, from additional cents to big bucks, depending on the average price of your offering in the marketplace, is often viewed as a primary indicator of your brand's market advantage and resulting equity.

Calculating your brand equity

Brands are worth money. As proof, John Stuart, one of the 20th century's great business leaders and a former CEO of the Quaker Oats Company, is quoted as saying, "If this business were split up, I would give you the land and bricks and mortar, and I would take the brands and trademarks, and I would fare better than you."

To figure out the equity of your brand so that you know the worth of the asset you're building, protecting, and leveraging *or* so that you understand your brand's possible sale price, use either or both of these two approaches:

- ✔ Assess the costs involved to establish or replace your brand.
- ✔ Assess the economic worth of your brand based on its market share advantage, price premium advantage, cost of sale advantages, and reputation.

Figuring out the cost of establishing or replacing your brand

One approach to estimating your brand's worth is to figure out what it would cost if you were to create your brand today or if the organization seeking to purchase your brand were to try to build your brand from scratch.

In assessing your brand from this angle, take the following into account:

- ✔ **The cost of creating your brand identity,** including
  - Name development and registration
  - Logo development and trademarking
  - Slogan development and trademarking
  - Domain name registration and establishment of web presence
  - Development of brand-identifying elements such as a unique and widely accepted color scheme, an olfactory signature or scent, a musical signature, and other elements that contribute to what your market understands to be the identity of your brand
- ✔ **The cost to achieve your current level of market awareness,** including
  - Advertising
  - Promotion
  - Digital presence
  - Publicity to achieve knowledge of your brand name, your brand message and promise, and your brand benefits and distinctions

✔ **The cost to attract and retain your current clientele,** including

- Advertising

- Promotions

- Lead generation

- Customer acquisition

- Relationship development

- Implementation of loyalty programs necessary to develop the level of customer retention and passion that contributes to your current levels of sales, repeat purchases, and positive reviews, ratings, comments, and word-of-mouth

Determining the economic value of your brand's premium market position

When businesses get ready to sell brands, often they begin by calculating the actual economic advantage of the brand. You can assess your own economic advantage by watching two indicators:

✔ **Price elasticity:** When your consumer demand remains high even when your prices go up, your brand enjoys pricing leeway known as *favorable price elasticity*. Price elasticity usually results from high brand value and usually leads to premium pricing.

✔ **Premium pricing:** To assess your brand's pricing advantage, determine how much extra consumers are willing to pay in order to purchase your branded product instead of the offering of a lesser-known or lesser-valued brand. This difference, multiplied by your sales volume, indicates the economic value of your premium market position.

In other words, high brand value leads to favorable price elasticity, favorable price elasticity leads to premium pricing, and premium pricing leads to higher brand equity.

To calculate the worth of your premium pricing position use this formula:

1. **Determine the price difference between your offering and generic offerings or offerings from lesser-known or less-respected brands.**

   For example, if a six-partner accounting firm sells time for $100 an hour and average rates in the firm's market area are $85, the accountants' price premium equals $15. Or if a bottled water product sells for $2.29 and competing, nonbranded products or products with lesser brands sell for $1.99, the branded water's price premium is $0.30.

2. **Multiply the price difference by the number of units sold.**

   If the six-partner accounting firm sells a total of 10,000 partner hours a year, its annual price premium equals $150,000 (100,000 hours × $15 price premium). If the bottled water producer sells 600,000 bottles a year, its annual price premium equals $180,000 (600,000 bottles × $0.30 price premium).

3. **Adjust your result to account for future brand performance projections.**

   These projections include the likelihood that customers will continue to behave in a similar manner in the future, that the brand's current economic reality is transferable to new owners, and that the brand's momentum will continue at its current pace. For example, if a service business commands premium pricing in large part due to the powerful reputation of the owner, and if the owner wants to sell the brand and depart the business, then the value of the price premium would likely be discounted by those considering a purchase of the brand.

When calculating the worth of a brand's premium price position, be aware that the number you arrive at is a valuation starting point, not the finishing line. The effect of future brand-building activities, market growth or retraction trends, actions of competitors, and other market realities affect whether the value of the price premium should be adjusted upward or downward in assessing the brand's worth.

Identifying evaluation experts

If you're thinking about selling your brand in full or in part, a good first step is to follow the advice in the preceding section so that you have a sense of what you believe to be your brand's worth. From there, you may have enough information to begin sale negotiations for a smaller brand, but for larger brands, it's worth it to call on professional assistance.

Evaluating the worth of a brand is both an art and a science. To obtain expert assistance, take these steps:

- ✔ Visit the website www.brandchannel.com, produced by Interbrand. Search the site for "equity evaluation" to reach case studies, white papers, and brand valuation advice. Go to the About Interbrand section and click "Our Work by Discipline" for information on Interbrand's brand valuation services.

- ✔ Contact brand development specialists in your market area to see if they're experts at brand valuation or to seek their assistance in reaching those who are.

- ✔ Conduct a web search for "brand equity valuation experts" to find resources for information and brand valuation.

Leveraging your brand equity

Leveraging your brand's equity is like boosting your next business opportunity with a loan from your own strong reputation.

When you have a valuable brand you're in a great position to take the credibility you've established and apply it to the launch of a new or related product or business — with instantaneous recognition thanks to the reservoir of goodwill and trust that resides in your brand identity and image.

Most leveraging opportunities take the form of

✔ **Brand extensions,** which extend the power of an established brand to a new but often related business or product line

✔ **Line extensions,** which add variety to the offerings of an established brand by extending the brand to new but closely related products

✔ **Licensing,** which essentially rents or leases your brand to another company that pays all expenses to produce and market a product that carries your licensed brand identity in return for a licensing fee and royalties on wholesale revenues

✔ **Cobranding,** which capitalizes on the mutual benefits of your brand and the brand of a promotional partner

Regardless of the approach, leveraging your brand into new opportunities requires careful planning and cautious implementation, covered in the second half of this chapter.

Protecting Your Brand Equity

For as long as you own your brand, you have to protect its value by following the same marketing approach you used to build the brand's equity in the first place, described in Chapter 2 and detailed in the first two parts of this book.

Chapter 9 includes advice for planning your brand launch, including how to set strategies for each of the four Ps in the marketing mix: product, pricing, promotion, and place (or distribution). As you build and protect your brand, regularly update your brand marketing plan, always monitoring these four strategic areas to be sure that all brand marketing decisions are consistent with your brand position, promise, and image.

✔ **Product:** If you adopt new product lines or make product adjustments, be sure they match your brand image and market position, including the quality for which your brand is known. While some brands have extended successfully into lower-level market positions, most success stories involve brand extensions that match the quality of the established brand image and market position.

✔ **Pricing:** Make all pricing decisions with your brand's market position and image in mind. Discounting is a popular way to win quick sales, but if your market position is that of the high-end, elite brand, a discounting strategy is probably also a quick way to ruin brand esteem.

✔ **Promotion:** Be sure all promotions are consistent with your brand identity. As brands mature, too often leaders loosen their grip, turning brand management over to those with less passion or understanding. The result is costly, brand-eroding diversion from the brand image and promise.

✔ **Place:** As you broaden your distribution — the way you get your product to your market — be sure to select channels that support your brand identity. Too many high-end brands have suffered by cutting distribution deals that send their best-branded offerings to warehouse outlets, later receiving a very cold shoulder from top-tier retailers with whom they'd built their reputations and clientele.

As if that weren't a long enough list to consider when protecting your brand equity, there's one more "P" to consider, and that's people — the employees who power your brand experience. Turn to Chapter 13 for plenty of advice on how to build brand spirit within your organization and how to achieve brand delivery excellence by developing a team of enthusiastic, knowledgeable, and passionate brand champions.

Planning for Product Innovations

Of the tens of thousands of new products that enter the retail arena each year, most die early deaths and few soar into the news as success stories. That's the bad news. The good news is that most of those that "make it" — those that beat the dire product start-up odds — have two things in common that, as a brand owner, you can leverage to your advantage.

The first common trait is that the innovation provides meaningfully different benefits from what exists in the marketplace. The second common trait shared by most successful new products is that they ride into the market on the magic carpet of a known name. That's why most bestselling new books are by known authors, and most top-selling new music releases are by known artists. Most successful new products either carry the names of known brands or are fueled by the powerful endorsements of known authorities or personalities. By gliding into the market on the current of an established brand, a new product debuts with the advantage of instant credibility, a strength that's basically borrowed from a brand name and reputation that may have taken years, decades, or even longer to build.

Leveraging a brand name is lucrative as long as you avoid some danger zones. If your new product doesn't align with your brand message and promise, or if it doesn't build on the emotional connection you've established with your customers, you can actually hurt your brand in the process of trying to help your new product.

Figure 15-2 illustrates the opportunities you can pursue as you aim to increase purchases by current customers and to attract new customers into your business.

	Current Customers		
E s t. P r o d u c t s	Reposition or revitalize your established products to increase purchases by current customers	Launch radically changed or altogether new products to increase purchases by current customers	**N e w P r o d u c t s**
	Reposition or revitalize your established products to attract purchases by new customers	Launch radically changed or altogether new products to attract purchases by new customers	
	New Customers		

Figure 15-2: Sales growth options.

© Barbara Findlay Schenck

Product innovations range from minor revisions to brand-new product introductions. Most new products fit into one of the following categories:

- **Brand extension:** When you introduce a new product or product line that supports your core brand message and promise while taking your brand outside its initial category, it's called a *brand extension*. A few examples include Starbucks Coffee Liqueur, Axe Face and Shave, and the Adidas training watch.

- **Line extension:** When you introduce a variation of your existing product or service that features the same characteristics and primary benefit of your established offering but with a new secondary benefit, it's called a *line extension*. Examples include Diet Coke, Crest Extra Whitening Toothpaste, and Dove Sensitive Skin Body Wash.

- **Repositioning:** When you present your established product in a way that causes consumers to think of it differently, expanding or altering its target market as a result, it's called *repositioning*. A few examples include St. Joseph Aspirin as a cardiac health treatment and Arm & Hammer Baking Soda as a cleaning, deodorizing and even cat litter box solution.

✔ **Revitalization:** When you make anything from a moderate to a radical product change to address evolving market realities with new packaging, benefits, pricing, or distribution, it's called *revitalizing*. A few examples include Kool-Aid Singles packets for making single servings of Kool-Aid, H&R Block TaxCut Online and Software for do-it-yourself tax preparation, and Tostitos Scoops for those preferring thinner, crispier, shaped-for-dipping version of Tostitos. (See Chapter 17 for more complete information on revitalizing your brand and offering.)

Some new products enter the market as new brand launches, following all the brand-introduction steps outlined in Chapter 9. Others take a profitable shortcut by entering the market as brand extensions or line extensions, riding in on the strength of an established brand identity.

As you leverage your brand, realize that you're working with a very valuable asset. In some ways, extending your brand is like taking out a home equity loan to underwrite a new investment. It's a great idea as long as the new venture you're funding doesn't shake the stability of your established asset. Before dipping into the reservoir of goodwill of your brand, look long and hard at the new product opportunity you're considering.

Tiptoeing into a Brand Extension

Most brands loan the value of their names in one of two ways:

✔ **Line extensions stretch the brand name to cover a new offering with new and different consumer benefits in the brand's current product category and consistent with the brand's established promise, position, and quality level.**

✔ **Brand extensions stretch the brand name to new product categories, usually in one of three ways:**

- By entering a new price or quality category in the same general product arena (such as a car company launching a new make and model)

- By entering a new but adjacent product category (such as Crest toothpaste moving into Crest toothbrushes or whiteners)

- By entering a completely new category (such as Nike introducing sunglasses or wearable technology)

Both forms of leverage — brand extensions and line extensions — come with some common advantages and risks.

✔ **On the plus side:**

- The new offering enjoys faster market acceptance at lower promotional costs than would be required if the product were to enter the market with a name consumers have never heard of.

- The extension allows the brand to reach current and new customers with a new offering capable of generating new sales revenue.

- Announcement of the new product allows the brand to strengthen and renew its brand message and promise in the marketplace.

✔ **On the minus side:**

- If the new product doesn't match the brand's position and promise, it can confuse customers and shake their confidence in the brand.

- If the nature of the new product causes the brand to drift from the brand's core message and promise, it can dilute the brand's strength and reduce brand loyalty and passion at the same time.

When extending your brand, the safest bet is to stay in your same product category or to stretch only so far as a complementary category. For example, a window manufacturer may safely extend its brand to screens and awnings.

Extending your name to a distant product category is the equivalent of making a loan to a risky venture, and any good banker will tell you that there's a reason why loan requests for risky ventures are routinely declined. When the profile of the applicant doesn't match the risk of the request, a bank loan officer simply says "no." When it comes to brand extensions, sometimes brand managers need to issue the same response.

If you see an opportunity to extend your brand into an altogether new category, proceed with caution, making certain that your brand promise still makes perfect sense in the new market arena. If it doesn't, either decline the new product opportunity, or seize it under the banner of an altogether new brand, following every step in the preceding chapters of this book. The section "Putting your extension idea through the hoops" later in this chapter helps you separate good extension ideas from brand-damaging ones.

Avoiding line-extension traps

Of the thousands of new products introduced each year, more than half are line extensions that carry the name and all the characteristics of an established brand while offering a distinct new advantage to the market.

When you extend your line, you seize a number of opportunities.

- ✔ You capture a greater share of your current customer's billfold by giving that person more reasons to buy from your business.

- ✔ You attract new customers by offering a new benefit and purchase incentive. For instance, adding a low-fat version of your product allows you to attract weight-conscious prospects. Offering single-sized portions allows you to serve one-person households and also to gain trial usage by those not willing to make larger-quantity purchases.

- ✔ In the retail arena, you expand brand presence by creating the need for more shelf space.

- ✔ Internally, you wring more profitability out of existing marketing and production investments.

Offsetting the upsides of line extensions are some major pitfalls to avoid:

- ✔ If the new product doesn't live up to brand expectations in terms of quality, market position, consumer preference, or brand promise, it erodes brand confidence in a hurry. Remember New Coke?

- ✔ If the new product extends your line to a mind-boggling and indistinct assortment, customers can become confused, which leads to selection dilemmas that result in no purchase at all.

- ✔ If people view the new offering as an improvement of an existing product in your line, they may purchase the new offering at the expense of the established offering (called *product cannibalization* and advisable only if you're trying to phase out the cannibalized product).

- ✔ If those inside your company aren't clear about the distinct attributes and target market for the new offering, or if they feel the new offering cannibalizes existing offerings, uncertainty and internal competition may result among the very people who should be championing your products.

Before extending your product line, answer the questions in Figure 15-3.

Looking before leaping into brand extensions

In many ways, an established brand is like a magic wand for new product introductions. But (there's always a hitch when something seems almost too good to be true) if you haven't done your homework, extending your brand into a new category can be a dangerous roll of the dice that an article in *AdWeek* described as "delusions of brandeur" and "mercilessly infecting otherwise healthy products."

LINE EXTENSION QUESTIONS TO ADDRESS
Why are you introducing a new product? What new benefits will the product offer?
Is the new product clearly related to your other offerings? Will customers quickly and clearly see both the relationship and the distinct differences?
How are the benefits of the new product distinctly different from the benefits of your current product or products?
Are the benefits of the new product ones that are meaningful and appealing to current and prospective customers?
Does your business have the financial and human resources necessary to create, produce, introduce, and market the new product without harming the strength of your established products?
Will the new product add enough new sales to offset any decreases in sales from existing products that may occur when customers shift purchases to the new offering?
Does the new product closely match the benefits of a competitor's established offering? If so, how will your product distinguish itself and win the purchase decision from existing and prospective customers?
Will the new product extend your line to the point that it becomes so varied it's confusing for customers to understand?
Is the new product completely consistent with your brand position (see Chapter 5) and your brand promise and identity (see Chapter 7)?

Figure 15-3:
Before
stretching
your line,
answer
these
questions.

© Barbara Findlay Schenck

What works? What doesn't?

Marketing graveyards are filled with brand extension failures. At the same time, business publications are filled with headlines heralding brand extension successes. In all cases, the new products started with good ideas, but from there, the paths went in vastly different directions.

In three steps, here's how you can steer your extension away from disaster and toward success:

1. **Make certain that there's a real market opportunity for your new offering.**

   Be sure your offering features innovations that result in meaningful value to customers. Also be sure the excitement for the new offering inside your business is equaled by excitement from those outside your business and in your target customer audience. Turn to Chapter 5 for advice on conducting market research and staking a market position for your offering.

2. **Make certain that your business has the staff, production, and financial resources necessary to support the new product without sacrificing the strength of existing offerings.**

3. **Make certain that your brand message and promise both extend to the new offering.**

   If the new offering isn't in complete alignment with the brand image held by those who know your brand, both your new product and your brand will suffer.

The illustration in Figure 15-4 comes courtesy of Prophet, a global brand consultancy specializing in branding and marketing. It shows how market opportunities, organizational capabilities, and brand relevance must converge to create a "sweet spot" for your brand extension.

Figure 15-4:
The conditions necessary for a feasible brand extension.

Courtesy of Prophet, a global consultancy specializing in branding and marketing

Don't ask your brand to stretch too far

When brand extensions fail, the downfall rarely stems from a lack of organizational ability or market opportunity. Most businesses stop themselves before stretching the ability of their staffs, production facilities, or management capability. And most businesses make sure that sufficient market potential exists before launching new products.

How elastic is your brand?

Brand elasticity is a term that describes a brand's capability to stretch into new product arenas without compromising the image or promise of what the brand offers in its market. A good example of a brand that successfully tested its elasticity is Dole, which for years was marketed as a brand for pineapples. Then research showed that consumers linked Dole to the broader concept of sunshine. Aha! Dole revitalized its brand (see Chapter 17) to stand for high-quality fresh fruit, vegetables, and other foods and extended its brand beyond pineapple to a wide range of products including sorbet, nuts, premium juices, and other offerings.

At the other end of the elasticity spectrum is Disney, which is so thoroughly perceived as a brand that represents family entertainment that it couldn't stretch into movies for mature audiences without creating confusion and conflicts in consumers' minds. That's why you see a second Disney brand — Touchstone Films — on movies that viewers may find too far outside the family entertainment category that they link to the Disney brand.

Most brand extension disasters occur when businesses try to stretch their brand identities into distant product categories where they lack relevance. In doing so, they basically expect the brand's followers to take a giant leap of faith. They assume that the consumer's belief in the brand as a preferred solution in product category A will translate into consumer trust in product categories B, C, and even X, Y, and Z.

Expecting your brand to stretch easily from category A to adjacent categories B and C may be reasonable. For example, asking consumers to believe that Oprah's magazine is a good launching pad for a hardcover book series obviously made sense. Longer stretches, however, get problematic. Remember when high-powered celebrities launched the Planet Hollywood restaurant chain? The effort required consumers to trust that great actors would be great restaurateurs. Shuttered restaurant sites prove otherwise.

Putting your extension idea through the hoops

Before proceeding with a brand extension, test the relevance of your brand to the new category by putting it through the process illustrated in Figure 15-5.

Figure 15-5:
Matching brand extensions to your brand identity.

Your Brand Image
Is it relevant to and enhanced by your new product idea?
If yes

Your Product Category
Does it cover or is it complementary to the category of your new product idea?
If yes

Your Brand Promise
Does it strengthen and is it strengthened by your new product idea?
If yes

Proceed to write your brand extension marketing plan. (See Chapter 9)

© Barbara Findlay Schenck

Rethinking subbrands

A *subbrand* is a brand that's closely tied to a parent brand but that has its own identity and values that distinguish it from the attributes of the top-level brand. If that definition confuses you, imagine what the concept of a subbrand does to the consumer!

Often a brand introduces a subbrand as a way to offer a lower-priced line without harming the esteem of the top-level brand; Four Points by Sheraton and United Airline's Ted are examples of subbrands.

Coauthor Bill Chiaravalle tells his Brand Navigation clients to proceed cautiously with subbrands.

For one thing, brands (whether top-level brands or subbrands) need esteem to succeed, and it's hard to build esteem out of an identity that begins as subordinate to something else. For another thing, subbrands confuse consumers and weaken brand management.

Bill goes so far as to say that there's really no such thing as a subbrand, at least not in the consumer's mind, which is where brands live. To the consumer, a brand is a brand, not a subset of a brand. As a brand manager, you should look at it the same way.

Bill's stance is reinforced by plenty of other brand thought leaders. James Burgin and Jon Ward, coauthors of *Branding For Profit* (Trump University Press), put it this way: "When it comes to brands, the consumer can only count to one." In today's overloaded marketing environment, the human mind takes in and remembers only so much, including one brand at a time.

For example, the consumer sees Diet Coke either as its own brand or as a flavor variety of the Coke brand, not as a subbrand of Coke. Likewise, consumers see Jetta and Passat either as their own brands or as flavors of VW.

The consumer keeps it simple, and as a brand manager, you should, too. When developing the branding strategy for a new product, rather than creating some second-cousin-once-removed relationship, ask "Does this product fit best as a flavor or variation of our established brand? Or does it have a unique enough set of attributes, or fit into a unique enough product category, that it should live under its own brand?" In any case, consider "subbrand" the wrong answer. The discussion of brand architecture in Chapter 2 can give you more information.

Cobranding Cautions

Cobrands capitalize on the benefits of two compatible brands that present similarly desirable attributes to consumers with similar profiles. Cobranding advantages include:

- ✔ Both brands benefit from the opportunity to appeal to a greater customer base than either may be able to reach on its own.

- ✔ Each brand stands to enhance its esteem by borrowing on the strength of the partner brand.

- ✔ The brands share marketing costs, resulting in cost savings for each.

- ✔ Each brand benefits from the perceived endorsement of the other.

Following are the potential dangers of cobranding:

- ✔ Brand management is complicated by the need to integrate the separate operating systems and management approaches of each brand.

- ✔ The cobranded offering can confuse consumers unless the link between the two brands is immediately obvious, sensible, and easy to understand.

- ✔ One brand can be diminished in stature if consumers consider the partner brand to be an incompatible match.

Cobranding efforts may involve strategic alliances in which two brands unite to reach common goals or cobranded promotions in which two brands team up to achieve short-term sales objectives. Efforts may also involve cobranded product introductions in which two brands bring their production and marketing efforts together to achieve a greater market impact than either could achieve alone.

Examples of cobranded product introductions include the Coach Edition of Lexus, the AT&T Universal MasterCard, and the Eddie Bauer Edition of Ford Explorer. Each leverages the esteem and attributes of both brands through a partnership that's a good fit in consumers' minds because the brands appeal to similar markets, offer similar quality, and represent similar benefits.

Before joining a co-branding partnership, be sure you can answer a strong "yes" to each of these questions:

- ✔ Are your brands compatible without directly competing with each other?

- ✔ Do your brands appeal to the same or very similar customers?

- Will both brands enhance their reputations through the partnership?

- Do customers, media, investors, and others respect both brands equally?

- Are the management and marketing styles of both brands compatible?

- Do you trust each other?

- Are all the details down on paper and signed by both parties, including the cobranding marketing plan, budget, timeline, and responsibilities?

- Can you explain the cobranded product or promotion in a sentence that will make sense to employees, customers, and others? Are both brands explaining it in exactly the same way?

Brand Licensing

Brand licensing is one of the most widely used ways to extend a brand, largely because it allows a brand to achieve new product introductions without gearing up operationally for the task. Instead, the brand licenses its name to a manufacturer that takes on all the production and marketing efforts of the new product.

When you *license* your brand, basically you rent your legally protected brand identity to another business that will manufacture and sell products carrying your name.

To the consumer, licensed products look just like branded products. So before you consider a license agreement, be sure the agreement will result in products that meet all the brand characteristics and avoid all the brand-damaging landmines detailed in preceding sections of this chapter.

Understanding licensing lingo

Brand licensing comes with a language of its own. The terms you hear most include the following:

- **Licensing:** Leasing a trademarked or copyrighted brand identity, including brand name, logo, tagline, or other form of brand signature, to another business, usually for use on a product or product line.

- **Licensor:** The owner of the brand and the renter of the rights.

- **Licensee:** The business renting rights to use the brand identity.

- **Contractual agreement:** The formal permission document that defines how the licensee may use the brand and how the licensor will be paid.

The contract should include specific usage purposes, limitations on applications, geographic area, time period, payment schedule, and terms. Rely on an attorney to draw up and review the agreement, and obtain formal signatures. Handshakes are great, but only *after* the ink is dry.

✔ **Royalty:** In most contracts, the licensee agrees to pay the licensor a guaranteed minimum payment plus a royalty on all sales that exceed the minimum payment amount.

Benefits of licensing

In a good licensing agreement, both parties benefit. The licensor gains the benefit of a brand extension and revenue (via royalties) without any investment in product development, production, or marketing. The license agreement provides a no-cost form of brand value leverage.

The licensee gains the benefit of the licensor's brand name, which lends immediate awareness, distinction, and trust to the manufacturer's product rollout. Without the need for any brand development investment, the licensor is able to achieve marketplace prominence and command a premium sales price thanks to the lease of the licensor's brand name.

Licensing steps to follow

Most license agreements result in what looks to the consumer like either a brand-produced product or a cobranded product. For instance, Disney licenses its name to Timex, and Timex makes watches featuring Mickey Mouse. The consumer thinks the two teamed up to make the watch possible, and they did, although it was likely through a licensing agreement rather than through a manufacturing and marketing partnership.

How your branded product gets to market is a behind-the-scenes issue that's invisible to consumers. The consumer simply sees the product, links it to your name, and decides whether the product enhances or diminishes your brand image. (The sections "Don't ask your brand to stretch too far" and "Putting your extension idea through the hoops" earlier in this chapter help you evaluate the match between licensing opportunities and your brand image.)

Give licensed offerings the same level of consideration and scrutiny that you give any other brand or line extension.

1. **Build, protect, and manage your brand and its esteem.** Otherwise, few licensees will find your name worth the lease price.

2. **Establish licensing guidelines.** Include how far you'll allow your brand to range — in terms of product categories, price range, and distribution channels — through licensed products.

3. **License only to well-managed, well-respected, and well-financed companies.**

4. **Limit licensing partners to one or only a few in each product category or geographic area.**

5. **Implement a comprehensive licensee training program to ensure that all licensed products are developed and marketed to your brand standards.** Most licensee training programs begin with education that immerses licensees in the brand image and usage guidelines. They also cover the steps licensees must take in order to gain approval of products, packaging, and any materials or communications that carry the brand identity.

6. **Monitor and protect the way your brand is presented via licensed products in the same way you protect its usage within your own organization.** Be vigilant regarding misuse of your brand identity or infringements on your license. Turn to Chapters 8 and 18 for help.

Chapter 16

Revitalizing Your Brand with a Full or Partial Makeover

In This Chapter

▶ Evaluating your need for a brand update

▶ Aligning your brand to current tastes, times, and market conditions

▶ Launching your revitalized brand

As you open to this chapter, the word *rebranding* is probably on your mind, but chances are good that *revitalizing* better explains the brand revision you're looking for.

Rebranding is the go-to term that marketers use when they talk about updating their brand identities and reputations. It involves basically erasing your current brand identity (along with much of the considerable value that goes with it) and starting the brand-development process all over again, following all the steps explained in this book.

Sometimes rebranding is called for (like following a major acquisition, a major image disaster, a merger, or a major change in business direction). For example, Phillip Morris rebranded itself as Altria to distance itself from the reputation of a tobacco company and Malaysia Air began talking about a rebrand after back-to-back air tragedies in 2014. More often, though, brand owners aren't in need of rebranding. Instead, they seek brand revitalizations to make their brand identities more contemporary, more competitive, and a clearer reflection of the businesses they represent.

In most cases, brands can be revitalized by retaining the core and valued elements of their identities while updating the execution with current styles of image, typography, and colors. For instance, when FedEx revitalized its logo over a decade ago, it did so by retaining and updating the symbol with fresher versions of the same basic colors and a cleaner expression of the thick sans-serif typography.

This chapter helps you to determine what kind of a brand revision you need and how far you want and need your identity update to go. Then it helps you plan the steps involved to make the changes you have in mind while protecting the brand value you've built to date.

Brands Grow Old, Too

Some brands age gracefully, gaining stature, esteem, and strength in the process. Others show their years in less distinguished ways, becoming out-of-step, a little dowdy, and no longer able to command the interest of those they most need to inspire — whether that means consumers, investors, employees, or other brand supporters.

With attention, many brands come back to life quickly. Some require only cosmetic attention — ranging from a design nip and tuck to a full brand facelift — along with some message and marketing realignment. Others need to be resuscitated with heroic rebranding efforts. Still others — a rare few — need to be put on life support while their owners prepare for their graceful departure from the big, branded world.

As evidenced by the fact that most brands never see their fifth birthdays but others live well into the second century of life, there's no timetable to rely on as you try to plot your brand's growth curve.

What you can count on, however, is that sooner or later your brand will go through all or most of the life-cycle stages illustrated in Figure 16-1.

Figure 16-1:
Life cycle of
a brand.

© *Barbara Findlay Schenck*

Spotting brand aging signs

Times change, businesses change, consumer interests change, culture changes, and sometimes brands need to change, too. To evaluate whether your brand may be in need of an update, ask the questions listed in this section on an annual basis, at the very least.

If you answer "yes" to these questions during your brand review, you definitely need to take action by following the steps detailed in the rest of this chapter.

Has your business changed dramatically?

Most rebranding or brand revitalizing is triggered by internal business changes. When the nature of your business changes, the nature of your brand changes, and realignment becomes necessary. To determine whether your situation merits branding attention, ask these questions:

- ✔ Have ownership or leadership changes led to a new company culture? If so, does your brand identity still accurately reflect your company mission, vision, and values?

- ✔ Has your product line changed, or are you about to add products that will dramatically alter your offerings? If so, does your brand promise still apply to every product and service you offer or plan to offer?

- ✔ Have you changed your distribution channels (how and where you offer your products)? If so, does your brand identity represent you well in all channels, particularly online?

Has your market changed dramatically?

To assess whether changes in your market environment have sapped your brand strength, ask these questions:

- ✔ Are you facing new or stronger competition? If so, how well do your brand identity, promise, and experience stand up to the challenge?

- ✔ Has your brand message and experience become out of sync with current consumer interests and tastes? If so, can you update your experience to make it compelling and competitive?

- ✔ Is your brand identity — your name, logo, tagline, and other identifying elements — out of step with design and cultural trends? If so, can you update your identity while retaining the highest-value elements?

Brand change-of-life warning signals

When your organization (the heart and soul of your brand) undergoes major change, most often your brand identity (the face of your brand) needs to undergo change as well. Otherwise, the core of your brand is out of alignment with the promise you make to your market, and a brand credibility crisis is likely to follow.

Likewise, when your market (the reason for your brand's being) undergoes major change, your brand probably needs to change, too. Otherwise your image is out of sync with market needs, tastes, and desires, and a brand relevance crisis is likely to follow.

To avoid a brand disaster, frequently scan your business situation for four warning signs that the strength of your brand may be at risk:

- Rapid business expansion
- Major product or channel diversification
- A merger or acquisition
- A brand identity that hasn't adapted to your changed business and market

The upcoming sections describe the symptoms of each of these brand-health red flags. Scan them, and then complete the questionnaire in Figure 16-2 to assess your brand's vulnerability.

Rapid expansion

In the race to roll out new products, seize new opportunities, open additional outlets, add new distribution channels, or expand into new market areas, your business can outgrow your brand identity. Suddenly, your core brand message is outdated, you can no longer keep your brand promise, and your brand experience is unpredictable. Even your name and slogan become inappropriate fits with the current realities of your business.

If your organization has experienced dramatic growth in the most recent six-month period, schedule a retreat — soon — to evaluate whether your brand identity still reflects the character, values, and attributes of your evolving business situation. Don't wait until an identity or credibility crisis sets in. Use the questions in Figure 16-2 as your assessment guide.

Questionnaire: Is your brand in need of an update?	
Is your name still an appropriate label for the business you've become, the promise you keep, and the markets you serve?	No = attention needed
Has your organization found it necessary to improvise adaptations of your brand name to make it an appropriate label for some of your offerings?	Yes = attention needed
Has your organization found it necessary to use alternate versions of your brand name, logo, and tagline in certain distribution channels?	Yes = attention needed
If the Internet has become a major distribution channel for your business and you weren't able to seize your business name as your domain name, are you successfully training customers to find you online under a different name?	No = attention needed
Does your staff understand and embrace the business you've become? When asked to describe your brand, do employees all give nearly identical answers?	No = attention needed
Do your customers understand and embrace the business you've become? Have your best customers stayed loyal and enthusiastic as you've grown?	No = attention needed
Has your brand experience begun to get unpredictable? (See Chapter 13 for help evaluating the experience you deliver.)	Yes = attention needed
Does your brand identity look dated, with a typestyle, ink colors, and graphic design that seem stuck in the past?	Yes = attention needed
Does your brand identity match the quality and sophistication of the business you've become?	No = attention needed

Figure 16-2: Uncovering brand-health red flags.

© Barbara Findlay Schenck

Major product, channel, or strategic diversification

The marketplace is in flux. Digital communications have upended how businesses communicate, present offerings, and even sell products. At the same time, market territories, even for small businesses, have expanded almost without limits. Even self-employed freelancers in home offices can now serve market areas that span the globe.

Amidst this change, brand owners refocus or change strategic direction — and brand identities — to adapt to their changing environments. Among the examples are businesses that have moved their bricks-and-mortar businesses online; businesses that have shifted emphasis to address environmental realities; and companies that have altered product lines, distribution approaches, and business strategies to serve global markets.

UPS is a case in point. Over the past decade, UPS shifted its emphasis from fleets of delivery trucks to teams of global logistics experts. In the process, the company changed its marketing message, redesigned its logo and website, and developed a new tagline to address the company's changed structure and market. In the 1990s, UPS marketed under the slogan, "The package delivery company more companies count on." Today, the company presents itself as "a leading global provider of specialized transportation and logistics services," eliminating reference to packages and shipping, instead opening the consumer's mind to the company's expanded market and capabilities.

BP (British Petroleum) is another business that restructured strategically and then realigned its brand accordingly. After multiple mergers and acquisitions, BP declared itself more than a petroleum company. It unveiled a revolutionary visual update, announced a transformation from "a local oil company into a global energy group," redefined itself as a "green" leader, and even changed the meaning of "BP" to stand for "beyond petroleum."

On the product-brand front, the cars we know as Nissan were called Datsuns until the mid-1980s when the manufacturer rebranded to align all its cars, in all global markets, under one brand name. In 2009, Microsoft rebranded its search engine Live Search with the easy-to-recall name Bing, invoking the sound made following a discovery: Bingo. And in our own backyard, the Oregon-based beverage brand Humm Kombucha was known as Kombucha Mama until the owners quadrupled production facilities, expanded distribution to serve a national market area, and unveiled a name that captured the essence of the brand as "a vibration of music and laughter. . .made with love and positive energy and the best ingredients on earth."

A merger or acquisition

When you hear the word *merger*, most often you're hearing a euphemism for the reality that one business has been acquired or taken over by another. On occasion, two businesses participate as 50-50 partners in a merger, but even then one company usually emerges as the dominant force.

Whether companies are acquired or merge, their brands rarely blend into one. Essentially, a brand is an organization's promise. If merged brands try to merge promises, most often they end up with a two-pronged promise that confuses consumers and rattles confidence.

In most acquisitions or mergers, the two organizations assess the value of each brand and the equity of each brand's identifying elements before adopting one of the following brand approaches:

- ✔ **The acquiring or dominant company keeps its name.** It emerges as the prevailing brand, often with a revitalized identity to reflect the benefits of the merger. (This is what happens in most cases.)

- ✔ **The seller's name prevails.** For example, when SBC acquired AT&T, it adopted the high-value AT&T name and updated the identity to appear more agile and youthful. Changes included a redesign of the brandmark to more closely resemble a globe — the market served by the new entity.

- ✔ **The combined brands merge their names.** This solution works but only once in a while. For example, FedEx acquired Kinko's and announced the new brand name FedEx Kinko's, but within years the merged entity was renamed FedEx Office. And then there's the Time Warner and AOL merger that resulted, briefly, in the merged brand name AOL/Time Warner, which confused consumers and investors alike until eventually the two entities separated back into independent brands: AOL and Time Warner. When Price Waterhouse merged with Coopers & Lybrand, the new brand name became PricewaterhouseCoopers, a memory test that was formally shortened to the brand name PwC in 2010.

- ✔ **A new brand name emerges with no apparent link to either of the merged brands.** For example, the name Verizon emerged from the merger, way back when, of Bell Atlantic and GTE.

A dated brand identity

In the low-budget start-up days, many businesses resort to brand identities that are either self-designed or whipped up by an aspiring artist recommended by the friend of a friend of a cousin of a brother-in-law. The result is usually a make-do identity created with all the best intentions in the world at a price that seemed right at the time.

Fast-forward several years, though, and what seemed to work fine at startup no longer represents the culture or sophistication of the organization or fits the nature of the market it serves or the environment in which it survives.

When that's the case, brand revitalization is in order, and it's a process you can't take lightly. Simply designing a great new brandmark isn't enough. At the very least, you need to take the following actions:

1. **Assess how much you want or need to change your identity.**

   Brand identity redesigns span the gamut from evolutionary to revolutionary depending on whether they move the current identity forward a little, a lot, or into an altogether new name and logo.

2. **Determine the brand identity assets that contribute the most value to your brand.**

   Assess and identify which identifying elements have the greatest marketplace awareness and affection so you know which aspects to protect and carry over to your revitalized identity. Turn to Chapter 3 for help with this task.

3. **Invest in the counsel and talents of a good brand designer as you weigh your existing brand strengths and consider your options.**

   Chapter 12 provides advice for interviewing creative firms, making selections, and getting design agreements in writing.

4. **Adopt a revitalized brand strategy that can represent your brand vision for at least ten years, which is about the maximum frequency that the look of a brand should undergo major change.**

Revitalizing because . . .

Revitalizing your brand presents a great opportunity to state anew what your brand stands for. As brands age, brand messages often get blurry; over time, people within and outside the business become unclear about a brand's identity, what distinguishes it from others, what unique attributes it offers, and what promise it makes.

Revitalizing lets you put a polishing cloth not only to your brand look but also to your brand message. You get the chance to say, "We are revitalizing our brand because . . ."

✔ We've expanded our market territory.

✔ We've added products or enhanced services.

✔ We've changed strategically to better address market realities, needs, and desires.

✔ We've grown through mergers, acquisitions, or meteoric success.

Brand revitalization lets you amplify the good news about what your brand has become. It gives you the chance to reunite everyone in your company and customer corps under a new, clearly stated brand message that gives you something to shout about.

Examining Your Brand's Health

Doctors require X-rays and lists of diagnostic tests before determining health conditions and issuing prescriptive remedies. Brands deserve the same treatment. Before "fixing" your brand, put it through a checkup:

1. **Start with a brand review, also called a *brand audit.***

2. **Determine how far you want or need your brand revision to go in terms of changes to your current brand identity.**

3. **Outline your brand revitalization plan by defining your goals, objectives, strategies, tactics, and measuring sticks.**

The following sections walk you through each step.

Conducting a brand review

A brand review takes your brand through many of the same steps you took when establishing your brand in the first place. (For an overview of the brand development process, see Chapter 3.)

As you review your brand's condition, give every one of the questions in this section the attention it deserves. Your answers will help you pinpoint where your brand is ailing so you can direct repair efforts toward fixing what's broken rather than overhauling strong and valuable brand attributes.

What do you want to achieve through your brand revitalization program?

Prioritize your goals by selecting from the following brand functions:

- Create greater awareness of your brand
- Enhance emotional connection with those in your target audience
- Clarify or redefine brand distinctions
- Build or rebuild credibility and trust
- Motivate product preference and purchases

Chapter 3 includes a worksheet that helps you assess how well your branding priorities are supported by your current brand strengths. If your brand is strong in your priority areas, your need for brand revitalization is low. If your brand is weak in the areas that are most important to your future success, however, your brand likely needs assessment, repair, and rejuvenation.

How well does your brand fit in your marketplace?

Answer these questions:

- How do others — including employees, customers, prospective customers, investors, and suppliers — perceive your brand?

- Why do people choose your brand? Are their reasons strongly compelling and adequately conveyed in your brand name, logo, tagline, and brand communications?

- What attributes do people believe distinguish your brand from competing brands? Are those the same attributes that you feel best differentiate your brand and its offerings?

- Are the distinguishing characteristics of your brand of increasing or decreasing interest to consumers?

- Is your brand well recognized among those you target as customers? When asked to name top contenders in your market category, do all, most, or few prospects cite your brand?

- Do your brand name, logo, and slogan appeal to current market and cultural tastes and trends?

See Chapter 4 for advice on how to conduct research to unearth the answers you need in the area of marketplace perception.

Is your brand an accurate reflection of your business?

All great brands share one important attribute: They're mirror images of the companies they represent. To assess how accurately your brand reflects your business, answer these questions:

- Does your brand identity mirror your business mission, vision, and values (see Chapter 6), or have ownership, leadership, or strategic changes made your brand identity out of date?

- Does your brand identity reflect the quality, character, personality, and voice of your business? (See Chapter 6 for help arriving at your answer.)

- Does your brand promise convey your strengths and distinctions, and is it believable and consistently reinforced through all brand encounters? (Refer to Chapter 6 again as you consider this question.)

- Do all products that you've added or that you plan to add fit well under your brand? Do the number of products and the nature of your offerings make sense to consumers? (Chapter 2 addresses brand architecture, and Chapter 15 touches on brand extensions.)

✔ Is your pricing a reflection of your brand image, message, and promise?

✔ Has your brand image been tarnished by events within or outside your control? (See Chapter 18 for help dealing with brand crises.)

Do customers and others accurately understand your brand?

Remember, your brand lives in the minds of others, so before you begin to revise your image, invest time and effort to discover what those who know your brand currently think of it. Answer these questions:

✔ Does the brand image that others currently hold in their minds reflect the image and competitive position you aspire to hold in your marketplace? (See Chapter 5 for help staking claim to your market position.)

✔ When customers rank the top competitors in your field, does the ranking of your brand fit with your desired level of market dominance?

✔ Does your brand attract the clientele you aspire to serve?

✔ Do those who work most closely with your business — including your employees, your business partners, your investors, and your most loyal customers — all describe your brand accurately?

Does your brand experience reinforce your desired brand image at all contact points?

Too often, brands undergo name or logo changes when what really needs fixing is the brand experience, starting with the way their products work.

People form opinions about a brand based on all contact with the brand, from marketing communications to staff encounter and, from the intricacies of the purchase experience to the experience of becoming a product owner. Determine whether your brand experience contributes to your desired brand image by answering these questions:

✔ Are your brand name, logo, communications, location, and experience consistent with the personality, character, message, and voice that you want associated with your business?

✔ When people encounter your brand, is the experience consistent, compelling, and competitive? (Turn to Chapter 13 for instructions on how to put your brand experience to the test.)

✔ Are your communications — from your ads to your website and social media pages to your phone, mail and in-person contacts — uniformly consistent in terms of look, voice, character, and brand message?

Does your brand compete well with the brands of dominant competitors in your market area?

As competitors enter your business arena, their brand offerings can change customer expectations. Determine whether your brand has remained current by answering these questions:

- ✔ Is your identity (your name, logo, tagline, and other identifying elements) distinctive and competitive in terms of quality, sophistication, and consistency?

- ✔ Are your website and social-media pages good representations of your brand and good reflections of your brand image? Is your brand findable and prominent in search results, which affect first impressions of your brand? Turn to Chapters 10 and 11 for advice.

- ✔ Is your brand promise clear, unique, and appealing when compared to promises extended by your competitors?

- ✔ Are your services outstanding compared to those of your competitors?

- ✔ Is your brand experience competitive and excellent?

Making the diagnosis: Retool or retire?

After you complete a brand review, the moment of decision arrives: Can your brand be revitalized, or do you need to put it out to pasture? To arrive at an answer, use the results of the brand review as you answer these questions:

- ✔ **Is your brand healthy?** Is it an accurate reflection of your business today? As you look at your plans and hopes for the next ten years, does your brand name, logo, promise, and message match your aspirations?

    If your answers add up to a resounding "yes," recommit to your brand, and also commit to a double-dose investment of time and money to see that it's well protected and well presented for years to come.

- ✔ **Is your brand ailing?** Has it lost its fit with your business and market? If so, is the gap between what your business has become and what your brand identity implies vast or narrow?

    If the alignment between your brand and your business is way off — if your brand is called Main Street Fix-It but you now offer business system reviews and solutions to a global market — you're facing an identity crisis, and complete rebranding may be in order.

    On the other hand, if the alignment between your brand and your business is only slightly amiss — if your name is Global Advertising but you now offer global clients strategic planning, branding, and message development services in addition to advertising production and placement — a name adjustment and a brand revitalization may be the extent of your needs.

✔ **Does your brand have high value?** (Chapter 15 can help you make your assessment.) If your answer is "yes," the worth of your brand as an established asset is reason enough to revitalize rather than rebrand.

By revitalizing — or updating and polishing your established brand — you realign it with changed conditions while also, and importantly, protecting the brand value you've built over the years.

By rebranding, you basically erase previously established value and start over again, building value from scratch. Rebranding is the way to go when the value in your existing brand is so low or in such negative territory that you're better off giving yourself the equivalent of a golf mulligan and taking an altogether new shot. If that's the case in your situation, turn straight back to Chapter 3, heat up your branding iron, and get ready to begin the branding process from square one.

Fixing a Broken Brand

Most brands break not because markets change but because businesses change.

Sometimes, names or logos need updating in order to keep pace with market realities, tastes, and cultural trends, but that kind of market-responsive change involves only a cosmetic update or name adjustment, not a brand overhaul.

Brand overhauls become necessary when business overhauls literally change a company's heart and soul. When the core of the business — the base of the brand — changes radically, the face of the brand — the brand's name, logo, and identifying elements — needs to change, too. Otherwise, there's a disconnect between what the brand says it is and what, in fact, the brand is. And *that's* a formula for credibility disaster.

Protecting your valuables

The most essential step in fixing or updating a brand is determining which brand assets carry the highest value in consumer minds. Brand assets include

✔ Your brand name

✔ Your brand's identifying elements, including your logo, your logotype or script, your tagline or slogan, your color scheme, your packaging, and brand signature items such as a unique scent (think Cinnabon), a musical signature (United Airlines' background music, for example), or even signature events that consumers link to your name

  ✔ Your brand's core message and promise

  ✔ Your brand's dominance in a defined market niche

  ✔ Your brand's link to key customer groups

The brand asset analysis worksheet in Chapter 3 can help you determine the value of each of your assets and whether or not the strength of your brand would be reduced if you were to change or eliminate the asset.

For instance, if you discover that your brandmark has low awareness or that its usage has been mismanaged over the years, you may determine that replacing your symbol will serve only to strengthen your image. On the other hand, if you find that consumers have high awareness and regard for your name, you should think long and hard before abandoning it. (As a case in point, think back to the 2010 disastrous Gap brand logo change.)

Making the change

Start the revitalization process after you take the following steps to determine which brand assets you should keep and which are dispensable:

1. **Get the leadership of your company involved right from the start.**

   The person who leads your company should lead or be involved in the brand revitalization or rebranding process. Otherwise, you're apt to face an uphill battle when it's time to adopt the new identity.

2. **Determine whether you'll refresh or revise your brand promise.**

   In essence, your brand is the promise you make to all who deal with you, your business, or your offerings. The degree to which you alter your promise in large part dictates the degree to which you alter your brand. (Chapter 6 has more information on brand promises.)

3. **Determine whether you need to alter your name, slightly or drastically, to fit your business, market, and sales channels.**

   Chapter 7 is all about naming your brand. Make it your guide if a new or different name is the next step in your brand's life.

4. **Decide whether you need to redesign your logo.**

   Chapter 8 has advice on logo design, including why to involve an experienced professional. As part of the redesign process, rewrite your graphic guidelines and your brand management policies (see Chapter 8).

5. **Decide how you'll refine your brand experience so that every encounter reinforces your revitalized brand message, strengthens your brand promise, and helps develop your desired image.**

6. **Relaunch your brand, starting within your organization and following the advice in Chapter 9.**

Don't leapfrog over this step. If you fail to gain understanding and buy-in from your internal team, nothing you do externally can save your brand from the ramifications.

7. **When your revitalized brand is known, accepted, and adopted internally (and not a moment before), take your brand public.**

   Begin with a publicity generation effort that shares the story of why you're making the change, how you're building on your brand's heritage while simultaneously embracing your brand's future, and how your new identity and brand strategy focus on a clear, strong, powerful vision. See Chapter 12 for publicity guidelines.

8. **Launch communications and promotions to announce and amplify the message of your revitalized brand (see Chapters 11 and 12).**

9. **Invest the time and dollars necessary to build and protect your revitalized brand's value (see Chapter 17).**

Ten mistakes to avoid when revitalizing

As you audit, update, and realign your brand to address your business and market realities, avoid some of the most common mistakes by spending a few minutes with this list of traps to avoid. The most common mistakes are

- ✔ Failure to enlist the head of your organization as the leader of your brand revitalization

- ✔ Failure to assess whether your product or your brand experience — and not your brand identity — may be what's hurting your brand's esteem in its marketplace

- ✔ Failure to enlist experienced professionals to help with research, name development, logo design, trademark registration, and brand communications

- ✔ Failure to inform your staff early on about why you're undertaking a brand revitalization

- ✔ Failure to protect your current brand assets as you revise your brand for the future

- ✔ Failure to maintain a *silent stage,* a time during which brand plans are held close to

the vest until they're adopted by management and ready for presentation to your organization's internal team (put in familiar terms, loose lips sink ships)

- ✔ Failure to introduce and win support internally before you let your revitalized brand story outside the confines of your organization

- ✔ Failure to reach your most loyal customers, investors, and suppliers with news of your revitalized brand before they learn about your brand changes through the grapevine or through social or mass media

- ✔ Failure to establish a brand-management plan that ensures continuous and consistent communication of your brand message and promise across all communication channels and at all consumer touch points

- ✔ Failure to introduce your revitalized brand with the fanfare it deserves

Part V
Protecting Your Brand

Think Big as You Register and Protect Your Name from Competitors

If your products or services will travel the world, think in global terms right from the get-go by following this advice:

- As you develop your brand identity, test its relevance and acceptance in other cultures and languages — especially in the cultures of countries where you plan to develop clusters of customers as a result of global offices, Internet marketing, or distributor relationships.

- If your products or services will travel national borders, obtain international trademark registrations in the very beginning, before others can beat you to the task. If you don't, someday when you seek to protect your brand in distant markets, you just may discover that your name has already been trademarked — but not by your organization.

- There's no such thing as a worldwide trademark, but you can file a single international application that allows you to apply for trademark registration in any of the more than 60 countries that participate in what's called the Madrid Protocol. For information, visit the World Intellectual Property Organization at www.wipo.int.

All the work you put into your brand will be for nothing if you don't defend it from attack and misuse. Head to www.dummies.com/extras/branding for bonus information on essential steps to take.

In this part . . .

- ✔ Keep your brand out of trouble by taking preemptive action against brand attacks and by fortifying it with all the necessary registrations and legal protections, including trademarks if your brand will travel across state or international borders soon or someday in the future.

- ✔ Protect your valuable brand asset by writing and enforcing an ironclad set of usage rules that cover everything from trademark-protection actions to social-media usage guidelines.

- ✔ Be ready to dodge dangerous and damaging brand-equity landmines by foreseeing potential threats to the strength of your brand and preparing a crisis-management plan that's ready to go (even though we hope you'll never need it).

- ✔ Know the steps to take should your brand suffer a value-eroding image hit. Be ready — just in case — to stage a brand rescue and recovery mission should your brand ever face natural or other disasters that shake the consumer credibility and brand relevance and worth.

Chapter 17

Defending Your Brand Legally and through Careful Usage

*F*or all their strengths, brands are vulnerable. They're susceptible to infringement by competitors who use disarmingly similar names or logos. Plus they're open to attack by friends and foes alike, who intentionally or innocently mess with your brand's identity and erode your brand strength in the process.

The reasons to protect your brand are many, but none tops the fact that when brands undergo competitive attack or weak management, marketplace confusion follows. And marketplace confusion is a high-risk condition for most brands.

This chapter helps you fortify your brand in two ways. First, it details how to take preemptive action by registering your brand identity so that others can't use it — or so you can take legal action if they do. Second, it lays out a plan for managing the presentation of your brand, beginning with usage guidelines and ending with usage enforcement.

Strong brands thrive under the careful watch of brand owners who never blink and who never turn a blind eye to brand management mishaps or transgressions. The old line "You snooze, you lose" could have been written as advice for brand managers. Vigilance is a prescription for brand strength and an antidote for brand erosion.

Immunizing Your Brand with Government Filings and Trademarks

The extent to which you protect your name legally depends on the size of your business, the size of your market area, and the vision you hold for your business. If you think that someday your brand will span state or national borders — or if you think that someday you may want to sell it to someone with aspirations of developing it into a national or global name — you should put every form of legal protection in place, the sooner the better.

The best time to protect your brand name is when you name your business, because your business name is likely to become your brand name, too. Turn to Chapter 7 for advice for choosing a name, screening to see that it isn't already in use, and registering it so it's unavailable to others.

The most common methods of name protection are

- Filing your business name with local government offices
- Establishing a trademark

Use the next sections as you proceed on both fronts.

Registering your name with local government offices

As you name your business, either you'll choose a name that includes the owners' legal surnames along with a description of the business or you'll choose what's called a *fictitious* or *assumed name,* which features a name other than your true name. In either case, filing your name with the right local government office is a necessary step. The process is straightforward and relatively easy.

Registering a business using the owners' legal surnames

If your business name includes the legal surname of each owner along with a generic description of your business (for instance, Smith, Jones, and Peterson Insurance), follow these steps:

1. **Find out where the database of registered business names is maintained in your state or region.**

   Contact the office of your county clerk or your secretary of state for help, or ask your attorney or accountant for instructions. Your banker can also point you in the right direction because financial institutions require name registration information when opening business accounts.

2. **Register your business name by completing a form and paying a fee.**

   When you're doing business under your legal name (such as John Johnson Plumbing), a name search isn't necessary. Simply register your name and open your business. But if you add a phrase such as "and Sons" or "and Associates" to your legal name (for example, John Johnson and Sons Plumbing), you need to register it as a fictitious or assumed name as described in the next set of steps because the name suggests that other owners are also involved.

Registering a fictitious or assumed name

Fictitious names or assumed names require registration following these steps:

1. **Confirm that no competing business has staked claim to the name you want.**

   Request a search of the assumed names database in all jurisdictions (usually that means counties) in which you want to register your name. Begin with the jurisdiction where your business is located and then add jurisdictions that cover each market area you plan to serve. Also consider searching the jurisdictions that cover the heaviest population areas of your state or region in case you want to expand into those areas.

   If the search reveals that your desired brand name is already in use by another business, head back to the drawing board, turning to Chapter 7 for naming advice.

2. **Register the name.**

   If the name you want is available, grab it. Fill out the forms and pay the required fees to register the name in your home region and in each region you plan to do business. Consider also registering the name in the regions that include your market area's greatest population counts to further protect it from use by competing businesses.

Obtaining a trademark

In the U.S., if your business serves only one state, you can inquire with the office of your secretary of state about a state trademark that prevents others from using a similar mark in your statewide area. However, the process for obtaining a state trademark includes no search of other state or federal registrations; therefore, your right to use a state mark could be preempted by discovery of prior use by a trademark owner with a federal registration.

A federal trademark provides broader protection than a state trademark and is important if your business serves or plans to serve a market area that crosses state or national borders. (A federal trademark is called a *service mark* if it protects the brand of a service rather than a tangible item.)

The process of obtaining a federal trademark is long, tricky, and important for two reasons:

- ✔ A federal trademark protects your brand identity from use by others.

- ✔ The process of obtaining a federal trademark steers you clear of the legal hot water that awaits if you obliviously try to use an already-trademarked name, logo, tagline, or other identifying brand element.

To obtain a federal trademark, plan to take these steps:

1. **Determine whether the brand identity you want to trademark is already in use as an established trademark.**

   Conduct a preliminary online search of the database maintained by the U.S. Patent and Trademark Office (USPTO). Go to www.uspto.gov, click on Trademarks, click on Trademark Search, and follow the instructions. (For information on international trademark protection, go to www.uspto.gov/main/profiles/international.htm.)

2. **If your desired brand identity appears to be available, hire an attorney who specializes in trademarks to conduct a more extensive search.**

   Don't try to proceed on your own; the trademark process requires professional expertise. (You can find details of the steps and costs involved in this extensive brand-identity search in Chapter 7.)

3. **If you get a green light from your attorney, move to secure a trademark as quickly as you can.**

   Establish your trademark through what's called *common-law usage* (see the next section) or through the rigorous process of obtaining a more-official and protective registered trademark (see the section "Obtaining a registered trademark" later in this chapter).

Trademarking through common-law usage

After you determine that the brand name, logo, tagline, or other identifying element that you want to protect isn't already protected, begin to establish a common-law trademark by using the letters *TM* in superscript (or *SM* if you're establishing a service mark) alongside the mark you're protecting. In the United States and countries with similar legal systems, announcing your trademark or service mark claim in this way lets you begin to accrue trademark rights through common-law usage.

In taking the common-law approach, be aware of these shortcomings:

- ✔ Common-law trademark protection is limited to the geographic areas in which your mark has actually been used.

- ✔ You don't have the protection of a federal registration if another party were to dispute your claim to your trademark.

✔ By using the trademark without undergoing the rigorous search and analysis of a formal trademark application, you may be liable for infringing upon someone else's registered mark. Even after your attorney screens and conducts a detailed risk analysis for your name, additional infringement issues can arise during the trademark application process that preclude your usage of the mark, which is why federal registration is the ultimate form of trademark protection.

Obtaining a registered trademark

To obtain a federally registered trademark, follow the steps described in the beginning of this section and in Chapter 7. The federal trademark process provides an especially important protection if you conduct or plan to conduct business across state or national borders. For information on federally registered trademarks, count on these resources:

✔ **For information on U.S. trademarks,** turn to the USPTO website at www. uspto.gov.

✔ **For information on obtaining trademarks in a number of countries through a single registration,** visit the World Intellectual Property Organization at www.wipo.int or go to the international property section of the USPTO website at www.uspto.gov/main/profiles/ international.htm.

Use the trademark designations *TM* or *SM,* in superscript, until your trademark is formally issued by the USPTO, at which time you can begin using the designation ®. Don't jump the gun and use the registered mark before your federal trademark is granted. Doing so is called *false use* and can result in denial of your federal registration.

As soon as you receive your federal trademark, give notice of your trademark in at least one prominent place in every brand communication:

✔ Use the symbol ® presented in superscript to the right of the trademarked name or symbol.

✔ Include *Registered, U.S. Patent and Trademark Office* (or the abbreviation *Reg. U.S. Pat. & Tm. Off.*), either in addition to or instead of the ® symbol.

Maintaining your trademark registration

After you obtain a trademark registration, kick your trademark protection efforts into high gear. If you don't, your trademark and all the work you put into obtaining it can fly right out the window.

Use it or abandon it

When you apply to register a trademark, the USPTO requires you to list the specific goods and services for which you seek the registration. For each area you list, you must be able to demonstrate *use in commerce,* which means that you must be able to provide evidence either that you're currently engaged in commerce in the areas listed or that you have good faith intent to use the mark in the areas listed on your registration application.

Using your mark in commerce means a couple of different things.

- ✓ **For trademarked goods:** The mark is placed on products, labels, packages, displays, or documents associated with the sale of goods that are sold or transported interstate.

- ✓ **For trademarked services:** The mark is used or displayed in marketing and selling services that are provided in more than one state.

Simply putting your mark on stationery products or using it in business presentations isn't enough to prove that it has use in commerce. You have to actually *use* the mark commercially in each of the categories covered by your application, and you have to keep using it. After three years of nonuse in any category, your trademark can be deemed *abandoned* and cancelled as a result.

To protect your trademark, work with and follow the advice of an attorney who specializes in trademark law. Be prepared to periodically assess that, in fact, your trademark is used in commerce in each of the usage categories for which it's registered. If you aren't using the mark in all its designated categories, amend your registration. Otherwise, you put your entire registration at risk.

Defend it or lose it

By obtaining federal trademark registration, you claim exclusive rights to use a name, symbol, tagline, or other identifying brand element. With that right, however, comes an obligation to use the mark continuously and consistently and to bar any usage that weakens your exclusive claim to the mark.

Follow all the trademark-protection advice provided by your trademark attorney and the USPTO, including these guidelines:

- ✓ **Don't use your trademark name as a verb, and don't allow it to be turned into an active word by adding *-ing.***

Consider this cautionary true story. The trademark for Windsurfer applied to a wind-propelled, surfboard-like apparatus patented by Californians Jim Drake and Hoyle Schweitzer in 1968. But after the term was presented as a verb — by using the word *windsurfing* to describe the sport of sailboarding — courts found the mark to be generic and no longer protectable as a trademark.

✔ **Do use your trademark as an adjective in front of the generic term for your offering, not as a noun that describes your offering. For example, Xerox copier and Macintosh computer are proper uses of trademarks.**

The story of the escalator illustrates what happens if you fail to follow this rule. The name *Escalator* was once a trademark of the Otis Elevator Company. However, instead of consistently using the mark as a descriptor (as in *Escalator brand moving stairs*), it was used as a noun (an escalator), and the trademark protection rolled right out of sight.

For a positive example of trademark protection, the owners of the Rollerblade mark have spent millions of dollars to educate consumers and competitors about how the mark can and can't be used. The gist of their message is that Rollerblade isn't a generic term for in-line skates, and rollerblading isn't a sport. Rather, Rollerblade is a trademark name of a company that manufactures in-line skates, and it's the brand of equipment you wear when you go in-line skating. Using the term in any other way puts the trademark at risk, and the makers of Rollerblade in-line skates pay dearly to ensure that doesn't happen.

✔ **Do accompany your trademark with the appropriate symbol: super-script *TM* for unregistered trademarks, superscript *SM* for unregistered service marks, and ® for registered trademarks or service marks in at least one prominent location in each brand communication.**

✔ **Do present your trademark consistently, with no variation in spelling and no addition of dashes or slashes.**

✔ **Do separate your trademark name from surrounding text by underlining it or by presenting it in bold, capital letters, or italics.**

If you slack off and use or allow others to use your trademark name as a verb or a generic label, you dilute your exclusive rights to the term and risk rights to your trademark as a result. See the sidebar "*Genericide*: A term only brand owners know and care about."

Shielding Your Brand from Misuse

Regardless of the form of legal protection you put in place to protect your brand's identity from misuse outside your company, you need to establish and adopt a set of well-crafted and carefully monitored usage guidelines and standards for use within your company.

Laying down the law with brand-usage guidelines

Chapter 8 includes advice for stipulating your logo usage guidelines. Beyond consistent logo usage, well-branded organizations establish style guidelines — *rules* may be a better word — for how their identities may be presented.

As you define how your brand can be presented, consider and cover all the points in this section.

Logo usage

To ensure that your logo always appears exactly to your specifications, begin by creating digital logo art files that can be scaled larger or smaller only as a single unit. By using these established files, designers and others can't take artistic liberties with logo elements.

Additional ways to protect your logo include

✔ Requiring that your logo be reproduced only from approved materials provided digitally or in reproduction-ready form by your organization

✔ Providing your logo in horizontal and vertical versions and stipulating that any alternative presentation must be approved prior to usage

✔ Defining how your logo may be placed in printed materials, including the smallest size in which it can be reproduced and the amount of open space that must surround it in order to protect its presentation

✔ Explaining allowable color treatments, including whether the logo can be reversed (to appear as a white image in a field of color) and the exact ink colors in which it can appear

Logo usage is covered in more detail in Chapter 8.

Typestyle

A quick way to unify the look of your brand presentation is to limit the typestyles or *fonts* that you allow in your ads, brochures, signs, packaging, or other materials. For best results, adopt and limit type usage to one or several fonts for use in headlines and one or several fonts for use in body copy or text.

As you choose typestyles, match how your communications look in print with the personality and character of your brand (see Chapter 6 for help defining your brand character). For example, if your brand personality is crisp and professional, you won't want to choose a typestyle that resembles cartoon captions or graffiti.

Copy guidelines

Write copy guidelines to define how your name can be presented and what words may and may not be used in association with your brand.

- ✔ Define which parts of your name or slogan must be presented in all capital letters or with an initial capital letter.

- ✔ Define when, if ever, your name may be abbreviated and, if so, what abbreviations are allowable.

- ✔ Prohibit using your brand name as a verb (with *-ing*) or as a noun. Think of your trademark name as an adjective that modifies a generic word that describes your product (for example, JELL-O gelatin).

- ✔ Prohibit using your brand name in plural or possessive form (in other words, don't add an *s* or *'s* unless your brand is trademarked in that form).

- ✔ Prohibit breaking and hyphenating your brand name at the end of a line.

- ✔ State whether and when your name must be accompanied by a designation such as Inc., Ltd., or LLC.

- ✔ Define which parts of your name or slogan must be accompanied by a trademark, service mark, or registered trademark symbol based on the advice of your trademark attorney.

- ✔ Define whether and how you want your marketing materials to carry a copyright notice (for example, © 2015 Your Brand Name, Inc.). For copyright information, go to www.copyright.gov.

Search online for "brand identity style guides" for examples of usage guidelines for established brands.

Social-media guidelines

Unless you've been without Wi-Fi the past few years you already know that social media is a breeding ground for brand disasters. A few errant words, a couple of misuses of the brand name, a comment out-of-tone for the brand voice, or a damaging post by a person identifiable as a brand representative can set the whole brand organization scrambling for image repair — which is the topic of Chapter 18.

If your brand doesn't already have a set of social-media usage guidelines, start assembling one now. For hundreds of examples, visit the Social Media Policy Database assembled by Social Media Architect Chris Boudreaux (socialmediagovernance.com/policies). You'll find links to the guidelines used by businesses, academics, nonprofits, and healthcare organizations, with examples covering everything from social media policy, blogging policy, Facebook comments policy, and more. A section of the site also leads to tips and templates.

At the very least, cover the following points in your guidelines:

✔ Provide those who will post on your behalf with a review of your brand statement and the brand image and promise all communications must uphold

✔ Clarify your policies regarding how staff members are allowed to post personal and professional updates.

✔ Regardless of how long your guidelines run, create an easy-to-understand overview that runs no more than a few pages long to be sure that everyone on your team reads at least the most important parts of your policy. Then hold personal training sessions to be sure the information is conveyed and received.

Enforcing brand-usage rules

Protecting your brand trademark takes a combination of preemptive, precautionary efforts followed by non-stop usage monitoring. You need to set and follow trademark protective actions — and you need to find and stop anyone who misuses or infringes on the brand you're aiming to protect.

Take every one of these actions:

✔ Put the appropriate brand protections in place, from filing your name with local government offices to registering your trademark.

✔ Define, formalize, and circulate your brand usage guidelines.

✔ Name and empower a department or person to monitor and enforce your brand usage guidelines (see the next section).

✔ Train your entire employee team about proper use of your brand and trademarks.

✔ Require all suppliers, marketing partners, licensees, or others who present or help you project your brand image to respect your trademark and to follow your brand-usage guidelines.

✔ Don't allow misuse or infringement of your brand and trademarks, either within or outside your organization. If you discover infractions, address them immediately.

✔ Monitor and manage your trademark registration to be sure you're using your mark properly in all registration categories, and to amend or renew your application as necessary to keep it accurate and current.

Genericide: A term only brand owners know and care about

If you own a trademark and aren't familiar with the term *genericide,* don't wait to get smart on the topic.

Genericide is the term for a trademark that becomes so widely and commonly used to refer to a category of products or services, rather than to the specific offerings of the trademark owner, that it becomes a generic term and therefore unprotectable. In blunt terms, that means the courts actually take away the brand owner's exclusive right to use the previously protected brand name. By most counts, only 5 percent of all brands lose their trademarks this way, but you don't want to make it into that elite circle.

Aspirin, once a Bayer trademark, was victim. So were the trademark names *linoleum, thermos, videotape, yo-yo, trampoline,* and even *heroin,* to name a few.

The thought that building a brand name to such prominence that it becomes synonymous with its category — like BAND-AID and Kleenex — sounds like the dream of marketing departments everywhere. To corporate lawyers, though, that level of popularity sets off alarms and triggers heightened efforts to assure that the brand name remains a specific identifier for a distinctive offering and that it doesn't slip into common use as a generic term.

That's why BAND-AID diligently presents its offering as BAND-AID® Brand Adhesive Bandages and Kleenex insists on usages such as Kleenex® Brand or Kleenex® Tissue, carefully distinguishing each brand as a provider of premium offerings in the categories where it reigns supreme.

Naming and empowering a brand cop

Your brand cop, also called a *trademark coordinator,* is the person (or department) that keeps your brand safe from misuse or infringements. Consider assigning the task to your marketing vice president or to a person in your marketing department. The brand cop's job is to enforce brand usage guidelines internally while also continuously monitoring for misuse of your brand from those outside your organization.

Following are the specific tasks this person should perform:

✔ **Train employees regarding use of your trademark and brand identity.**

Training should take place at the time of hiring and again whenever the brand is updated, extended, or in any way revised. Providing printed or online versions of usage guidelines isn't enough; plan face-to-face meetings and in-person presentations to demonstrate and personally explain your brand presentation. Then provide printed or online versions of the guidelines for ongoing reference.

- ✔ Review brand materials for consistency with brand presentation.

- ✔ Review (with your attorney) plans for copromotions or license agreements to be sure that they uphold your trademark and brand presentation rules.

- ✔ Monitor use of your trademark by those within your organization, watching for any of the trademark violations noted in the section "Defend it or lose it" earlier in this chapter.

- ✔ Watch for misuse of your mark by other organizations that may try to use or misuse your mark or to adopt a mark that closely resembles yours and causes marketplace confusion as a result.

Search online for unauthorized usage by entering your trademark name as well as violations of your name — such as your name as a verb — in search engines. Study the search results as well as the ads that appear alongside the results to see if your mark is being used erroneously.

- ✔ Take action against trademark abuses.

- ✔ Keep records of trademark usage and trademark enforcement.

Should your trademark ever be questioned, you want to be able to prove that, in fact, your trademark was used in commerce in each category covered by the application and that it was aggressively protected and defended, both within and outside your organization.

Chapter 18

Taking Action When Bad Things Happen to Good Brands

In This Chapter

▶ Watching for brand-damaging landmines

▶ Preparing for the worst, just in case

Sometimes brands make news for the worst reasons. In spite of great planning and a million good intentions, brands can run into trouble due to anything from bad decisions to bad management to bad luck. When they do, the situation requires action, *ASAP.* The alternative — waiting around while you try to wish the problem away — is a formula for a public relations disaster. This chapter is about righting wrongs, should they happen. It's also about steering clear of the biggest brand-eroding problems brand-owners encounter.

If all goes well, you'll follow the crisis-preemption steps and never need to implement the crisis-management advice in this chapter. But be read just in case. Your preparation and ability to respond promptly could be the key to rescuing your brand's reputation and equity.

Caution Ahead: Avoiding Brand-Equity Landmines

Beware. Most brand-damaging events fall into one of these categories:

▶ **A lapse in social responsibility:** For example, think of the apparel brands that have been tainted by news coverage of unsafe working conditions in manufacturing facilities. Other social-responsibility lapses result from worker mistreatment, environmental damage, human-rights violations, or other harmful actions.

✔ **A lapse in corporate behavior:** Scan the financial news for too many examples of brands caught cooking the books, violating regulations, skimping on safety procedures, or using loopholes to maximize shareholder value, devastating their brand reputations and minimizing their brand equity in the process.

✔ **A lapse in the behavior of a high-profile executive, spokesperson, or brand representative:** Names are probably popping up in your mind as you read this sentence. From star athletes to celebrities to politicians to church, association, or corporate leaders, personal transgressions (to use the term popular in *mea culpa* admissions) turn into scandals that ruin personal brands, for sure, while also damaging the branded organizations led or represented by those making news for the worst of reasons. While major personal scandals are the most obvious behaviors to hurt brand images, an insensitive comment, a poorly timed social-media post, or a political or social stance counter to customer opinions are equally capable of shattering brand support.

✔ **Death or sudden departure of a high-profile corporate leader:** For example, consider the impact of Dr. Robert Atkins's death on Atkins Nutritionals, Inc. Within days of Atkins's untimely death from a fall on an icy sidewalk, headlines asked, "Is the Atkins brand toast?" The answer came through loud and clear two years later when the company filed for Chapter 11 bankruptcy court protection.

✔ **Product failures, malfunctions, or dangers:** Whether real or perceived, and whether the result of human errors, inadequate or overlooked quality procedures and controls, violations of procedures, circulation of misinformation, consumer misunderstandings, or out-and-out product sabotage, when people lose trust in a brand's offering, trust in the brand is simultaneously endangered. See the sidebar in this chapter, "Pushing through the pain," for a summary of how product tampering can trigger a brand disaster that sincere and skillful crisis management can overcome.

✔ **Natural or manmade disasters or accidents:** These events can range from earthquakes or fires to snipers or terrorist attacks.

The best offense is a good defense. Before planning how to handle brand threats, take some time to plan how to avoid them if you can.

To defend yourself, you need to take two essential steps:

1. **Identify potential threats.**

   Go through the preceding list to identify the kinds of threats that may take a toll on your brand reputation. Then assess the likelihood of those threats actually occurring. For any threat that appears to loom large, reduce vulnerability by establishing systems and protective actions that steer your organization away from the potential risks.

2. **Prepare a brand-crisis-management plan.**

   Decide who will lead and serve on the crisis-management team, what communication procedures will be followed, and the steps that will get a clear, consistent message out to all affected audiences.

Identifying potential threats

While your business environment is calm, take time to imagine some of the worst-case scenarios your brand may face. Then assess how significantly each threat could affect the strength of your brand and business. Take these steps:

1. **Consider potential brand threats that may negatively impact your brand image.**

   Refer to the preceding list of brand-damaging event categories to prompt your thinking.

2. **Rank the likelihood of each brand threat occurring.**

   For instance, a privately held service business with no shareholders and no production facilities has a low likelihood of encountering a threat from a lapse of corporate behavior. If that same business is headed by an owner with a high-profile, jet-set lifestyle, however, the likelihood of a real or perceived lapse of personal behavior may be high.

3. **Determine which of your brand attributes would be most affected should your brand encounter each potential brand threat.**

   For example, if your business has to deal with news of a product failure, brand attributes such as safety, precision craftsmanship, or quality would be affected. If it suffers from a lapse of the leader's personal behavior, and if part of the brand's image is reliant on the leader's reputation for trustworthiness and integrity, a brand crisis could easily follow.

4. **Rank the impact of each attribute that may be affected on the overall strength of your brand.**

   For example, if your brand is known primarily for its safety record and suddenly sustains a safety lapse, the impact on brand strength would be high. Brand damage is always worst when the damage hits closest to the promise and attributes for which the brand is known and respected.

 Use the chart shown in Figure 18-1 as you assess the likelihood that various potential threats will impact attributes that are important to the strength of your brand image. Wherever you see a likely brand threat to a high-value brand attribute, take preventive action by fortifying systems and procedures in order to avoid the lapse and the brand-shaking crisis it would likely trigger.

EVALUATING IMPACT OF BRAND THREATS ON BRAND STRENGTH				
In any row that you check "high" in both the Likelihood and Impact columns, the brand threat is both real and potentially highly damaging.				
Potential Brand Threat	✔ Likelihood Low Medium High	Which of your brand attributes would be most affected by the brand threat? (Performance, Design, Prestige, Reliability, Safety, Comfort, Luxury, Expertise, and so on)	✔ Impact of the affected attribute on your brand strength Low Medium High	
Lapse of social responsibility (due to hiring policies, vendor policies, production processes, human rights, and so on)	☐ ☐ ☐		☐ ☐ ☐	
Lapse in corporate behavior (due to accounting discrepancies; violation of environmental or other regulations; violation of trust of consumers, employees, investors, stockholders, and others)	☐ ☐ ☐		☐ ☐ ☐	
Lapse of personal behavior of high-profile owner or leader, spokesperson, or other brand representative (due to legal issues, personal troubles, and so on)	☐ ☐ ☐		☐ ☐ ☐	
Death or sudden departure of corporate leader	☐ ☐ ☐		☐ ☐ ☐	
Product failure, malfunction, or danger (whether real or rumored)	☐ ☐ ☐		☐ ☐ ☐	
Natural or human-caused disaster or accident that affects business access, product delivery, or safety of consumers and employees.	☐ ☐ ☐		☐ ☐ ☐	

Figure 18-1: Assessing threats to your strongest brand attributes.

© Barbara Findlay Schenck

Taking preemptive strikes against brand threats

After you complete the chart in Figure 18-1, pay special attention to any rows in which you've checked "medium" or "high" in both the second and fourth columns. These rows indicate areas where your brand faces a strong likelihood of encountering a threat that could shake its reputation to the core.

For each high-risk, high-impact threat, develop a two-pronged strategy to reduce the risk while also developing a capability to deal with the threat should it happen. Go so far as to share your preemptive plans with those who have a stake in your brand — from employees to customers to suppliers to investors.

For example, Berkshire Hathaway is a publicly traded company controlled by Warren Buffett, one of the most renowned and richest investors in the world. When it comes to Berkshire Hathaway's brand attributes, the wisdom and wit of Warren Buffet soar to the top of the list. As a result, the departure of Buffett, who has run the company since 1965, is a valid brand threat from which the company doesn't run or hide. Berkshire Hathaway annual reports include "Succession Planning" sections. One included the paragraph, "As owners, you . . . also want to know what happens if I should die tonight." The rest of the section details how the company is prepared to handle the transition in a way that protects the security of the company and shareholder investments. It ends with the assurance, "We have an outstanding group of directors, and they will always do what's right for shareholders. And while we are on the subject, I feel terrific."

Take a straightforward approach when owning up to and addressing your own brand threats. Follow these steps:

1. **Face facts.**

   Where you know you face a risk, admit it. Trying to wish danger away is never a decent strategy. If you're vulnerable because of lax production policies, admit it. If the public places high confidence in your beloved but aging leader, admit it. The same goes for any other possible threat that could endanger a key attribute of your brand or that could strike at the essence of what your brand promises and stands for. Wherever you think a threat could be lurking, shed light on it. Dare to imagine worst-case scenarios and begin planning to avert the threat and minimize the danger it could cause.

2. **Gather a team to discuss risks and responses.**

   Form a brand-threat management committee to consider potential threats. Involve not just brand-management staff but also managers from customer service, production, financial management, and other departments. Discuss what kinds of events could trigger a brand threat and how each can be preempted.

3. **Take preventive action.**

   If the threat is real and the risk is high, address it head-on. Enact new policies. Install new procedures. Establish a succession plan. Create evacuation procedures. Address high-risk behaviors. Take whatever steps are necessary and effective to face up to and reduce or eliminate vulnerabilities that could damage your brand image.

Be Prepared: Planning to Dodge Brand Threats and Missteps

Today, bad news transmits virally at the speed of Internet connections. If the worst happens and your brand reputation is attacked by internal or outside forces, be ready to move immediately to get in front of the story, to remedy the problem, and to assure the public that it won't happen again.

Public relations professionals talk about a *golden hour* during which you can control the news and move quickly to save your brand image from disaster. Yet too many companies spend the first hour following a brand threat wringing their hands, pointing fingers, and trying to figure out the steps to take. By the time they're ready to move, the story is out of their control and being told by others, often with inaccuracies and from perspectives that damage the brand even further.

Commit to developing a brand-crisis-management plan that includes these components:

- **Who's who** on your crisis-management team, including who will serve as the primary and secondary spokespersons, who will provide legal or technical advice, and who will help staff the plan.

- **Whom to contact** in the event of a crisis. Prepare a list with home, office, fax, and cellphone numbers; email addresses; and mailing addresses for

  - Emergency and security contacts
  - Top executives and managers
  - Business and financial partners
  - Media contacts

> - Employees
> - Key contacts in your community, industry, and distribution channels
> - Key customers

✔ **What to say,** including what happened, what you're doing to make it right, and how it won't happen again — all in terms that describe your concern for the public and not simply your actions to minimize corporate or brand loss. Remember, you can't plan your exact message in advance, but you can plan what your message needs to convey.

✔ **What your strategy is,** including plans for releasing the news, establishing and staffing physical and online media centers, staying active and responsive on social media, handling heightened interest through expanded and even back-up phone and online capacity, and providing ongoing updates regarding how you're working to remedy the problem and prevent it from recurring.

The following sections cover each of these components in more detail.

Compiling a list of who's who

To activate a crisis-management program at lightning speed, know in advance exactly who will serve on your management and communication team. Fill the roles explained in each of the following sections.

Primary spokesperson

Each communications crisis needs one calm, knowledgeable person to serve as a spokesperson who presents facts, fields questions, and provides an interface between the media and the brand. In small businesses or organizations, the CEO or the owner often takes on spokesperson responsibilities simply because no one else in the organization has a high enough profile to fill the role. In larger organizations, the person who serves as the communications expert (usually the vice president or director of public relations) assumes the task.

When other qualified candidates are available, many organizations avoid naming the CEO as primary spokesperson. The reasoning behind naming someone other than the CEO is sound: If media representatives are trained to deal with the CEO, they won't settle for statements from a secondary spokesperson. As a result, if the CEO isn't available, media representatives may hold their questions, and potentially damaging information lapses may occur as a result.

As you appoint your spokesperson, be sure he or she is trained in your brand story and message as well as in media relations, including how to conduct and manage interviews and media coverage. Also be sure the spokesperson is

✔ Capable of communicating and presenting information well

✔ Comfortable and experienced in front of cameras and in media interviews

✔ Knowledgeable about your organization

✔ Credible, trustworthy, and an empathetic representative to those both within and outside your organization

✔ Able to inspire confidence and explain issues clearly and without jargon

✔ Aware of the full scope of the issue and the range of experts who can provide additional information to reporters

✔ Calm, sincere, and likeable

Avoid naming a lawyer as the primary spokesperson. Doing so indicates that you have legal concerns, which translates to guilt in the minds of consumers.

Secondary spokesperson

Your primary spokesperson can't always be on-call, so name a back-up spokesperson with similar capabilities so that a fully informed person is always available to media and others.

If your primary spokesperson is your CEO, be sure that your secondary spokesperson is a high-level company officer or owner who shares similar clout. Otherwise, media representatives will want to wait to talk with the CEO, potentially costing your brand an opportunity to provide breaking news and facts to the public.

Expert advisors

Depending on the nature of the brand crisis, you may need to involve representatives from various outside organizations to provide specific information on anything from medical to legal to police activities.

Ask each outside organization to name its own primary and secondary spokespersons rather than making comments through a list of different representatives. This arrangement helps you limit the number of people who are explaining the crisis to the public. Otherwise, people hear bits and pieces of the story from a mind-boggling number of representatives, triggering confusion and a lack of confidence in your story, business, and brand.

Your CEO

Regardless of whether your CEO serves as the primary crisis spokesperson or not, he or she must lead the response to a brand threat, getting involved in the very first moments and signing off on every element of the communication plan so that no second-guessing or finger-pointing occurs along the way of dealing with the problem.

Knowing who to call

In advance of any crisis, prepare a crisis communication contact list that contains full contact information for the following:

- ✔ **Internal contacts,** including executives, crisis team members, managers, employees, union representatives, and others
- ✔ **Emergency contacts,** including police, security, and government offices
- ✔ **Media contacts,** including reporters, bloggers, and editors at local, national, international, and trade or industry media outlets that have an interest in news of your organization
- ✔ **Investor and analyst contacts,** ranging from local bankers to your shareholders to investors or potential investors
- ✔ **Community and industry contacts,** including your local chamber of commerce, industry or trade association, key partners, subcontractors, and competitors
- ✔ **Business partners,** including customers, suppliers, and distributors
- ✔ **Special interest contacts,** including those that lead environmental, safety, consumer, or other groups that take an interest in your business

List the sequence in which contacts should be made to ensure that those who most need to know are reached immediately and before all others. Also make sure that copies of the contact list are readily available in multiple locations inside and outside your business, including in the offices of your CEO, communications or public relations director, top-level executives, and in password-protected online files.

Working out what to do and say

The first priority of every brand manager is to avoid brand crises in the first place. That's why it's important to regularly assess and take proactive steps to defend against the kinds of threats that are likely to attack your brand strength. The chart in Figure 18-1 helps you with this task.

Sometimes, though, in spite of the best efforts, bad things happen to good brands. Should your brand face a crisis, be ready to launch defensive action.

A single set of advice applies to *all* crisis situations: Tell the truth, be as complete as possible, issue statements immediately, and aim to restore trust as quickly as possible.

Instead of wasting precious moments debating what to do, take the following actions immediately:

1. **Activate your emergency communication system by contacting those who need to know first about the threatening event.**

2. **Convene your brand-crisis communication team.**

   Immediately assess the situation. Determine how the situation affects customers or others. Also determine whether the situation affects your organization legally, financially, administratively, operationally, or in other ways.

3. **Craft the message you'll deliver to explain what happened and what your organization will do to address the situation and restore safety and confidence.**

   When writing your message, limit it to a few sentences. If you can't explain the situation in seconds, people aren't able to grasp and understand it, and they'll turn to others for what may be erroneous explanations. Prepare a message that meets these criteria:

   • It has no more than three key points that explain the situation, each summarized in fewer than ten words. For each point, prepare up to three supporting facts that your spokesperson can provide as additional explanation.

   • It includes no industry jargon or words that can't be understood by someone with an eighth-grade education.

   • It's relevant and delivered in terms that matter to those who are affected by the situation. This isn't the time to talk about how your organization is affected. This is the time to show you care about all affected parties and are dealing with the situation on their behalf.

4. **Name who will serve as your primary spokesperson and secondary spokesperson and what additional experts you will need to call on to explain the situation.**

5. **Make a list of a dozen or so of the toughest questions you think your spokesperson will be asked.**

   For each question, prepare and rehearse a short response that includes the name of the person who can provide additional legal, technical, or other specific information.

6. **Have your message and your prepared answers to anticipated questions reviewed and approved by those responsible for the affected functions as well as by your company's CEO and legal team.**

7. **Prepare a news release that explains the situation.**

   Tell who, what, where, when, why, and how you're dealing with the situation, using your approved message and Chapter 12's advice on writing releases.

8. **Make your announcement and distribute your news release as quickly as possible.**

   Notify employees and all organization insiders immediately before or at the same time that you release the story to news media. In addition to circulating your prepared release, deliver a concise statement that summarizes key points and focuses on the steps you're taking to achieve a positive outcome for all affected parties.

9. **Open a media center where you can meet with reporters in a location that allows them access to the story yet provides adequate distance from the hub of activity so that they don't overhear unplanned comments.**

10. **Activate an emergency website, or add designated pages to your online pressroom to present breaking news and background information.**

    See Chapter 12 for assistance in building an online pressroom.

11. **Constantly update and distribute information that provides situation and response updates, including steps your organization is taking to ensure the safety of people and products.**

    Remain consistent, forthright, available, and responsive to all who are affected or who have questions or concerns.

12. **When the crisis subsides, assess the impact on your brand and begin work immediately to restore your brand strength by following the steps detailed later in this chapter and in Chapter 16.**

Pushing through the pain

One of the most legendary examples of a successfully implemented crisis management plan comes out of the early 1980s, when packages of Tylenol Extra Strength capsules were maliciously filled with cyanide-laced capsules, resealed, and placed on retail shelves in the Chicago area.

Johnson & Johnson, parent company of McNeil Consumer Products Company, the maker of Tylenol, learned of the crisis through the kind of phone call no brand owner wants to receive. A Chicago news reporter called to report that people weren't just sick but were dying from poisoned Tylenol product.

Johnson & Johnson wasted no time in launching a crisis response. The company immediately convened a crisis strategy team charged with devising a response to two questions (in this order): How do we protect the people? And how do we save the product?

First, the team used the media to alert consumers nationwide not to consume any form of Tylenol until further notice. They withdrew all

(continued)

(continued)

Tylenol packages from Chicago-area shelves and stopped all advertising and production. When a tainted product was found outside the Chicago area, they went a step farther and pulled every bottle of Tylenol from every retail shelf nationwide. Simultaneously, Johnson & Johnson offered to exchange all purchased Tylenol capsules with Tylenol tablets, at a potential cost to the company of millions of dollars.

The financial impact on Johnson & Johnson was enormous, but the focus of the company's efforts remained firmly on consumer safety rather than on dollars lost. It established hotlines and issued a constant stream of news updates. Not once did the company spotlight the fact that it had nothing to do with the tainted product. Instead, it put up a $100,000 reward and worked with the police, FBI, and other government agencies to help find those responsible, all the while working internally to devise tamper-proof packaging to protect against such a disaster recurring in the future.

Within months, Tylenol returned to pharmacies and retail shelves, this time wrapped in triple-safety sealed packaging. To bring consumers back to the brand, the company circulated coupons to be applied to new purchases of Tylenol. It launched a new ad campaign, and more than 2,000 salespeople were enlisted to make presentations to members of the medical community to inspire support for the product reintroduction.

Tylenol quickly reclaimed 27 percent of the pain-reliever market and today is one of the top-selling over-the-counter drugs in the United States. This fact is a strong testament to the way Johnson & Johnson rapidly responded to the crisis by taking responsibility, putting consumer safety first, working with the media, and, ultimately, recovering from the greatest brand crisis in the pharmaceutical industry.

Acting with speed, calm, consistency, and unwavering customer focus

A long string of high-profile public-relations crises have taught some of indisputable lessons:

✔ **Don't wait to address the problem.** The longer you stay silent, the longer you allow others to frame the story and spread their version of the facts, rumors, or even conspiracy theories, with damage escalating with each post, tweet, or newscast. Brand silence gets translated to mean a lack of control or a lack of concern. Either is devastating to brand trust. Instead, learn what happened, know how the problem is being addressed or corrected, know where and how the news is spreading, and replace conjecture with facts and solutions.

✔ **Don't try to trivialize or, even worse, cover up the issue.** With 24-hour news and split-second social media commentary, there's no such thing as a "blip on the radar screen" when it comes to brand missteps. When public awareness and concern about a brand problem or misstep is high, the story likely won't go away until the issue is adequately addressed and overcome. Being anything less than honest about the extent of the problem creates a situation that requires further elaboration or even backtracking, nicking away remaining brand credibility with each revised comment. Instead, take responsibility. Briefly communicate what happened, what you're doing to right the wrong, and how you'll prevent the problem from reoccurring.

✔ **Don't say *no comment*.** If you truly can't comment due to legal or other restrictions, admit you're unable to make a statement. Otherwise, explain that the issue isn't related to the topic at hand, or that you have nothing to add, which is an apt response to a question that's already been asked and answered repeatedly. Saying *no comment* is the worst of all answers because in the ears of others it sounds an awful lot like *guilty as charged*.

✔ **Spread your response to the story through the same media channels where the bad news is spreading.** If your brand mishap is trending on Twitter, sending a news release to traditional media outlets adds nothing to the conversation that's taking place. For an example worth following (though we hope you won't need to), consider the Domino's response to a disgusting video featuring two uniformed employees enacting our worst fears about behind-the-scenes food prep. Within 48 hours and, unfortunately, a million views, Domino's countered by uploading its own video. With cameras rolling, the Domino's USA president apologized, thanked members of the online community for making the corporation aware of the video, and announced that even though the employees claimed their video was a hoax, Domino's was taking the issue "incredibly seriously," shutting down and sanitizing the location and instituting a review of hiring practices to avoid similar problems in the future. The brand also gave the whistle-blowers coupons worth approximately a year's worth of free food. Other than wasting 48 hours between the crisis and the response, Domino's delivered a superb reaction that, most agree, saved the brand's reputation.

In a crisis, silence isn't golden

Today, brand crises go viral within seconds, so be prepared to launch a rapid response.

Chances are good someone has video or photos of what happened (a too-long list of NFL brand crises come to mind) so trying to minimize or fictionalize the damaging event is nearly sure to backfire.

Social media has turned the rumor mill into a high-speed transmission channel, so in a crisis be ready to speak up immediately and honestly or be prepared to let others tell their version of the story in your absence. Tiger Woods demonstrated what happens if you wait weeks and then hold a no-questions-allowed news conference, and the Catholic Church provided evidence of what happens to brands that try to ignore or minimize problems.

Even if unaddressed disastrous news slips from the front pages or trending topics, brand strength nearly always goes with it.

Following crisis communications do's and don'ts

Whether you're in the throes of a brand crisis or simply preparing your organization for such a situation, use this checklist of advice as you prepare to face up to public concern:

- ✔ Do be caring and genuinely concerned.

- ✔ Do take responsibility.

- ✔ Do explain the situation immediately in a few sentences that can be widely understood by the general public.

- ✔ Do prepare a concise message and share it within your organization so that everyone is talking from the same page and telling the same truths.

- ✔ Do be prepared to present complete back-up information and explanations upon request, but don't offer more information than requested or you risk confusing the message.

- ✔ Do avoid jargon or language that the general public doesn't understand.

- ✔ Do keep your employees informed of all new developments.

- ✔ Do plan and share remedies for the situation and controls that will prevent it from recurring.

- ✔ Do answer questions in a way that allows you to reiterate the key points of your approved message.

- ✔ Do prepare updated background information and news releases prior to each new announcement or major interview.

- ✔ Do realize that the spokesperson should provide facts that have been assembled and confirmed by your organization and its expert resources and should stick to the approved points.

- ✔ Do limit the number of people who explain the crisis to the public. Include only your primary spokesperson, a secondary spokesperson, and a handful of designated expert spokespeople from within or outside your organization who are selected to explain legal, medical, technical, or other aspects of the situation.

- ✔ Do rehearse presentations and responses to anticipated questions.

- ✔ Do follow up immediately on all information requests.

- ✔ Do refer questions requiring technical or legal responses to the designated expert spokespeople.

- ✔ Do stay calm and positive and demonstrate genuine care and concern.

✔ Don't veer from approved messages.

✔ Don't say *no comment* or ask to be off the record.

✔ Don't respond to negative questions by repeating negative phrases. Instead, address the issue in positive terms.

✔ Don't delay responding to media. If you need additional time, schedule a return call shortly, by which time you should have the appropriate information to share.

Picking Up the Pieces Post-Crisis

After the crisis — after you've moved quickly and transparently to explain, address, and overcome the problem facing your brand, two major steps remain: Following up on promises made during the crisis response and rebuilding brand trust that was weakened during the ordeal.

Following up on promises made

When the heat of the moment passes, details remain to be addressed:

✔ Provide any information that was promised to reporters, bloggers, customers, investors, or other stakeholders who were aware of or affected by the brand crisis.

✔ Create and circulate a summary of recovery efforts and corrective measures. Externally, circulate information that audiences will find reassuring, useful, or simply interesting. Internally, circulate assessments of how well your crisis response worked and what additional preventative measures or response plans should be addressed, and how such improvements are being planned.

Above all else, offer thanks and issue compensation, rewards, or praise as appropriate to those who helped you address and overcome a threat not just to your brand but to the people your brand is fortunate to serve.

Rebuilding trust

On an ongoing basis, monitor what's being said about your brand. Then double your brand-monitoring efforts following a brand threat.

At the very least, increase the frequency at which you study search results for your brand name. Set up Google Alerts (google.com/alerts) to receive email messages each time the brand name or terms you want to study are mentioned online. Also, use free services such as Social Mention (www.socialmention.com) and Topsy (www.topsy.com) to monitor social media for mentions. Plus, do your own searches using browsers and search boxes on social networks to find recent references to your name or to terms that reference the recent crisis you've been through.

Use your findings to guide development of responsive communications. If your brand promise has been endangered, create programs to reactivate the pledge you make to your market. For example, Domino's followed its brand crisis by launching a "Pizza Turnaround" campaign, and the Lean-In organization launched a paid internship program after it faced a damaging barrage of criticism in response to an ad seeking unpaid internship applications.

Never forget: Your brand is your most valuable asset. Constantly protect, defend, and strengthen it, whether that means realigning your brand to address changing market situations or, in the most drastic of circumstances, rebranding it with an entirely new identity if — and this is the rare circumstance — the damage done is irreparable. Make Chapter 16 your brand-repair guide.

Part VI

The Part of Tens

For a list of the ten traits that top brands share, visit www.dummies.com/extras/branding.

In this part . . .

- ✔ Review ten things you need to know about personal brands, including why they matter and why you need one whether you're part of a branded business, whether you're building your own branded business, or whether you're developing a private practice, freelance business, or one-person consulting firm that relies on the strength of your personal name and the reputation of your unique expertise and offerings.

- ✔ Clue into the ten biggest branding mistakes to steer clear of, each accompanied with advice to adopt and remedies to follow. From avoiding a weak brand launch to confusing a logo with a brand to underestimating the value of brand protections and brand experiences, get familiar with the most frequent brand-breakpoints so you know what problems to avoid and where and how to build brand value instead.

- ✔ Memorize a round-up of branding truths ranging from what brands are to how they're built, what makes and keeps them strong, where they live and grow, and how names, logos, and brand experiences fit into the process of creating, maintaining, and forever building value for your brand — the single most valuable asset your business owns.

Chapter 19

Ten Signs that Your Personal Brand Needs Attention

In This Chapter

▶ Reviewing ways personal branding overcomes success obstacles

▶ Making personal branding a personal priority

There's a reason personal branding is a priority of the most successful people you know, whether they operate as freelancers, independent consultants, small business owners, corporate executives, employees in well-branded businesses or organizations, or leaders of every stripe. Those who achieve their goals and ascend to the top of their fields benefit from highly regarded reputations — personal brands — that pave the way for their success.

Personal branding is how you manage your reputation and interactions to develop positive impressions in the minds of those you want to influence. Through personal branding, you positively affect how people react to you, how they fit you into their hierarchy of interests and needs, and how they view you as an asset, a leader, a star in your field.

Tick through the ten points in this chapter to determine whether your personal brand is in need of attention. Then make Chapter 4 your guide to follow.

You're Not Making Your Personal Goals

If you're not getting the promotions, interviews, publicity, customers, or opportunities you want, chances are your personal brand is part of the problem. The image others hold, or what they discover when they inquire about you or search for you online, may be blocking the positive responses you seek.

Personal branding is how you manage your reputation and interactions to develop positive images in the minds of those you want to influence. It does so in two ways:

✔ **Personal branding creates an internal force:** Through the personal branding process you figure out what you're best at and how you want to be perceived by others. You set personal goals and the roadmap you'll follow to reach them. You lock in on how to present yourself. As a result, you gain self-confidence about your strengths, your goals, your target audience, and the unique personality, expertise, and message you want to consistently cultivate and convey.

✔ **Personal branding creates an external force:** Through personal branding, you help others form good first and lasting impressions about who you are and what you stand for, your expertise, your unique benefits and value, and what they can count on you to do best. You help them gain trust in your attributes and abilities every time they encounter you or any information about you, especially online, where those you want to influence often form their first impressions.

You Think Personal Branding Sounds Self-Absorbed

Intentionally or not, you have a personal brand. It's whatever people believe about who you are and what you stand for based on what they've personally experienced, what they've heard from others, or what they've seen online.

If you think the term *personal branding* sounds somehow self-centered, call it *reputation management* instead. Either way, it's essential to your success.

Through personal branding, you positively affect the beliefs about you that arise in the minds of others when they encounter you or your name. You help them understand the value you deliver. You help them see, how you fit into their hierarchy of interests and needs. You enhance how they view you as an asset, a leader, and a star in your field. As a result, you improve how they react when they encounter you or your name and as they decide whether or not to involve you in their lives.

You Can't Say What You're Best At

Personal branding begins with knowledge about what you want people to believe about you and what, in fact, they currently believe. To get started, take these steps:

✔ **List five words you'd like associated with your image.**

✔ **Look through recent compliments, testimonials, endorsements, and recommendations for words others use when describing your strengths.**

✔ **Ask people you know and work with to name the first five words that come to mind when they think of you.**

When you've decided what you want to be known for, and after you've determined what, in fact, you're currently known for, the process of personal branding helps you close the gap and align the images held by others with the images you want them to have and hold.

Search Results for Your Name Are Few and Far Between

These facts are from Chapter 4 and worth repeating in this roundup of personal branding motivations:

✔ Google handles more than a billion name searches daily.

✔ Nine of 10 job recruiters use social networks to find candidates, and three of four check search results and social-media profiles.

✔ Nearly everyone now gathers information online or through word-of-mouth when pursuing personal or business relationships.

When people enter your name into a search box, the results influence their opinions about who you are, what you stand for, and how outstanding you are in your field. Check yourself out:

✔ Do you own the all-important first search result for your name?

✔ Do you dominate the first page of results, with links to positive content all the way down the page?

If the results for your name search are few, outdated, or embarrassing, get busy establishing online presence that helps those you want to influence see and believe that you're a valuable force of influence in your field. Turn to Chapters 10 and 11 for advice to follow.

Links to Your Name Are Dated, or Worse

This malady may be the single biggest kick-in-the-seat-of-the-pants for those in need of personal brand repair. Online self-sleuthing is often called *ego surfing,* and few can live comfortably with results that reflect poorly on who they are and how they want to be perceived.

If you don't like how you look online, consider this advice:

✔ **Lack of online presence:** If a search for your name leads to no, few, or deeply buried results, make online presence a top personal branding goal. Start by launching a personal blog or website and creating profiles on major social-media networks, including Google+ and LinkedIn profiles, as both appear prominently in search results. See Chapter 10 for advice.

✔ **Outdated, irrelevant, or embarrassing online presence:** If results for your name search don't support your desired brand image, make development of links to current, favorable content part of your personal branding program. By achieving positive mentions on high-traffic, reputable sites you can push unfavorable links onto second, third, or subsequent screens, where they're less likely to be seen.

To make the most of your efforts, make all links findable by using one version of your name everywhere, from your business cards to your personal introductions, to your domain name and social-media profiles.

You Freeze Up When It's Time to Introduce Yourself

If you draw a blank when you have a chance to introduce yourself, you're missing out on the only chance you'll have to make a great first impression. Personal branding helps you land on the words to use. Cover these points:

✔ What you do and for whom, using keywords or terms people are likely to use when searching for people like you

✔ A sense of the kind of information and expertise people can count on receiving from you

✔ A sense of your personality

✔ A thought-provoking, interesting, likeable indication of why you're credible, trustworthy, and worth associating with, along with interesting facts about what you're into and what you've done that's cool and brag-worthy — without actually bragging

As you introduce yourself, remember that in today's attention-deprived world you get only seconds to make others want to learn more. To be ready for any situation, prepare your personal introduction in several forms:

✔ A 30-second introduction you can use face-to-face, whether in business meetings, networking events, or chance encounters with those who can be instrumental to your personal or business-building goals

✔ A 160-character, 20-word introduction you can use to win interest and convey who you are on social-media pages and other online sites

> ✔ 50-, 100-, and 500-word versions of your introduction you can rapidly select from to share when people ask for your biographical information

Your Connection Invitations Get Ignored

If your job applications are routinely bypassed, your social-media invitations get no response, your phone calls don't get returned, or your pitches always come in behind those of the winning contender, your personal brand may well be part of the problem.

People respond positively to those they believe will have a positive impact on their own lives and goals. Give thought to these questions:

> ✔ What do people think when they meet you or see or hear your name?

> ✔ What do they learn if they ask around or search for your name online?

> ✔ What do they see if they look at your social-media pages?

> ✔ What impression do they get from their first contact with you, whether that contact comes through an email message, a letter, a phone call, a résumé, a personal encounter, or some other form of introduction?

Turn to Chapter 3 as you take a candid look at your brand image and what may be blocking the responses you're seeking from others.

You Aren't Sure Which to Promote: Your Personal or Your Business Brand

Most people present two brands at once: their personal brand and the brand of their own or their employer's business. As you present both brands, maintain balance between the two so that each reinforces without eclipsing the other.

The following questions will help you decide if you need to pay special attention to boosting the visibility and strength of either your personal or your business brand:

> ✔ **Assessing your personal brand:** If you sold your business or left your current job tomorrow, is your personal brand strong enough to move with you into new opportunities? Have you developed a reputation based on your personal abilities and the distinct value you consistently deliver, or is your reputation built primarily on your current employer and business title and therefore not easily transportable to future opportunities? If your personal brand isn't well-defined and transportable, it needs work.

> ✔ **Assessing your business brand:** If you own your own business or hold a key position in your employer's business, is the business brand you represent strong enough to survive without the power of your personal brand behind it, should you decide to leave the business? If your personal brand is so strong that people know and trust you more than your business, your business brand needs attention.

Flip to Chapter 4 as you work to keep your personal and business brands in balance and as you plan ways to cross-promote the two.

You Need but Don't Know How to Ask for Referrals and Recommendations

Good words from respected and trustworthy sources can be key to success in reaching your personal branding goals. Instead of just waiting for praise, reach out and request recommendations, following these steps:

✔ Tell why you're reaching out and the reason you're asking for a recommendation. For example, "I'm preparing to announce my new book and would like my website and promotional material to include kudos from respected authors like you who are familiar with my work." This gives your request context, allows you to share a compliment, and conveys that the request is carefully targeted.

✔ Tell what kind of recommendation you're hoping to receive. For example, "Would you help by writing a couple of sentences that mention my expertise and your experience working with me? I'm including a few recent comments as examples that might make my request easier to fulfill." This saves the request recipient time and guides development of a recommendation that suits your needs.

✔ State your timeline. For example, "I'm hoping to receive your comment by the end of next week, along with the website you'd like me to link to your name." This makes your request clear and mutually beneficial.

You Want More Awareness, Credibility, and Recognition in Your Field

Personal goals are the best reason of all to kick your personal branding efforts into high gear. Follow the steps in Chapter 4 and use the advice throughout this book as you get specific about what you want to accomplish, how you want to be known, and the strategy you'll follow to differentiate yourself, develop awareness, win credibility and trust, and gain the reputation and influence that affects your success in every aspect of your life.

Chapter 20

Ten Branding Mistakes and How to Avoid Them

Some brands get off to great starts. Some are wobbly from the get-go. Others start well and then lose their way through lack of focus, discipline, and follow-through on brand strategies, brand promises, and reliably consistent brand experiences.

This chapter describes ten branding mistakes to steer clear of, each accompanied by tips to keep your brand moving continuously in the right direction, constantly gaining esteem and equity as a result.

Thinking of Branding as a Quick Fix

The mistake: When business is down, when customer interest ebbs, or when competition surges, the idea of branding masquerades as some miracle cure for transforming perceptions and jump-starting success. In the heat of the moment, otherwise cool-headed professionals begin to believe that a cosmetic fix — a new logo and maybe a new name, tagline, or message — will remedy all that ails the bottom line. It doesn't work that way, though, because a successful brand has to go all the way to the core of an organization.

The remedy: Before you create or alter the face of your brand, be sure you're creating an accurate reflection of what's at the base of your brand. The part of your brand that rises into public view — your name, logo, and marketing materials — must mirror the mission, vision, values, culture, leadership, and management that lies at the heart and soul of your organization. Otherwise, a credibility crisis looms large.

Chapter 6 helps you define the essence of your organization and how it operates and then guides your thinking as you put your brand promise, brand character, and brand identity into words. Then, and only then, are you ready to name your brand, design your logo, and create marketing materials and a brand experience to convey your brand accurately and successfully in your world. The process isn't quick, but it's worth it!

Starting with a Weak Brand Identity

The mistake: Weak identities appear in the form of names that limit the scope and success of the brands they represent. Or they're displayed as logos that at-a-glance convey they were created on shoestring budgets by organizations with little chance of competing with big, established businesses.

As long as the brands represented by weak names and logos are satisfied to remain in the confines that their identities dictate, all's well. But if they want to expand into more competitive spheres, their weak identities are heavy anchors dragging down their success.

The remedy: Invest the time and money required to develop a strong name and logo when you first establish your brand. Remember these points:

- ✔ **In most cases, your name will live as long as your business does, so choose, register, and protect a name that your brand can grow with over years and decades.** Great brand names travel through time, trends, markets, and even strategic redirections. Settle on a name that conveys your brand promise, supports your brand image, and that's unique, pleasant to say, and easy to recall — all without confining your brand to a specific product or market area. (Chapter 7 has naming advice.)

- ✔ **Your logo will become the immediately identifiable face of your brand, so make it a strong, simple, unique design that reproduces well in all forms of communication.** Chapter 8 provides a guide to logo design along with the strong recommendation that you seek professional design assistance. When the time's right to update your look, turn to Chapter 16 for tips on how to revitalize your logo so that it remains a contemporary representation of your brand.

Forgetting the Branding Rule of One

The mistake: Businesses that barely have the budgets and staff required to build one brand try to build two or more. In doing so, they dilute the expertise and funding they can devote to any one brand and build strength for none.

The remedy: Unless you're sure that you have the marketing budget and expertise required to build and support multiple brands, stick to what we call the Rule of One: Build one brand for your business rather than a business full of many brands. Apply the Rule of One by following this advice:

✔ Build a single brand that can preside over all your offerings.

✔ Introduce each new product or service as an offering under your one-and-only brand. This strategy allows each new product to capitalize upon the credibility of your brand while boosting the strength of your brand through the success of each new offering.

Chapter 2 has tips on how to manage a number of products under your one-and-only brand, and Chapter 7 can help you develop a family of names under one brand umbrella. Chapter 15 offers advice for leveraging the power of your brand through new products, cobranded offerings, and licensing opportunities.

If you decide to create separate brands for individual products or services, build a separate business unit for each new brand. Separate business units allow each offering to stand on its own, drawing on its own resources and building independent value that you can spin off or sell in the future.

Failing to Differentiate

The mistake: If you can't tell customers what you do best, they have no reason to choose your offering and good reason to opt for a different, more distinct solution. Or if they think that all available offerings deliver the same value and quality, they'll simply buy whatever's most easily available at the lowest price.

The remedy: Find a distinguishing characteristic that causes your offering to excel over alternatives and build your brand around that point of difference.

Chapter 5 helps you find your brand's unique position in the marketplace. Chapter 13 guides development of a customer experience that reinforces your point of difference at every point of encounter with your brand.

Failing to Launch Your Brand with Fanfare

The mistake: Even business owners that love groundbreakings, ribbon cuttings, grand openings, and lavish celebrations underestimate the importance of staging a brand launch. If you fail to introduce your brand with a formal launch you lose a great one-time opportunity to make news about your brand identity, point of difference, promise, and message.

The **remedy:** Launch your brand from the inside out, bringing every aspect of your business into alignment with your brand promise, personality, and character before you raise the curtain and introduce your brand in your marketplace (see Chapter 9). Chapters 10, 11, and 12 are full of information on how to take your brand to public audiences via publicity, advertising, social media, and digital communications.

Failing to Protect and Defend

The **mistake:** Brand owners get complacent. They fail to obtain or defend trademarks, lock up domain names, write brand usage guidelines, or enforce brand-usage rules. Before long, brand names are in jeopardy, brand consistency is at risk, and brand value plummets.

The **remedy:** Protect your brand in three important ways:

1. **File your name with appropriate government offices and obtain brand trademarks if your sphere of business crosses state or national boundaries.**

2. **Establish, adopt, and enforce usage guidelines so that those within or outside your organization don't tamper with your brand identity.**

3. **Address every brand-usage infraction, without fail.**

Check out Chapter 17 for advice to follow in order to defend your brand.

Believing that What You Say Is More Important Than What You Do

The **mistake:** Even with the best name and logo, the most awesome brand launch, and brand marketing materials that win best-of-show in creative competitions, brands suffer if they don't live up to their promises.

The **remedy:** Realize that your brand is either made or broken not by what you say but by what you do. People base their brand impressions upon the caliber and consistency of their own experiences. To establish and maintain the kind of brand experience that builds passion, loyalty, and brand value, follow the advice in Chapter 13 and take these steps:

1. **Identify every point of customer contact within your brand experience, including pre-purchase encounters, purchase and product usage, and post-purchase communications and service.**

2. **Evaluate each point of contact to see that you present your brand message, promise, look, and tone consistently and without fail.**

3. **Identify and correct any points of contact where the brand experience falls even slightly short of your brand promise.**

4. **Regularly audit your brand experience to ensure against brand-eroding communication or service lapses.**

Losing Brand Consistency

The mistake: Brand owners get bored. They get tired of their looks and messages, so they start improvising. They begin fiddling with their names, revising their logos, or trying out new brand voices or personalities. Just like that, consistency goes out the window. With it goes the ability to convey the brand's identity and promise with the kind of clarity that had inspired confidence in everyone from employees to consumers to investors and others.

The remedy: Realize that to build and maintain a strong brand, you have to be consistent. Follow this advice:

- Insist on uniform presentation of your logo (see Chapter 8).

- Put your brand promise into words (see Chapter 6) and make sure it's kept at every point of encounter with your brand, whether with customers, employees, suppliers, associates, or prospects.

- Define and stay true to your brand character, which is the look and voice that conveys the personality of your organization.

- Create brand-usage guidelines to be followed by everyone who produces marketing materials for or speaks on behalf of your business, and then name a brand cop to keep everyone's efforts in line (see Chapter 17).

If your brand needs updating, don't do it in a haphazard or ad hoc fashion. Follow the brand revitalization process outlined in Chapter 16.

Asking Your Brand to Stretch Too Far

The mistake: A good brand extends its name to an iffy product or to a product that contradicts the brand message and promise, confusing customers and eroding the brand's emotional connection with its loyal following.

The remedy: Extending your brand to a new offering is a smart, lucrative action only if you extend within your brand's reach, either remaining in your established product category or moving into categories that are very compatible with your the offerings for which your brand is known.

As you consider brand extensions, consider these two cautions:

- ✔ Be sure that any new products that carry your brand identity match up with consumer expectations of your brand in terms of quality, market position, and brand promise.

- ✔ Be careful that your new offering isn't so similar to an existing offering that customers can't tell the difference. Unless you're intentionally trying to phase out the established product, a lack of distinction between the two can confuse customers, causing them to buy the new product instead of the established product (called *cannibalization*) or creating selection dilemmas that result in no purchase at all.

Leveraging your brand into new product or market categories is one of the most valued perks of brand development. It allows you to capitalize on the reputation you've built over time and apply it to new ventures that benefit from instant awareness and competitive advantage. Chapter 15 provides a good overview for how to seize brand extension opportunities without stretching your name to the breaking point.

Ignoring Brand Aging Signs

The mistake: When brands get stuck in times past, brand owners are often the last ones to notice. They're so busy fending off competitors and working to attract and keep business that they fail to notice when their brand identities no longer reflect the essence of their businesses, or when their brand experiences become out of step with marketplace tastes and trends.

The remedy: On a regular basis, put your brand through the equivalent of a physical to see if its age is starting to affect its health. Chapter 16 outlines symptoms to watch for, including:

- ✔ Major ownership or leadership changes that alter your mission, vision, values, or strategic direction

- ✔ Major changes to your product line or distribution channels

- ✔ Major changes to your market situation, including significantly increased competition or major shifts in customer preferences and behaviors

- ✔ A merger or acquisition

- ✔ A brand that no longer reflects your changed business and market

- ✔ A brand message, experience, or identity that's become dated and out of sync with cultural trends and customer interests and tastes

Some brands benefit from minor cosmetic repair and message realignment, whereas others require more significant revitalization or even total rebranding. Turn to Chapter 16 for help as you conduct a brand assessment and plan what kind of a brand revision, if any, is in order.

Chapter 21

Ten Branding Truths to Remember

In This Chapter
▶ Understanding the traits of great brands
▶ Benefiting from great brand experiences

*T*he best name, logo, ads, and efforts can't compensate for a weak brand. But what's a brand? And how do you build a strong one? The ten truths presented in this chapter summarize the key points you have to know.

Branding Starts with Positioning

Your *position* is the birthplace of your brand. It's the unique space in the consumer's mind that only your offering can fill. You need to determine and stake your position before you develop the brand that will live there.

Positioning is the process of finding an unfulfilled want or need in the consumer's mind and addressing it with a distinctively different and ideally suited offering.

Remember these rules about positioning:

✔ **Your position must be open.** Otherwise, you'll need to dislodge an existing brand — and that's big and costly challenge to tackle.

✔ **Your position must be based on a unique point of difference that's believable, meaningful, and attractive to consumers.**

✔ **Your point of difference must be one that you can deliver with such consistency that every experience with your brand reminds customers of why they chose and remain loyal to your brand.**

Chapter 5 helps you determine and stake claim to the position for your brand.

A Brand Is a Promise Well Kept

Brands are promises that people believe in.

You establish a brand, in essence, by building trust in a promise about who you are, what you stand for, and what unique and meaningful benefits people can count on you to deliver.

You build your brand by reinforcing your promise every time people come in contact with you or with any facet of your organization — whether as customers, prospects, investors, employees, suppliers, friends, neighbors, or others; whether in person, online, through word-of-mouth, or through personal experiences; whether before, during, or after a purchase; and whether they're interacting with you, your staff, your products, your marketing or social messages, or any other form of encounter.

Your promise is the pledge upon which you stake your brand reputation. For help defining your promise, turn back to Chapter 6.

Branding Happens from the Inside Out

The way you present your brand to the world has to align perfectly with the values and purpose of your organization. Otherwise, your brand messages and promise won't sync with the identity that resides at the core of your business, and people will sense the lack of credibility and tune out your marketing efforts as a result.

To arrive at a brand that accurately reflects the essence of your organization, begin the branding process by writing three essential statements:

- ✔ **Your vision statement,** which defines the long-term aspirations of your organization and the ultimate good you aim to achieve.

- ✔ **Your mission statement,** which defines what you do for others and the approach you'll follow to achieve your vision.

- ✔ **Your brand statement,** which defines what you do and the positive difference you promise to make in the lives of those you serve.

Chapter 6 includes statement templates and step-by-step advice to follow in writing these statements. Chapter 9 helps you win understanding and buy-in for your brand within your organization before you announce it to the outside world.

Consistency Builds Brands

After you're clear about what your brand stands for, be prepared to reinforce it by delivering your product, promise, and brand experience with total consistency. Doing so puts the odds strongly in your favor that you'll win out over brands that shift with the wind, regardless of how beautifully they've polished their identities or their marketing materials.

Create a brand that customers can recognize and count on by

- ✔ Displaying a consistent look
- ✔ Projecting a consistent brand character
- ✔ Delivering a consistent level of quality in all communications, products, and services
- ✔ Staying consistently true to what your brand is, stands for, and promises

The chapters in Part III help you present your brand through publicity, advertising, social media, and online communications. Chapter 13 guides development of an unfailingly consistent brand experience.

People Power Brands

Brands are made or broken by human encounters that either advance or erode brand promises. Passionate employees and passionate customers — in that order — power great brands. If you develop brand understanding, enthusiasm, and commitment within your organization, customer understanding, enthusiasm, and commitment will follow.

A great brand name, logo, promise, and communication program are essential ingredients for brand success, but nothing tops the need for an internal team of brand champions, beginning with the leader of your organization and including every single person who affects the consumer's experience with your offering.

Turn to Chapter 13 as you prepare to suit up and train a team capable of delivering a brand experience that ignites customer passion for your brand.

Brands Live in Consumers' Minds

When people see your logo or hear your name, they automatically conjure up impressions and memories that determine what they believe about you. Their notions may be the result of firsthand encounters with you, your products, or organization. Their notions may be based on communications they've seen or heard — anything from your ads to displays, signs, news articles, even your identity on Little League hats. Their notions may result from web searches, social-media posts, or secondhand recaps of other customers' experiences that are passed along online or by word-of-mouth.

Regardless of whether the beliefs customers hold about you are many or few, good or bad, or accurate or inaccurate, they comprise the image of your brand and they influence how people think and buy.

Your brand image lives in your customers' minds whether you intentionally put it there or not. Good branding is how you make sure that the brand image you have is the brand image you want. The chapters in Part III provide tips and best practices for capitalizing on every brand communication opportunity.

Brand Names and Logos Are Like Keys that Unlock Brand Images

Your brand is a set of memories that's tapped each time people see or hear your name.

The right name establishes your brand from the day it's announced, and it grows with your business and your vision as you reach into new market areas, new geographic regions, and even new product areas.

A great brand name should

- ✔ Reflect the brand character of your business.
- ✔ Describe your offering and convey an association to the meaning of your brand.
- ✔ Convey or be consistent with your brand promise.
- ✔ Be easy and pleasant to say and unique and memorable so that, over time, it appreciates into an asset that you can harvest through premium pricing, licensing, or even a sale to a new owner.

Naming your brand is the most challenging, momentous, and necessary phase in the process of branding. Count on Chapter 7 to walk you through the steps involved. Then turn to Chapter 8 as you begin the process of designing a logo to serve as the visible face of your brand.

Brand Experiences Trump Brand Messages

In branding, what you say pales in comparison to what you do.

When consumers gravitate to one brand over the others, their decisions are rarely based on reactions to marketing messages alone. Instead, people rely on their own experiences or on what they've learned about the experiences of others. They choose and stay with brands that they believe will keep their promises based on what they've personally seen and sensed.

To create a brand experience capable of moving markets and instilling loyalty, be ready to convey and reinforce your brand promise through every encounter with your organization — from the office of the CEO down and from the first inquiry to the final service call. If one portion of the experience falls short of consumer expectations — from one poorly handled phone call to one erroneous invoice — your brand image suffers.

"Be the brand" isn't just talk; it's the key to branding success. To develop a team of brand champions prepared to deliver a great brand experience and to put your brand experience to the test, turn to Chapters 9 and 13.

Brands Need to Start and Stay Relevant

To win and keep a slot in the consumer's mind, your brand needs to begin and remain credible, competitive, current, and relevant to customer wants, needs, and interests. That means you need to tune in to market conditions, consumer preferences, and cultural trends not only when you establish your brand but also on a regular basis as your brand ages.

Markets change, and businesses change. When they do, brands that remain stuck in times past pay a high price in terms of credibility and competitiveness.

Follow the advice in Chapter 5 to conduct customer and competitive research before you launch your brand and afterward. Then use Chapter 16 as your guide as you determine what kind of brand update may be in order — from an evolutionary revitalization of your brand name, logo, and look to a revolutionary, full-scale rebranding following a major merger, acquisition, or redirected business strategy.

Either way, the revised brand strategy that you adopt should represent your brand vision for at least ten years, which is about the frequency that brands should undergo major change.

Brands Are Valuable Assets

In the world's most successful businesses, the brand is often the most valuable single asset. When companies with great brands are sold, the value of the brand often accounts for as much as half of the sale price. Plus, brand value translates into everyday economic benefits, including

- Premium pricing and reduced price sensitivity
- Lower costs of sales and promotions
- Higher market share
- Reduced threat of competition
- Greater employee satisfaction
- Higher recognition by consumers, industry leaders, media, investors, and analysts

Count on the information in Chapter 15 to help as you assess the value of your brand, as you plan how to protect and leverage brand value, and as you pursue brand extensions, licensing, and cobranding opportunities.

Index

About the Authors

Bill Chiaravalle knows brands and how to build them. His background includes 11 years with world-renowned brand strategy and design firm Landor Associates, where he served as Senior Designer, Design Director, and Creative Director, working on branding programs for the Audubon Society, American Express, AT&T, Bacardi, Bell Atlantic, California State Lottery, Danone, Delta Airlines, FedEx, Four Seasons Hotels, Gatorade, Hyatt Hotels, IBM, Microsoft, Motorola, NEC, P&G, Radio Shack, San Francisco Zoo, Smucker's, Sunkist, Trinchero Winery, United Airlines, the University of California, and many others. Did we already say he knows brands?

He now serves as Principal and Creative Director of his own firm, Brand Navigation, where he assists clients large and small in telling and marketing their brand stories, products, and services. A partial list of Brand Navigation clients includes the Annenberg Foundation, Ghirardelli, Hartmann Luggage, Krusteaz, Microsoft, Linfield College, Park Hyatt, National Geographic, and World Vision.

Bill was born in San Francisco and received his training at the Academy of Art University in San Francisco. He has been honored with branding, design, and industry awards, including AIGA, American Advertising Federation, Dupont International Packaging Design Awards, Logo Lounge, Print Magazine, and the San Francisco Art Directors Club. Away from brands, he enjoys spending time with his wife, Leila, swimming, enjoying fine dining and jazz music, learning to speak Italian, and traveling the West to visit his four adult children. To reach his company online, go to www.brandnavigation.com.

Barbara Findlay Schenck is a business strategist who has spent her career helping individuals, companies, and organizations shape their businesses, brands, messages, and marketing plans. She's worked internationally in community development, served as a college admissions director and writing instructor in Hawaii, and cofounded an advertising agency that ranked as one of the Northwest's Top 15 at the time of its sale. Since then, she's authored or co-authored *Small Business Marketing Kit For Dummies, Business Plans Kit For Dummies, Selling Your Business For Dummies*, and *Branding For Dummies*. She also writes marketing and branding articles for national and international businesses and media sites, speaks at conferences, and presents live, online, and taped marketing, branding, and business-planning workshops and programs.

When she's not helping entrepreneurs plan, start, brand, market, or sell their businesses, she's likely traveling, golfing, enjoying time with her husband, Peter, or trekking to the San Francisco area to visit their son, Matthew. Reach her through her website, www.bizstrong.com.

Authors' Acknowledgments

Where to begin?

We start with heartfelt thanks to the long list of businesses and organizations that have entrusted their brands and business hopes to each of us over the years. This book, in great measure, shares solutions and advice learned through your success.

We also give special thanks to John Wiley & Sons, Inc., for allowing us this opportunity to explain branding in the famous format of the world's most famous book brand. Acquisitions Editor Stacy Kennedy, Senior Project Editor Alissa Schwipps, Copy Editor Caitie Copple, and Technical Editor Jonlee Andrews made the making of this book a pleasure.

Additionally, we each offer personal acknowledgements.

From Bill: In addition to developing brands for over 20 years, I've been involved in the design of more than a thousand book covers in my lifetime. But I'd never considered writing one — until Barbara Schenck approached me. Thank you, Barbara and Peter; you have been kind advocates for almost a decade. Thanks also to my longstanding teammates and friends at Brand Navigation: DeAnna, Mark, and Mike. Without you, designing brands wouldn't be as possible, or as much fun.

Special thanks to my children, Heidi, Wil, Michael, and Laura, who love me regardless of my obsession with brands.

And, most of all, to my beautiful wife, who is not only my business partner but my friend and the love of my life. You complete me.

From Barbara: Deep thanks to Bill for agreeing to coauthor this book and for adding so significantly to its value. This book confirms why people say yours is the smartest voice in any branding conversation.

Immeasurable gratitude, also, to those who make all the joys and successes in my life possible: My husband, Peter, and our son, Matthew.

Above all, we both extend deep thanks to every reader who selects this book as a brand-building guide. As you enter or travel farther into the world of branding, you carry all our best wishes with you.

Publisher's Acknowledgments

Acquisitions Editor: Stacy Kennedy

Senior Project Editor: Alissa Schwipps

Copy Editor: Caitie Copple

Technical Editor: Jonlee Andrews

Project Coordinator: Erin Zeltner

Cover Image: ©iStock.com/somchaij

Apple & Mac

iPad For Dummies,
6th Edition
978-1-118-72306-7

iPhone For Dummies,
7th Edition
978-1-118-69083-3

Macs All-in-One
For Dummies, 4th Edition
978-1-118-82210-4

OS X Mavericks
For Dummies
978-1-118-69188-5

Blogging & Social Media

Facebook For Dummies,
5th Edition
978-1-118-63312-0

Social Media Engagement
For Dummies
978-1-118-53019-1

WordPress For Dummies,
6th Edition
978-1-118-79161-5

Business

Stock Investing
For Dummies, 4th Edition
978-1-118-37678-2

Investing For Dummies,
6th Edition
978-0-470-90545-6

Careers

Job Interviews
For Dummies, 4th Edition
978-1-118-11290-8

Job Searching with Social
Media For Dummies,
2nd Edition
978-1-118-67856-5

Personal Branding
For Dummies
978-1-118-11792-7

Resumes For Dummies,
6th Edition
978-0-470-87361-8

Starting an Etsy Business
For Dummies, 2nd Edition
978-1-118-59024-9

Diet & Nutrition

Belly Fat Diet For Dummies
978-1-118-34585-6

Personal Finance
For Dummies, 7th Edition
978-1-118-11785-9

QuickBooks 2014
For Dummies
978-1-118-72005-9

Small Business Marketing
Kit For Dummies,
3rd Edition
978-1-118-31183-7

Mediterranean Diet
For Dummies
978-1-118-71525-3

Nutrition For Dummies,
5th Edition
978-0-470-93231-5

Digital Photography

Digital SLR Photography
All-in-One For Dummies,
2nd Edition
978-1-118-59082-9

Digital SLR Video &
Filmmaking For Dummies
978-1-118-36598-4

Photoshop Elements 12
For Dummies
978-1-118-72714-0

Gardening

Herb Gardening
For Dummies, 2nd Edition
978-0-470-61778-6

Gardening with Free-Range
Chickens For Dummies
978-1-118-54754-0

Health

Boosting Your Immunity
For Dummies
978-1-118-40200-9

Diabetes For Dummies,
4th Edition
978-1-118-29447-5

Living Paleo For Dummies
978-1-118-29405-5

Big Data

Big Data For Dummies
978-1-118-50422-2

Data Visualization
For Dummies
978-1-118-50289-1

Hadoop For Dummies
978-1-118-60755-8

Language & Foreign Language

500 Spanish Verbs
For Dummies
978-1-118-02382-2

English Grammar
For Dummies, 2nd Edition
978-0-470-54664-2

French All-in-One
For Dummies
978-1-118-22815-9

German Essentials
For Dummies
978-1-118-18422-6

Italian For Dummies,
2nd Edition
978-1-118-00465-4

e Available in print and e-book formats.

Math & Science

Algebra I For Dummies,
2nd Edition
978-0-470-55964-2

Anatomy and Physiology
For Dummies, 2nd Edition
978-0-470-92326-9

Astronomy For Dummies,
3rd Edition
978-1-118-37697-3

Biology For Dummies,
2nd Edition
978-0-470-59875-7

Chemistry For Dummies,
2nd Edition
978-1-118-00730-3

1001 Algebra II Practice
Problems For Dummies
978-1-118-44662-1

Microsoft Office

Excel 2013 For Dummies
978-1-118-51012-4

Office 2013 All-in-One
For Dummies
978-1-118-51636-2

PowerPoint 2013
For Dummies
978-1-118-50253-2

Word 2013 For Dummies
978-1-118-49123-2

Music

Blues Harmonica
For Dummies
978-1-118-25269-7

Guitar For Dummies,
3rd Edition
978-1-118-11554-1

iPod & iTunes
For Dummies, 10th Edition
978-1-118-50864-0

Programming

Beginning Programming
with C For Dummies
978-1-118-73763-7

Excel VBA Programming
For Dummies, 3rd Edition
978-1-118-49037-2

Java For Dummies,
6th Edition
978-1-118-40780-6

Religion & Inspiration

The Bible For Dummies
978-0-7645-5296-0

Buddhism For Dummies,
2nd Edition
978-1-118-02379-2

Catholicism For Dummies,
2nd Edition
978-1-118-07778-8

Self-Help & Relationships

Beating Sugar Addiction
For Dummies
978-1-118-54645-1

Meditation For Dummies,
3rd Edition
978-1-118-29144-3

Seniors

Laptops For Seniors
For Dummies, 3rd Edition
978-1-118-71105-7

Computers For Seniors
For Dummies, 3rd Edition
978-1-118-11553-4

iPad For Seniors
For Dummies, 6th Edition
978-1-118-72826-0

Social Security
For Dummies
978-1-118-20573-0

Smartphones & Tablets

Android Phones
For Dummies, 2nd Edition
978-1-118-72030-1

Nexus Tablets
For Dummies
978-1-118-77243-0

Samsung Galaxy S 4
For Dummies
978-1-118-64222-1

Samsung Galaxy Tabs
For Dummies
978-1-118-77294-2

Test Prep

ACT For Dummies,
5th Edition
978-1-118-01259-8

ASVAB For Dummies,
3rd Edition
978-0-470-63760-9

GRE For Dummies,
7th Edition
978-0-470-88921-3

Officer Candidate Tests
For Dummies
978-0-470-59876-4

Physician's Assistant Exam
For Dummies
978-1-118-11556-5

Series 7 Exam For Dummies
978-0-470-09932-2

Windows 8

Windows 8.1 All-in-One
For Dummies
978-1-118-82087-2

Windows 8.1 For Dummies
978-1-118-82121-3

Windows 8.1 For Dummies
Book + DVD Bundle
978-1-118-82107-7

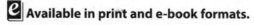

Available in print and e-book formats.